# THE FIELD GUIDE
## TO NORTH AMERICA'S

# BREWERIES
*And*
# MICROBREWERIES

# THE FIELD GUIDE
# TO NORTH AMERICA'S

# BREWERIES

*And*

# MICROBREWERIES

by
Bill Yenne

**Crescent Books**
New York/Avenel, New Jersey

This 1994 edition published by Crescent Books, distributed by Random House Value Publishing, Inc., 40 Engelhard Avenue, Avenel, New Jersey 07001.

Random House
New York • Toronto • London • Sydney • Auckland

Produced by Brompton Books Corporation, 15 Sherwood Place, Greenwich, Connecticut 06830

ISBN 0-517-10232-3

8 7 6 5 4 3 2 1

Printed and bound in China

Designed by Tom Debolski

## PICTURE CREDITS
All of the illustrations in this book appear through the courtesy of the companies whose products, facilities and artwork are depicted with the following exception:
Photo on page 186 © Bill Yenne

**Page 1:** *These gleaming copper brew kettles are part of Coors' 18-million-barrel flagship brewery in Golden, Colorado.*

**Page 2:** *A delighted couple enjoy the renowned hospitality offered at Pike Place Brewery, Seattle, Washington.*

**Below:** *Molson Breweries has operated a brewing plant on this site in Montreal for over two centuries.*

# CONTENTS

### INTRODUCTION
### 6

### USING THIS GUIDE
### 17

### THE NORTHEAST
### 20

### THE MIDDLE ATLANTIC AND SOUTH
### 40

### THE MIDWEST
### 58

### THE MOUNTAIN WEST
### 84

### SOUTHERN CALIFORNIA
### 102

### NORTHERN CALIFORNIA
### 110

### OREGON
### 130

### WASHINGTON AND ALASKA
### 142

### WESTERN AND PRAIRIE CANADA
### 150

### EASTERN CANADA
### 162

### GLOSSARY
### 184

# INTRODUCTION

I n the 1870s, there were 5000 breweries in North America, and as late as 1945 there was a home-town brewery in practically every city, each brewing products whose brand names spoke to the hometown pride of the local community. After World War II, however, there was a great consolidation in the brewing industry. As the national brands expanded their distribution, local breweries began to disappear. Where there were once thousands of breweries in North America, the number had dwindled to a few dozen by the 1970s.

By this time, there was so little variety available that North American beer, especially that brewed in the United States, was regarded around the world as a uniformly tasteless beverage that had little in common with world-class beers other than alcohol content. This had, of course, not always been the case. Brewing in North America had a long, rich history. This history began with the Indians of Mexico and the American Southwest, but most of our present traditions arrived with the European immigrants. The English brought their top-fermenting ale yeasts with them and immediately established breweries in the Colonies. By the time of the American Revolution, ales and porters had become a well-developed part of daily life, and most landowners were as likely to have a brewhouse on their grounds as a stable. In fact, both George Washington and Thomas Jefferson were home brewers.

In 1840, the first wave of German immigrants introduced bottom-fermenting yeasts to North American brewing, and we soon became a continent of lager drinkers. By the turn of the century, the advent of a continental railroad network and the invention of artifi-

Above: *A vintage turn-of-the-century label for Labatt's India Pale Ale. Labatt was founded in London, Ontario in 1853 and is still headquartered there.*

**Opposite:** *The Gordon-Biersch Brewery in Palo Alto, California is the epitome of the modern brewery/restaurant.*

cial ice making made possible the rise of megabrewers like Schlitz, Pabst and Anheuser-Busch. They became large, regional brewers, and by World War II were all in a position to launch truly national brands. With the rise of the national brands, however, small local and regional brewers suffered, and many disappeared as nearly everyone attempted to create pale lagers that would appeal to as wide an audience as possible.

In the 1980s, thanks to changes in state laws and changes in the tastes of the beer-buying public, new hometown breweries—known as 'microbreweries'—began to appear in cities and towns from Maine to California. By the 1990s, there were nearly 500 new breweries in the United States and Canada. The advent of microbreweries and brewpubs in the United States and certain parts of Canada was probably the most exciting event in the history of North American brewing since Prohibition was repealed in 1933. For the first time in over a century, the number of brewing companies in North America began to increase. In the United States the number of breweries increased from 53 in 1983, to 190 in 1988 and to over 400 in 1994. The microbrewery revolution has given North Americans a vastly wider selection of styles and varieties of fresh, domestically produced beers than has been available since the nineteenth century. It also signaled a return to the concept of regional, and even neighborhood, breweries, an idea that was thought to have perished at the end of World War II.

Unlike regional breweries which attempted, and failed, to compete with the national brands in the 1950s and 1960s, today's smaller breweries brew specialty beers with unique characters and much richer flavors than any of the national brands. While these styles do not appeal to the same millions that buy Budweiser and Miller Lite, North America's two leading brands, many have attracted large and enthusiastic followings.

The richness, freshness and unusual variety of the new brews appealed to a generation of consumers who had just begun to experiment with imported specialty beers. This same generation had also come of age after the heyday of local and regional brands, most of which had become defunct prior to the 1970s. The microbreweries were starting up in a market which was, with few exceptions—like Anchor in California and Stevens Point in Wisconsin—almost devoid of small, regional specialty

*Above: The Anheuser-Busch brewery in St Louis was once the largest single brewhouse in North America. The brewing company, however, is still the largest in the world.*

*Opposite top: Established in 1829, Yuengling & Son is the oldest brewery in the United States.*

*Opposite bottom: Miller Brewing's 8.5-million-barrel flagship plant in Milwaukee, Wisconsin. Miller is North America's second largest brewer.*

brewers. American brewing history was repeating itself. A new generation began to discover and take pride in local brews, just as their grandparents had.

By definition, a *microbrewery* was originally considered to be a brewery with a capacity of less than 3000 barrels, but by the end of the 1980s this threshold increased to 15,000 barrels as the demand for micro-brewed beer increased severalfold, and microbreweries ceased to be 'micro.'

At the same time, a whole new type of brewery appeared on the scene. Known as *brewpubs*, these new institutions were similar in scale to the microbreweries, but by definition were literally pubs or taverns that brewed their own beer on the premises.

Until the 1980s, as a holdover from Prohibition laws, it was illegal in most states and Canadian provinces to both brew beer and sell it directly to the public on the same site. Subsequent changes in local laws have rescinded these outdated restrictions and have made it possible for brewpubs to become more widespread. Ironically, brewpubs were once very much a part of American history. During the seventeenth century many

of the original establishments in places such as New Amsterdam were, in fact, brewpubs.

A brewpub differs from a microbrewery in that its primary market is under its own roof. Some brewpubs bottle their beers for sale to patrons and for wholesale to retailers, while some microbreweries also operate brewpubs, so the distinction between the two is somewhat blurred. Both, however, share a commitment to their own unique beers, and most brewpublicans entered their trade out of a love for brewing and an interest in distinctive beer styles.

The microbrewery revolution started with the now extinct New Albion Brewing of Sonoma, California, which was founded by Jack McAuliffe in 1976. The patron saint of the revolution, however, was certainly Fritz Maytag, who purchased 70-year-old Anchor Brewing in San Francisco in 1965 with the express purpose of developing specific and unique specialty beers. Maytag was probably the last person to wish such a mantle upon himself, yet he is almost universally cited by those who followed McAuliffe's lead.

**Below:** *The microbrewery movement spread to Colorado with the founding of the Boulder Brewing Company in 1980. Their picturesque 10,000-barrel brewery was opened in 1984.*

At the same time that McAuliffe was starting New Albion, there was a growing public awareness of a variety of beer styles, such as ales, wheat beers and stouts, that were rare or even unknown in the United States, and imports were becoming increasingly popular, particularly in major cities such as Seattle, Portland, San Francisco and New York. It became common to see as many as one dozen draft handles in taverns. It was in fact this interest in European beer styles—nurtured in the 1970s—that was a catalyst for the microbreweries of the 1980s.

After New Albion was born, it would be several years before the microbrewery revolution began to spread. In 1980 River City Brewing opened in Sacramento, California and Sierra Nevada Brewing opened in nearby Chico. While River City survived only a few years, Sierra Nevada is now one of the largest of North America's new generation of microbreweries.

The first brewpub in Oregon, a state that was destined to play a pivotal role in the microbrewery revolution, opened in 1984. The Hillsdale Brewery, founded by Portland bar owner Mike McMenamin, along with his brother Brian, would become the anchor for the largest chain of brewpubs on the continent. Portland was also the city where Henry Saxer had started the first western brewery outside of San Francisco in 1852, which in turn had become Henry Weinhard's brewery, and later the flagship of Blitz-Weinhard. Between 1984 and 1985, Portland became a multi-brewery town for the first time in a century, with four breweries located within a one-half mile area on the city's northwest side. McMenamin and Blitz-Weinhard (now flying the Heileman flag) were joined by the Columbia River Brewery, the new Portland Brewery (not related to the Portland Brewing Company, which operated between 1905 and 1928) and the Widmer Brewing Company.

The microbrewery movement spread to Colorado in 1980 with the opening of the Boulder Brewing Company, and to New York state as William Newman began brewing in Albany the following year. Two microbreweries opened in Washington state during 1982: the Red Hook Ale Brewery in Seattle and Yakima Brewing & Malting, which is coincidentally located in the heart of the best hop-growing region in North America.

The brewpubs began to follow the microbreweries as the laws prohibiting them were repealed. Mendocino

Above, at top: *San Francisco's Anchor Brewing Company, rescued from collapse by Fritz Maytag in 1965, is now the very model of an efficient, small regional brewery.*

Above: *Anchor's Old Foghorn is a barleywine-style ale.*

Brewing, which was established in the appropriately-named village of Hopland, about two hours north of San Francisco, opened in 1982, and was followed two years later by Buffalo Bill Owens' brewpub in Hayward, across the Bay from San Francisco. Allen Paul opened San Francisco Brewing—the city's first brewpub since Prohibition—in the old Albatross Saloon in 1986. There was a rush of new brewpubs opening throughout the United States.

The style and ambience of brewpubs varies greatly. In a sense, San Francisco Brewing is the definitive American pub. It is small and compact, with a carved mahogany bar and antique Indian 'Oompah' palm fans on the ceiling. Located in a neighborhood that has been a beer drinkers' gathering place since the Gold Rush era, it has the comfortable, well-worn feel that makes it easy to believe that it was one of the first bars to reopen after the 1906 earthquake, which it was. It is home to both local characters and visitors from hundreds of miles away who are following the brewpub trail through the West.

While most brewpubs specialize in what Allen Paul of San Francisco Brewing describes as 'pub food'—sandwiches, burgers and snacks—the brewpub is no longer necessarily a 'pub' in the traditional sense. The definition of brewpub has now been stretched to include full service restaurants that brew beer. This trend is indicative of the recognition that beer is just as important a complement to fine cuisine as wine. This is particularly true now that American brewers are producing a much wider variety of beer styles, each of which has a character that complements a particular type of food. These may include more familiar ales, porters and lagers, but can also range from the cherry beer produced by the Lakefront Brewery in Milwaukee, which is delightful with desserts or game, to the beer brewed in Newport, Oregon by Bayfront Brewing, which uses barley roasted over a wood fire. The result is a beer which is perfect with smoked sausages, any type of barbecue or the wonderful smoked oyster pizza served in Bayfront's brewpub.

On the other end of the brewpub spectrum there is the Oldenberg Brewery and entertainment complex on Buttermilk Pike in Fort Mitchell, Kentucky, across the Ohio River from Cincinnati. The name 'entertainment complex' truly tells the story. With perhaps 50 times the square footage of San Francisco Brewing or most typ-

**Above, at top:** *Buffalo Bill's of Hayward, California became one of the first three brewpubs to open in the United States since Prohibition when it opened in 1983.*

**Above:** *Thomas Kemper Weizen Berry is a handcrafted lager beer flavored with natural raspberry juice.*

ically modest brewpubs, Oldenberg is really a beer drinkers' amusement park. The centerpiece is an immense beer hall with a 65-foot ceiling that seats 650 people and offers live entertainment. The Oldenberg complex also houses the American Museum of Brewing History & Arts, which owns the largest brewing memorabilia collection in the world.

Meanwhile, the Gordon-Biersch Breweries in Palo Alto, San Francisco, San Jose and Pasadena, California are good examples of brewpubs which are really *full service restaurants* that also brew beer. Begun in 1988, they not only feature the beer of Dan Gordon, who spent five years in the brewing engineering program at the Technical University of Munich, but also the kitchen expertise of noted chefs.

Although today the area stretching south from western Oregon and Washington to the San Francisco Bay Area contains the largest concentration of brewpubs and microbreweries in North America, the revolution has spread to every corner of the continent—from Florida Brewing in Miami, to the Granite Brewery in Halifax, Nova Scotia; to Schirf Brewing in Park City, Utah, to Alaskan Brewing (formerly Chinook) in Douglas, Alaska. Milwaukee, once the proud capital of American brewing, experienced the demise of both Schlitz and Blatz, but saw the rise of the Lakefront and Sprecher microbreweries.

As microbreweries were beginning to flourish, the public's heightened awareness of distinctive specialty beers created an expanded market for smaller regional brewers whose existence predated the microbrewery revolution. This is certainly true of breweries from Anchor Brewing of San Francisco to August Schell Brewing of New Ulm, Minnesota, which was founded in 1860 and which survived the 1862 Sioux uprising because of August Schell's own personal rapport with the tribe.

In the major markets of the Northeast, unlike those of the West, the trend in the mid-1980s was toward *contract* brewing rather than toward microbreweries. Philadelphia, New York and Boston each saw the development of a major local brand that was actually brewed *under contract* somewhere else. Contract brewing typically involves off-site production using a recipe developed by the brewing company's owner, usually with the help of a brewing consultant such as Dr Joseph Owades of the Center for Brewing Studies in San Fran-

Above, at top: *The Gordon-Biersch Breweries not only feature quality beer that is brewed on-site, but also the kitchen expertise of noted chefs.*

Above: *The Oldenberg Brewery in Fort Mitchell has been called a beer drinkers' amusement park. It features a beer hall that seats 650, live entertainment, and the largest brewing memorabilia collection in the world.*

cisco, who has helped any number of small brewing companies to get their start.

One of the first and best known contract brewers was Jim Koch, a Boston entrepreneur whose family was involved in the Fred Koch Brewery, which was established in Dunkirk, New York in 1888. Wanting to create a beer which could compete with the best German beers and pass the Reinheitsgebot (German Purity Law), Koch formed his Boston Beer Company in 1985 to produce Samuel Adams Lager. Named for the eighteenth century Boston patriot and home brewer, 'Sam Adams' passed the Reinheitsgebot test and was actually sold in West Germany before Koch expanded his marketing in the United States beyond the Boston area. Brewed under contract by Pittsburgh Brewing until Koch opened his own brewery near Boston in 1987, Sam Adams is now available throughout the United States and is the best-selling beer made by any of the new North American brewing companies that have started since 1980.

*Above: Jim Koch's Samuel Adams Lager was brewed under contract by Pittsburgh Brewing until his Boston Beer Company opened their own brewery in 1987. 'Sam Adams' is now the best-selling beer produced by a new North American brewery started in the last decade.*

Both of Philadelphia's initial 'house' brands—Jeff Ware's Dock Street and Tom Pastorius' Pennsylvania Pilsener—were originally contract brewed, but both had opened their own breweries by 1990, and Ware now operates brewery/restaurants in both Philadelphia and Washington.

Perhaps the largest of the contract brewers in the East has been the FX Matt Brewing Company of Utica, New York. Originally founded in 1853, the company that had long been famous for its own Utica Club brand initially contract brewed for Dock Street of Philadelphia, in addition to Long Island Brewing of Montauk, New York, Old New York Maine Coast Brewing, Brooklyn Brewery and Monarch Brewing of Brooklyn, as well as William S Newman Brewing of nearby Albany, which opened as a microbrewery in 1981 but found the demand for its beer outstripped its on-site capacity.

In New York City the first new brewing companies in town after the microbrewery revolution began were Old New York, whose Amsterdam Amber is brewed under contract by FX Matt in Utica, New York, and Manhattan Brewing, a brewpub opened in 1984 in a former Consolidated Edison substation on Thompson Street in the city's Soho district. Manhattan Brewing closed in 1992, but was back in business by 1994. A second New York brewpub, the Zip City, opened in 1991.

This trend toward contract brewing has proven to be beneficial to older, regional breweries as well because of the new business they have experienced and from the fresh ideas they have obtained through contact with enthusiastic entrepreneurs.

The initial trend toward contract brewing in the East, which was looked down upon by western micro-brewers, gradually changed as brewers such as Koch, Ware and Pastorius opened their own facilities. At the same time, a good many important microbreweries, with in-house brewing present at start-up, have opened in the Northeast.

These include Catamount Brewing in White River Junction, Vermont; DL Geary Brewing in Portland, Maine; Mass Bay Brewing in Boston, Massachusetts; and Old Dominion Brewing in Ashburn, Virginia. Washington, DC, meanwhile, is home to Capitol City Brewing, an extraordinary brewery/restaurant.

The success of the microbreweries, and certainly the quality of the beers they are producing, is due in part to

*Above, at top: Francis Xavier Matt II, president of FX Matt Brewing. This company is perhaps the premier contract brewer in the eastern United States.*

*Above: Saranac is FX Matt's flagship line of premium beers.*

the establishment in 1975 of a brewing course in the Food Sciences Department at the University of California's Davis campus, which is located halfway between San Francisco and Sacramento. Under the able direction of Dr Michael Lewis, the department evolved into the American School for Malting and Brewing Science & Technology, which has in turn graduated brewmasters who have become employed not only by many of the microbreweries, but by large, established breweries as well. For example, several of the people brewing beer at the Anheuser-Busch facility in nearby Fairfield are graduates of Dr Lewis's courses.

As the twentieth century draws to a close, North American brewing is enjoying a renaissance. Total consumption remains relatively constant, but per capita consumption of beer, as opposed to high-alcohol beverages, is the highest that it has been since before Prohibition. In the 1990s, after four decades of decline, the number of brewers has multiplied six-fold in less than a decade, and the demand for noteworthy specialty beers continues to grow.

The North American brewing industry in the 1990s is in much the same place that the American wine industry was two decades before. It is producing truly world-class beers and finally receiving the recognition that it deserves. Many of the finest restaurants now have *beer* lists prepared with the care and consideration once reserved for their *wine* lists. When New York's Plaza Hotel offers a beer list, it is profoundly clear that beer is getting its due!

While the microbreweries brew far less beer than the megabreweries, by the end of the 1980s they had started to make serious inroads in the North American market against European specialty beers, because they are true world-class beers and because they are much *fresher* than any imported beer.

The spectrum of beer styles being brewed today in North American is nothing short of incredible. Not only is there the best selection of lagers in over half a century, but North Americans are able to choose from ales and wheat beers, and brewers are producing distinctive stouts and have even helped to revive the art of porter brewing, which had all but died out even in England. Brewers are also developing more esoteric beer styles. Best of all, there are fresh local beers of every style being brewed in virtually every corner of the continent.

**Above:** *The products of Connors Brewing* **(top)** *and Okanagan Spring Brewery* **(above)**—*two fine examples of Canada's burgeoning microbrewery industry.*

**Opposite:** *The sight of the numerous taps at the San Diego Brewing Company is paradise to the eyes of thirsty beer drinkers.*

# USING THIS GUIDE

**I**f this guide had been produced 20 or 30 years ago, it would have been much smaller, but the listings would have remained relatively constant for the better part of a decade. However, today's brewery and microbrewery scene is in a constant state of change and evolution. There are major brewing companies that have existed for over a century and major microbreweries that have been solidly in place since the mid-1980s, but there are also new microbreweries and brewpubs coming on line almost monthly, and there are several older ones that go out of business every year. Further, existing microbreweries, and especially brewpubs, frequently add or delete brands from their lists. This is especially true with brewpubs which do not have money invested in labels or in establishing brands in the retail market. Against this backdrop, we have tried to assemble the most comprehensive directory possible.

The listings are organized by region. Those establishments listed as being adjacent to pubs, brewpubs or brewery restaurants are open to the public during typical day and evening hours. Most breweries and microbreweries offer tours, but these are not continuous and may be offered only once a day, once a week or by appointment only. People wishing to view the brewing process or purchase samples of beer being produced are advised to contact each establishment directly for details about its operations.

We have been able to provide more information about some breweries than others. Those with more information listed are usually older and have a longer history, or play a larger role in regional or national markets, or have supplied more data to us in response to our questionnaires.

We have also endeavored to note gold and silver medals awarded by the Great American Beer Festival. The GABF has been held in Denver, CO every year since 1983, and awards have been made in specific beer style categories since 1987. The GABF is by no means the definitive rating system for United States beers—only *you* can judge for yourself what you beers you like best—and indeed, many brewing companies choose not to participate in the GABF competition. The GABF is, however, the largest competitive beer tasting in North America and thus the closest thing there is at this moment to being an industry standard for judging the quality of beer brewed by United States breweries. Other, also prestigious, awards are indicated for Canadian brewers.

As I noted in the 1990 edition of *Beers of North America*, any list of breweries and microbreweries is a snapshot of a dynamic, evolving industry at the moment that it is taken. The book is the result of numerous and ongoing field studies and a continuous review of periodicals relating to beer and the brewing industry. In addition to this, questionnaires were sent to every brewery in North America and to the home offices of major brewing companies. To keep abreast of changes in the brewery and microbrewery scene, readers are referred to two excellent periodicals: *The Celebrator Beer News* (PO Box 375, Hayward, CA 94543) and *World Beer Review* (PO Box 71, Clemson, SC 29633).

**Below:** *Golden Bear Lager is produced by Golden Pacific Brewing of Emeryville, California.*

# THE NORTHEAST

**Samuel Adams:** See Boston Beer Company (Boston, MA) and Philadelphia Brewing (Philadelphia, PA)

**Allegheny Brewery:** See Pennsylvania Brewing (Pittsburgh, PA)

## Andrew's Brewing
RFD #1 Box 4975
Lincolnville, ME 04849

This brewery was founded by Andy Hazen in 1992.

Annual production: 300-400 barrels

Flagship brand: Andrew's Old English Ale

Major top-fermented brands: Andrew's Old English Ale, Brown Ale, St Nick Porter

## Anheuser-Busch
200 US Highway 1
Newark, NJ 07101

This brewery was started by Anheuser-Busch in 1951.

Annual production: 9,900,000 barrels

Other breweries owned by the same company: See Anheuser-Busch, St Louis, MO for a list of Anheuser-Busch breweries.

Flagship brand: Budweiser

Major bottom-fermented brands: Budweiser, Bud Light, Bud Dry, Bud Dry Draft, Michelob, Michelob Light, Michelob Dark, Natural Light, Busch, Busch Light, King Cobra, O'Doul's Elephant Malt Liquor, Carlsberg, Carlsberg Light

See Anheuser-Busch, St Louis, MO for a list of medals awarded to Anheuser-Busch beers.

## Anheuser-Busch
221 Daniel Webster Highway
Merrimack, NH 03054

This brewery was started by Anheuser-Busch in 1970.

Annual production: 3,200,000 barrels

Other breweries owned by the same company: See Anheuser-Busch, St Louis, MO for a list of Anheuser-Busch breweries.

Flagship brand: Budweiser

Major bottom-fermented brands: Budweiser, Bud Light, Michelob, Michelob Light, Michelob Dark, Natural Light, Busch

See Anheuser-Busch, St Louis, MO for a list of medals awarded to Anheuser-Busch beers.

## Anheuser-Busch
2885 Belgium Road
Baldwinsville, NY 13027

This brewery was started by Anheuser-Busch in 1983.

Annual production: 8,200,000 barrels

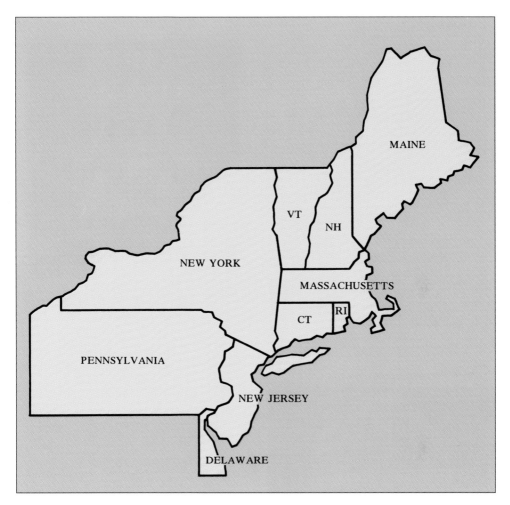

Other breweries owned by the same company: See Anheuser-Busch, St Louis, MO for a list of Anheuser-Busch breweries.

Flagship brand: Budweiser

Major bottom-fermented brands: Budweiser, Bud Light, Michelob, Michelob Light, Michelob Dry, Busch, LA

See Anheuser-Busch, St Louis, MO for a list of medals awarded to Anheuser-Busch beers.

## Arrowhead Brewing
1667 Orchard Drive
Chambersburg, PA 17201

This brewery was founded by Fran Mead in 1991.

Annual production: Under 500 barrels

Flagship brand: Red Feather Pale Ale

## Atlantic Brewing Company
Lompoc Cafe & Brewpub
30 Rodick Street
Bar Harbor, ME 04609

This brewery was founded by Jon Hubbard and Doug Maffucci in 1991. The bar originated a year prior to the brewery and is named for the Old Lompoc Cafe, featured in the WC Fields film *The Bank Dick*. After beginning by selling local beers, Maffucci decided to add a brewery.

Annual production: 1000 barrels

Flagship brand: Bar Harbor Real Ale

Major top-fermented brands: Bar Harbor Blueberry, Coal Porter, Lompoc Pale Ale

Major seasonal brands: Ginger (Rogers) Wheat, Tree Frog Stout

## Bar Harbor Brewing
Route 3, Otter Creek
Bar Harbor, ME 04609

This brewery was founded by Tod Foster in 1990.

Annual production: 160 barrels

Flagship brand: Cadillac Mountain Stout, Thunder Hole Ale

Major top-fermented brands: Cadillac Mountain Stout, Thunder Hold Ale

Major seasonal brands: Brewer's Choice Mild Ale, Harbor Lighthouse Pale Ale

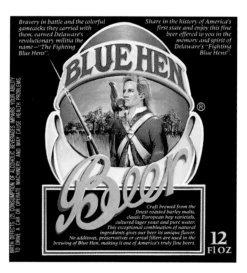

## Blue Hen Beer Company
PO Box 7077
Newark, DE 19714

This contract beer company was founded in 1987 by Jeff Johnson.

Annual production: None. This beer is produced by Gibbons (Wilkes-Barre, PA)

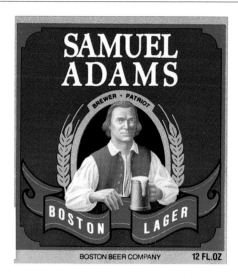

## Boston Beer Company
30 Germania Street
Boston, MA 02130

The company was founded by James Koch in 1984, with the beer contract brewed by Pittsburg Brewing and first placed on sale in 1985. In 1987, Koch moved production to his own brewing facility in Boston.

Jim is the sixth generation of Koch brewmasters. His great-great-great-grandfather brewed beer 150 years ago in Germany, and his great-great grandfather founded a brewery in St Louis in 1860, where he brewed Louis Koch Lager. Jim's father, Charles Joseph, Jr, began as an apprentice brewmaster in 1942, and in 1948 he received his degree from the Siebel Institute. Within the next few years, those breweries began to close as large nationals took over the beer business from small local and family breweries. Jim's father left the beer business that had supported his family for nearly 150 years. Luckily, the Koch family story of brewing did not end there. In 1983, to his father's consternation, Jim Koch decided to leave his highly paid management consulting job to continue his family's brewing tradition. Although he was convinced of his son's folly, Jim's father eventually retrieved Louis Koch's recipe from the attic. After a year spent brewing test batches, Jim introduced to

Americans a taste of beer that had all but disappeared. Samuel Adams Boston beers were named for Samuel Adams (1722-1803), Boston's famous statesman, patriot and brewer.

Annual production: 450,000 barrels

Other brewery owned by the same company: Jim Koch also has an interest in Philadelphia Brewing (Philadelphia, PA).

Flagship brand: Samuel Adams Boston Lager

Major top-fermented brands: Boston Ale, Honey Porter, Cranberry Lambic, Samuel Adams Cream Stout

Major bottom-fermented brand: Boston Lightship

GABF Gold Medals: Samuel Adams Boston Lager (European Pilsener), 1987, 1990; Boston Lightship, 1988; Samuel Adams Boston Stock Ale, 1989; Samuel Adams Double Bock (Dopplebock), 1990; Dusseldorf Style Altbiers, 1992

GABF Silver Medals: Samuel Adams Boston Ale (Dusseldorf Style Altbier), 1991; German Wheat Ales, 1992; Samuel Adams Octoberfest (Amber Lager), 1993

**Boston Beer Works:** See Slesar Brothers Brewing (Boston, MA)

Major top-fermented brands: Bavarian-style Weizen Ale, Belgian Cherry Ale, Harwood's 'Almost Original' Porter, Light Rye Ale, Rauch Boctoberfest, St Nick's Nectar Barley Wine, Uncle Rodney's Oatmeal Stout

Major bottom-fermented brands: Amber Lager, Golden Lager

Major seasonal brands: Christmas Dark, Mardi Gras Bock, Oktoberfest, St Nick's Nectar Barley Wine

**Budweiser:** See Anheuser-Busch (St Louis, MO)

## Buffalo Brewing

Abbott Square Brewpub
1830 Abbott Road
Lackawanna, NY 14218

This brewery was founded in a former roller rink by Kevin Townsell in 1990.

Not to be confused with Buffalo Bill's California pub, this establishment is one of two related pubs located near Buffalo, NY.

Annual production: 8500 barrels

Other breweries owned by the same company: Buffalo Brewpub (Williamsville, NY), Rochester Brewpub (Henrietta, NY)

Flagship brand: Buffalo Lager

## Brown & Moran Brewing

#417-419 River Street
Troy, NY 12180

The company was founded by James Moran in 1990 and brewing began in 1992.

Major top-fermented brands: Limberick's Irish Red Ale, Weisse Beer

Major bottom-fermented brands: Blizzard Bock, Buffalo Lager, Buffalo Lager Light, Pils

Major seasonal brand: Oktoberfest

## Buffalo Brewpub
6861 Main Street
Williamsville, NY 14221

This brewpub was founded in 1986. Not to be confused with Buffalo Bill's California pub, this establishment is one of two related pubs located near Buffalo, NY.

Annual production: 7000 barrels

Other breweries owned by the same company: Buffalo Brewing/Abbott Square Brewpub (Lacakwanna, NY), Rochester Brewpub (Henrietta, NY)

Major top-fermented brands: Amber Ale, Buffalo Bitter, Nickle City Dark, Oatmeal Stout

Major bottom-fermented brand: Weiss

Major seasonal brands: Oktoberfest Lager, Kringle Beer

**Busch:** See Anheuser-Busch (St Louis, MO)

## Cambridge Brewing
1 Kendall Square, Building 100
Cambridge, MA 02139

This brewery was founded in 1989. The owner and master brewer is Phil Bannatyne.

Annual production: 2000 barrels

Flagship brands: Belgian Tripel, Cambridge Amber, Charles River Porter, Regatta Golden, Tall Tale Pale Ale

Major seasonal brand: Belgian Tripel

GABF Gold Medal: Belgian Tripel, 1992

## Catamount Brewing
58 South Main Street
White River Junction, VT 05001

Founded by Stephen P Mason in 1987, Catamount Brewing is the first commercial brewery to operate in Vermont since 1893. Initial distribution included only Vermont and New Hampshire, but has been expanded to other New England states since 1988.

Annual production: 13,000 barrels

Flagship brand: Catamount Amber

Major top-fermented brands: Catamount Amber, Catamount Gold, Catamount Porter

Major seasonal brands: Catamount Christmas Ale, Catamount Bock, Catamount Octoberfest

GABF Gold Medal: Catamount Gold, 1989

## Chapter House Brewpub
400 Stewart Avenue
Ithaca, NY 14850

The brewpub was established in 1992 in a bar that has existed since 1939.

Annual production: Less than 500 barrels

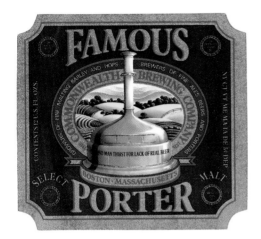

## Commonwealth Brewing
138 Portland Street
Boston, MA 02114

Founded by Richard Wrigley in 1986, Commonwealth Brewing was the first brewpub to open in Massachusetts since Prohibition. The new owner is Joe Quattrocchi; general manager, Bill Goodwin; brewer, Tod Mott; and chef, Larry King.

Annual production: 1850 barrels

Flagship brand: Boston's Best Burton (bitter)

Major top-fermented brands: Amber Bitter, Blonde Ale, Burton Ale, Golden Ale, Old Ale, Porter, Stout

Major seasonal brands: ESB, IPA, Smoked Dunker-Weizen, Wheat

## Dock Street Brewing
Brewery & Restaurant
Two Logan Square
18th & Cherry Streets
Philadelphia, PA 19103

The company was founded in 1986 by Philadelphia chef Jeffrey Ware and the beer was contract brewed until Ware opened his own Philadelphia brewery/restaurant in 1990.

Annual production: 10,000 barrels

Other brewery owned by the same company: Dock Street Brewing Company (Washington, DC)

Flagship brands: Dock Street Amber, Dock Street Bohemian Pilsner

Major top-fermented brands: Amber, IPA, Porter

Major bottom-fermented brands: Bock, Bohemian Pilsner, Dortmunder, Dunkel, Helles, Pils, Weiss

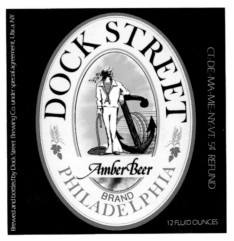

## Eastern Brewing
334 North Washington Street
Hammonton, NJ 08037

This brewery was established in 1933 at the end of Prohibition as Eastern Beverage Corporation. It has brewed under a wide variety of mainly budget brand names—including Colonial, Fox Head, Garden State and Tube City—over the ensuing years.

Annual production: 400,000 barrels

Major bottom-fermented brands: Canadian Ace, Milwaukee Premium, Old German

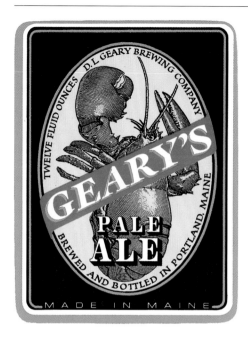

## DL Geary Brewing

38 Evergreen Drive
Portland, ME 04103

This brewery was founded by David Geary in 1986.

Annual production: 9000 barrels

Flagship brand: Geary's Pale Ale

Major top-fermented brands: Geary's Pale Ale, Hampshire Special Ale

Major seasonal brand: Hampshire Special Ale

## Genesee Brewing

445 St Paul Street
Rochester, NY 14605

The company was founded by Jacob Rau in 1878 and it is now America's largest family-operated, regional brewery. While Genesee beers are sold in only 24 states, the company is ranked seventh largest among all the brewing companies in the United States.

Annual production: 70,000 barrels

Subsidiaries of the same company: Fred Koch Brewery (Golden Anniversary Beer, Golden Anniversary Light), Shea's Brewery (Michael Shea's Irish Amber, Michael Shea's Black and Tan), Dundee's Brewery (JW Dundee's Honey Brown Lager)

Flagship brand: Genesee Beer

Major top-fermented brands: Genesee Cream Ale, 12 Horse Ale

Major bottom-fermented brands: Genesee Beer, Genny Light Beer, Genesee NA (Non-Alcoholic), Genny Ice Beer

Major seasonal brand: Genesee Bock Beer (January)

GABF Gold Medal: Koch's Golden Anniversary Beer, 1987; Black Horse Ale, 1988; Genesee Cream Ale, 1990, 1991

GABF Silver Medal: 12 Horse Ale, 1988; Genesee Cream Ale, 1987, 1988, 1993

## Gibbons/Stegmaier Brewery

The Lion, Inc
700 North Pennsylvania Avenue
Wilkes-Barre, PA 18703

The company was founded as the Luzerne County Brewing Company in 1905 and became Lion Brewing in 1910. It became The Lion in 1933 and has used the Gibbons, Stegmaier and Pocono brand names since that time.

Annual production: 250,000 barrels

Flagship brand: Gibbons

Major bottom-fermented brands: Gibbons, 1857, 1857 Dry, 1857 Light, Bartels, Esslinger, Liebotschaner, Lionshead, Stegmaier, Stegmaier Light

## Gritty's (Gritty McDuff's) Brewpub
396 Fore Street
Portland, ME 04101

This brewpub was founded near the Portland waterfront by Richard Pfeffer and Ed Stebbins in 1988.

Annual production: 1600 barrels

Flagship brand: McDuff's Best Bitter

Major top-fermented brands: McDuff's Best Bitter, Black Fly Stout, Portland Headlight Pale Ale

Major seasonal brands: Halloween Ale, Summer Wheat Ale

## Hartford Brewery
35 Pearl Street
Hartford, CT 06103

This brewpub was founded by Les Sinnock and Phil Hopkins in 1991.

Annual production: 1000 barrels

Major top-fermented brands: Thirty-six recipes, six on tap at all times. Arch Amber and Alet Pitbull Golden are stock ales. All varieties of ale, from Golden to Brown to Porter, Stout, Strong and Scotch, are served.

## John Harvard's Brew House
33 Dunster Street
Cambridge, MA 02138

This brewpub, located on Harvard Square, was founded by Gary F Gut and Grenville Byford in 1992.

Annual production: Under 500 barrels

Flagship brand: John Harvard's Pale Ale

Major top-fermented brands: Nut Brown Ale, Export Stout, 'Old Willy' India Pale Ale

Major bottom-fermented brands: All American Light Lager, Cristal Pilsner, Bockbier

Major seasonal brands: Mid-winter's Strong Ale, Celtic Ale

**Heurich:** See Olde Heurich (Washington, DC)

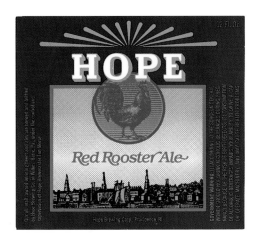

## Hope Brewing
669 Elmwood Avenue
Providence, RI 02907

This company was founded in 1988, with the beer produced under contract in Wilkes-Barre, PA by The Lion, Inc.

Flagship brand: Hope

Major top-fermented brand: Red Rooster Ale

Major bottom-fermented brands: Hope Lager, Hope Light Lager

Major seasonal brands: Bock Beer, Christmas Ale, Oktoberfest Beer

## Ipswich Brewing
25 Hayward Street
Ipswich, MA 01938

This brewery was founded by Paul Sylva, James Beauvais and James Renallo in 1992.

Annual production: 6000 barrels

Other brewery owned by the same company: Smuttynose Brewing Company, Inc

Flagship brand: Ipswich Ale

Major bottom-fermented brands: Ipswich Ale, Ipswich Dark Ale

**Iron City:** See Pittsburgh Brewing (Pittsburgh, PA)

## Jones Brewing
254 Second Street
Smithton, PA 15479

This brewery was founded by Welsh immigrant William B 'Stoney' Jones in 1907 as the Eureka Brewing Company. The brewery's original brand was Eureka Gold Crown, but because Stoney Jones habitually made personal sales calls to taverns in the area, it came to be known unofficially and later officially as 'Stoney's Beer.' Until recently, the brewery was operated under the presidency of William B 'Bill' Jones III.

Annual production: 100,000 barrels

Flagship brand: Stoney's

Major bottom-fermented brands: Esquire Extra Dry, Stoney's, Stoney's Light, Stoney's N/A Brew

GABF Silver Medals: Stoney's Lager, 1991; Stoney's Light Lager, 1991; Esquire Extra Dry Lager, 1993

## Kennebunkport Brewing (Federal Jack's Brew Pub)
8 Western Avenue, #6
Kennebunk, ME 04043

This brewpub was founded by Fred Forsley in 1992, who owned Federal Jack's restaurant.

Annual production: 500 barrels

Other brewery owned by the same company: The Shipyard Brewery (Portland, ME)

Flagship brand: The Shipyard Export Ale

Major top-fermented brands: The Shipyard Bluefin Stout, The Shipyard Goat Blue Light

Major seasonal brands: IPA, Prelude Ale, Winter Ale

**Koch:** See Genesee (Rochester, NY) and Boston Beer Company (Boston, MA)

## Latrobe Brewing
119 Jefferson Street
Latrobe, PA 15650

Latrobe Brewing was established in 1893 at a time when the town's only other brewery was located at St Vincent's Abbey and operated by Benedictine monks. The brewery at St Vin-

This brewpub was founded by Ray McNeill in 1991 in one of Brattleboro's oldest wood frame buildings, which has served as both the fire station and police station.

Annual production: Under 500 barrels

Major top-fermented brands: Big Nose Blond, Dead Horse India Pale Ale, Duck's Breath Bitter, Firehouse Pale, James Brown, McNeill's Special Bitter, Oatmeal Stout, Slopbucket Brown

Major bottom-fermented brands: Bohemian Pilsner, Bok Beer, Doc Feelgood's Pils, Payday Beer

## Manhattan Brewing

40-42 Thompson Street
New York, NY 10013

The brewery was founded in 1984 by Robert D'Addona in a former Consolidated Edison electrical substation. It closed in 1992 but reopened in 1993 under new ownership.

Annual production: Up to 40,000 barrels

Flagship brand: Manhattan Gold

GABF Gold Medal: Manhattan Gold Lager, 1989

GABF Silver Medal: D'Agostino Fresh, 1989

cent's closed in 1898 after 42 years of operation, but the brewery that took the name of the town survives to this day. The flagship Rolling Rock brand is named for the nearby Rolling Rock Estate, a horse ranch. An intriguing detail about Rolling Rock is the presence of the mysterious '33' symbol that appears on the back of the bottle. The company itself cannot remember why it was put there in the first place because the product was introduced in 1939. However, among the most popular answers to the riddle are that Prohibition was repealed in 1933; there are 33 words on the back of the 12 ounce Rolling Rock bottle; or that there are 33 letters in the ingredients of Rolling Rock—water, malt, rice, corn, hops and brewer's yeast.

Annual production: 1,000,000 barrels

Other brewery owned by same company: Latrobe is a subsidiary of Labatt's USA.

Flagship brand: Rolling Rock

Major bottom-fermented brands: Rolling Rock Light Beer, Rolling Rock Premium Beer

**The Lion, Inc:** See Gibbons/Stegmaier (Wilkes-Barre, PA)

**McDuff's:** See Gritty's (Portland, ME)

## McNeill's Brewery
90 Elliot Street
Brattleboro, VT 05301

## Mass Bay Brewing

306 Northern Avenue
Boston, MA 02210

This brewery was founded by Rich Doyle and partners in 1986, with the first beer delivered in June 1987.

Annual production: 13,000 barrels

Flagship brand: Harpoon Ale

Major top-fermented brands: Harpoon Ale, Harpoon Dark, Harpoon IPA, Harpoon Stout, Harpoon Winter Warmer

Major bottom-fermented brands: Harpoon Golden Lager, Harpoon Light, Harpoon Octoberfest

Major seasonal brands: Harpoon Stout (spring), Harpoon IPA (summer), Octoberfest (fall), Winter Warmer (winter)

## FX Matt Brewing (West End Brewery)

811 Edward Street
Utica, NY 13502-4092

This major regional brewery was founded by Charles Bierbauer as the Columbia Brewery in 1853. The company was taken over in 1888 by Francis Xavier Matt I, and organized as West End Brewing. The brewery was renamed for FX Matt in 1980, 22 years after his death. The brand name Utica Club, which was introduced for the soft drinks produced by the company during Prohibition, became so popular that it was retained afterward for West End's beer products.

Annual production: 800,000 barrels

Flagship brand: Matt's Premium Lager

Major top-fermented brand: Saranac Black & Tan

Major bottom-fermented brands: Freeport USA, Matt's Light, Matt's Premium Lager, Saranac Adirondac Lager, Saranac Golden Pilsner, Utica Club

Major seasonal brand: Season's Best Holiday Amber

GABF Gold Medals: Matt's Premium Lager, 1984; Saranac Adirondac Lager, 1991

GABF Silver Medal: Saranac 1888 All-Malt Lager (Continental Pilsener), 1987

**Michelob:** See Anheuser-Busch (St Louis, MO)

## Mountain Brewers

Box 140, Route 4
The Marketplace
Bridgewater, VT 05034

The brewery was founded in 1989 and expanded in 1992.

Annual production: 13,000 barrels

Flagship brand: Long Trail Ale

Major top-fermented brands: Brown Bag Ale (draft only), Long Trail IPA, Long Trail Kölsch, Long Trail Stout

GABF Gold Medal: Long Trail Ale, 1991

GABF Silver Medals: Long Trail Ale, 1990; Northern Light, 1991

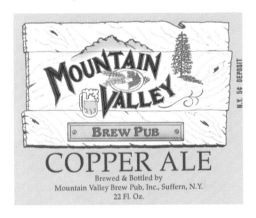

## Mountain Valley Brewpub

122 Orange Avenue
Suffern, NY 10901

This brewery/restaurant was founded by Lon Lauterio and Lisa Cantillo in 1992.

Annual production: 1200 barrels

Flagship brand: Copper Ale

Major top-fermented brands: Christmas Ale, Copper Ale, Pale Ale, Porter, Stout, Wheat Beer

Major bottom-fermented brands: Amber Lager, Golden Lager

Major seasonal brands: Blonde Double Bock, Christmas Pale Ale, Maibock, Oktoberfest, Rauch Bier

## New England Brewing Company

25 Commerce Street
Norwalk, CT 06850

The original New England Brewing Company was founded in 1897 and, like most breweries, closed during Prohibition. It was reopened in 1936 by J Harold Murray, the stage personality, and finally closed in 1940.

This brewery was founded in February 1989 by Marcia and Richard King to 'bring fresh quality beer back to the region.' New England's beer is brewed in small batches with ingredients of the highest quality. Inspired by the discovery that handcrafted beers have a wonderful taste and great character, the Kings added a full range of seasonal beers. The brewery continues to expand to meet the growing demand throughout the Northeast, and plans are underway to build a new brewery in the historic section of South Norwalk. The new facility will house German copper brewing kettles, a New England Brewing Museum and a brewpub where the brewing process can be seen firsthand.

Annual production: 5000 barrels

Flagship brand: Atlantic Amber, Gold Stock Ale

Major seasonal brands: Oatmeal Stout (January-May) Light Lager (spring-summer), Holiday Ale (November-January)

GABF Gold Medal: Atlantic Amber, 1993

## New Haven Brewing
458 Grand Avenue
New Haven, CT 06513

The brewery was founded by Mike Gettings in 1989.

Annual production: 6000 barrels

Flagship brand: Elm City Connecticut Ale

Major seasonal brands: Belle Dock Barley Wine Style Ale

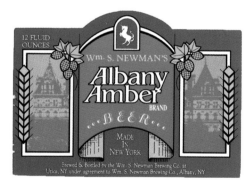

## William S Newman Brewing
84 Chestnut Street
Albany, NY 12210

Founded by William S Newman in 1981, the brewery was the first microbrewery in the East and, incredibly, the first new company to establish a brewery in New York State since Prohibition. Older breweries had changed hands or built new plants during that period, but all of the more than 700 previous breweries in New York had roots before 1934, and the majority of those had both opened and closed prior to Prohibition.

Serving as head brewer, William S Newman himself brewed the company's products in a brewhouse whose 6500-barrel capacity certainly made it one of the nation's smallest. However, demand for Newman's products eventually increased to the point where he closed the brewery in 1988 and moved to contract production at FX Matt (Utica, NY).

Major brands: Albany Amber Ale, Newman's Albany Amber Beer, Newman's Tricentennial Pale Ale, Newman's Winter Ale.

## Northampton Brewery
Brewster Court Bar & Grill
11 Brewster Court
Northampton, MA 01060

This brewery was founded by Peter Egelston in 1987.

Annual production: 1000 barrels

Major top-fermented brands: Golden, Northampton Amber, Old Brown Dog, Pale Ale, Porter

Major seasonal brands: Bock, Holiday Ale, Oktoberfest, Weizen

## Old Marlborough Brewing
Marlborough, MA 01752

Old Marlborough Brewing was founded in 1989 by Larry Bastien and three partners: Joseph Cunningham, AJ Morgan and Barry McCarthy.

Their Post Road Real Ale—named for the old New York to Boston thoroughfare—is produced under contract by Catamount Brewing in White River Junction, VT.

Annual production: Under 500 barrels

GABF Silver: Post Road Real Ale, 1989

**O'Doul's:** See Anheuser-Busch (St Louis, MO)

## Otter Creek Brewing
74 Exchange Street #1
Middlebury, VT 05753

This brewery was founded by Lawrence Miller in 1991.

Annual production: 6000 barrels

Flagship brand: Copper Ale

Major bottom-fermented brand: Helles Alt Beer

Major seasonal brands: Hickory Switch Smoked Amber Ale, Mud Bock Spring Ale, Stovepipe Porter, Summer Wheat Ale

## Ould Newbury Brewing
227 High Road
Newbury, MA 01951

This brewery was founded by Joseph Rolfe in 1992.

Annual production: 500-1000 barrels

Flagship brand: Yankee Ale (amber ale)

Major top-fermented brand: Ould Newbury Porter

Major seasonal brands: Summer Wheat, Ould Newbury Spiced Ale (November-December)

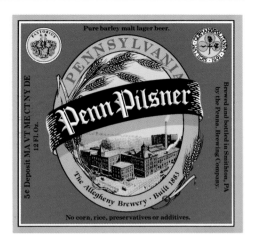

## Pennsylvania Brewing
Allegheny Brewery & Pub
800 Vinial Street
Pittsburgh, PA 15212

The company was founded by Thomas V Pastorius in 1986. After working in Germany for 12 years, Pastorius returned home to Pennsylvania with the idea to locally produce world-class German beers. In 1986, he founded the Pennsylvania Brewing Company, the first microbrewing company in Pennsylvania, and introduced his flagship brand, Penn Pilsner, at City Tavern in Philadelphia. The beer was contract produced while Pastorius worked to restore the historic Eberhardt & Ober Brewery buildings in Pittsburgh and to install a new brewery there. The brewery opened in 1987, followed by a beer hall and brewpub in 1989, which was expanded in 1992.

Annual production: 10,000 barrels

Flagship brand: Penn Pilsner

Major top-fermented brands: Altbier, Weizen, Weizen Bock

Major bottom-fermented brands: Kaiser Pils, Penn Pilsner, Penn Light Lager, Penn Dark

Major seasonal brands: Maezen (spring), Oktoberfest (fall), Celebrator Bock (Christmas)

GABF Gold Medals: Penn Light Lager, 1990, 1993

## Philadelphia Brewing
## Samuel Adams Brewhouse
1516 Sansom Street, 2nd Floor
Philadelphia, PA 19102

This brewpub was founded by Jim Koch with David and Judy Mink in 1989. It is a partnership of Koch's Boston Beer Company, makers of Samuel Adams, and the Sansom Street Oyster House.

Annual production: Under 500 barrels

Other brewery owned by same company: Jim Koch also owns Boston Beer Company (Boston, MA).

Major top-fermented brands: Ben Franklin's Gold, Poor Richard's Amber

GABF Silver Medal: George Washington's Porter, 1989

## Pittsburgh Brewing
3340 Liberty Avenue
Pittsburgh, PA 15201

The Pittsburgh Brewing Company, which is literally the trunk of the family tree of Pittsburgh brewers, traces its roots to the brewery founded by Edward Frauenheim and August Hoevler in 1861. The original brewery evolved into the Iron City Brewing Company by 1888, and in 1899 it was one of 21 brewing companies to merge into the Pittsburgh Brewing Consortium. Some of the other breweries were: Baeuerlein Brewing (1845-1934), Eberhardt & Ober Brewing (1852-1952), Earnest Hauch's Sons (1849-1904), Isaac Hippley & Sons Enterprise Brewery (1859-1899), Keystone Brewing (1887-1920), Philip Lauer (1874-1899), John Nusser's National Brewery (1852-1900), Frank Ober & Brothers (1858-1904), Phoenix Brewing (1845-1920), John Seiferth & Brothers (1865-1899), Herman Staub (1831-1920), Wainwright Brewing (1818-1920) and Michael Winter & Brothers (1874-1920). In 1986, the company became part of the Bond Group, owned by Australian entrepreneur Alan Bond, which at that time also owned Australia's Swan Brewing.

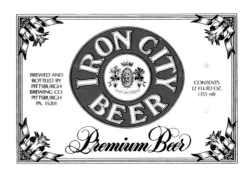

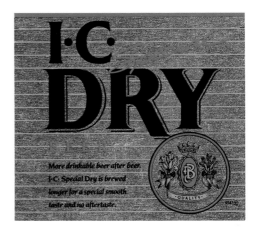

Annual production: 1,200,000 barrels

Flagship brand: Iron City Beer

Major brands: American, American Light, Iron City Beer, IC Special Dry, Iron City Light, Keene's Old Dutch, Old German, PBC Classic, PBC Classic Light

## Portsmouth Brewing
56 Market Street
Portsmouth, NH 03801

This brewpub was founded by brewer Peter Egelston in 1991, a co-founder in 1987 of Northampton Brewery (Northampton, MA).

Annual production: Under 500 barrels

Major top-fermented brands: Black Cat Stout, Blond Ale, Pale Ale

Major bottom-fermented brands: Amber Lager, Golden Lager

Major seasonal brands: Black Cherry Stout, Cranberry Holiday Ale, May Bock, Octoberfest

## Rochester Brewpub
800 Jefferson Road
Henrietta, NY 14623

This brewpub was founded in 1988.

Annual production: Under 500 barrels

Other breweries owned by the same company: Buffalo Brewing/Abbott Square Brewpub (Lackawanna, NY), Buffalo Brewpub (Williamsville, NY)

Major top-fermented brands: Amber Ale, Buffalo Bitter, Nickel City Dark, Oatmeal Stout, Pale Ale

Major bottom-fermented brand: Buffalo Pils

Major seasonal brands: Kringle, Octoberfest, Weiss

## Rohrbach Brewing
315 Gregory Street
Rochester, NY 14620

This brewpub was founded by John Urlaub in 1992 in the historic Old German House, a famous public house dating from 1908.

Annual production: Under 500 barrels

Major top-fermenting brand: Old Nate's Pale

Major bottom-fermenting brands: Gregory Street, Highland Amber

Major seasonal brands: Pilsner, Porter, Wheat

**Rolling Rock:** See Latrobe Brewing (Latrobe, PA)

**Schlitz:** See Stroh Brewing (Detroit, MI)

## C Schmidt & Sons
127 Edward Street
Philadelphia, PA 19123

The brewery was founded by Robert Coutrenny in 1859. C Schmidt & Sons of Philadelphia (not to be confused with the former Jacob Schmidt Brewing of St Paul, MN, which is now known as Minnesota Brewing) was acquired by Christian Schmidt in 1863 and has used its present name since 1892.

Annual production: 1,000,000 barrels

Flagship brand: Schmidt's

Major bottom-fermented brands: Christian Schmidt's Rheingold Extra Dry, Rheingold Extra Light, Schmidt's Bavarian

Major seasonal brands: Schmidt's Bavarian, Schmidt's Bock

## Seven Barrel Brewery
West Lebanon, NH

This brewpub was founded in 1993 by Greg and Nancy Noonan.

Annual production: 60 barrels

Other brewery owned by the same company: Vermont Pub & Brewery (Burlington, NH)

Major top-fermented brands: Old Number 7, New Dublin Brown Ale, Pale Ale

Major bottom-fermented brand: Wolf Roads Pilsner

## Slesar Brothers Brewing
Boston Beer Works
61 Brookline Avenue
Boston, MA 02215

This brewpub was founded by brothers Joe and Steve Slesar across the street from Fenway Park in 1992. Brewers include Bryan E Hoak, Paul G Hogan and Steve Slesar.

Annual production: 3500 barrels

Flagship brand: Boston Red

Major top-fermented brands: Acme Light, Bambino Light Ale, Blueberry, Buckeye Oatmeal Stout, Fenway Pale Ale, Hercules Strong Ale, Kenmore Kölsch

Major bottom-fermented brands: Amber Lager, Boston Beer Works Eisbock, Boston Beer Works Oktoberfest, Boston Victory Bock, Golden Lager, Pawtucket Pilsner

Major seasonal brands: Boston Beer Works Winter Works, Christmas Dark, Mardi Gras Bock, Oktoberfest

**Stegmaier:** See Gibbons/Stegmaier (Wilkes-Barre, PA)

**Stoney's:** See Jones Brewing (Smithton, PA)

## Stoudt Brewing
Box 880, Route 272
Adamstown, PA 19501

The brewery, and the adjacent Black Angus Brewery House Restaurant, were founded by Carol Stoudt in 1987.

Annual production: 3000 barrels

Flagship brand: Stoudt's

Major bottom-fermented brands: Adamstown Amber, Stoudt's Golden Lager, Stoudt's Pilsner, Stoudt's Weizen

Major seasonal brands: Bock, Dark, Doppelbock, Fest, Raspberry Wheat, Stout

GABF Gold Medals: Stoudt's Weizen, 1989, 1990; Bock Oktoberfest, 1990; Oktoberfest Maerzen, 1991; Pilsner, 1993

GABF Silver Medals: Stoudt's Golden Lager, 1988; Dortmunder Export, 1990; Doppelbock, 1991; Bock, 1993

## Straub Brewery
303 Sorg Street
St Mary's, PA 15857

The brewery was founded by Captain Charles Volk in 1872 as an extension of his City Hotel. It was taken over by Peter Straub, Volk's former

Brewed and bottled by the Stoudt Brewing Company, Adamstown, PA 19501.
Not pasteurized—keep refrigerated. 750 ml. (25.36 ozs.)

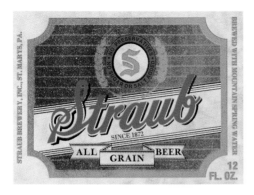

also operates breweries in Longview, TX; St Paul, MN; Tampa, FL; and Winston-Salem, NC.

Flagship brands: Schlitz, Stroh's

Major bottom-fermented brands: See Stroh Brewery (Detroit, MI) for list of Stroh brands.

Major seasonal brands: See Stroh Brewery (Detroit, MI) for a list of Stroh brands.

GABF Silver Medal: Signature, 1988

brewmaster, in 1876, and thereafter, except for two years (1911-1913) as the Benzinger Spring Brewery, the brewery has carried the Straub name.

Annual production: 40,000 barrels

Flagship brand: Straub

Major bottom-fermented brands: Straub, Straub Light

## Stroh Brewery
7880 Stroh Drive
Fogelsville, PA 18051

This brewery was founded by Schaefer Brewing (aka Piel Brothers) in 1972 and it became a Stroh Brewery in 1980 when Stroh purchased Schaefer.

Annual production: 4,500,000 barrels

Other breweries owned by same company: Stroh, which is headquartered in Detroit, MI,

## Sunday River Brewing
1 Sunday River Road
Bethel, ME 04217

The brewery, along with the adjacent Moose's Tale Pub and Restaurant, was founded by Grant Wilson and Hans Trupp in 1992.

Annual production: 1100-2000 barrels

Flagship brands: Black Bear Porter, Sunday River Alt

Major top-fermented brands: Mollyocket IPA, Pyrite Golden Ale, Redstone Ale

Major seasonal brands: Brass Balls Barleywine, Eisbock, Reindeer Rye, Stone Ridge Stout

## Syracuse Suds Factory

210-216 West Water Street
Syracuse, NY 13202

This brewpub was founded by Al Smith in 1993 in a building whose back steps were once used for unloading cargo from Erie Canal barges.

Annual production: Under 500 barrels

Major top-fermented brands: Amber Ale, Pale Ale

**Utica Club:** See FX Matt (Utica, NY)

## Vermont Pub and Brewery

144 College Street
Burlington, VT 05401

This brewpub was founded by Greg and Nancy Noonan in 1988.

Annual production: 975 barrels

Other brewery owned by the same company: The Seven Barrel Brewery (West Lebanon, NH)

Flagship brand: Burly Irish Ale

Major top-fermented brand: Dog Bite Bitter

Major bottom-fermented brand: Bombay Grab IPA

Major seasonal brand: Maple Ale

GABF Gold Medal: Auld Tartan Wee Heavy Strong Ale, 1993

**West End:** See FX Matt (Utica, NY)

**Wharf Rat:** See Oliver Breweries (Baltimore, MD)

## Windham Brewery

6 Flat Street
Brattleboro, VT 05301

This brewery/restaurant, which incorporates the Latchis Grille, was founded in 1991 in the basement of the 1938 art deco Latchis Hotel.

Annual production: 252 barrels

Major top-fermented brands: Moonbeam Ale, Ruby Brown Ale

Major bottom-fermented brand: Whetstone Golden Lager

Major seasonal brands: Frankenspice Xmas Ale, Oktoberfest

## Woodstock Brewing

20 St James Street
Kingston, NY 12401

The brewery was founded by Nat Collins in 1991 in a building near the edge of Kingston's Stockade section, settled by the Dutch in the seventeenth century, and the site of the first meeting of the state senate during the American Revolution. The brick structure that houses the brewery was built around 1830 as the Hermance Foundry.

Annual production: 1200-1500 barrels

Flagship brands: Big Indian Porter, Hudson Lager

Major top-fermented brands: Big Indian Porter, Roundout Stout, St James Ale

Major bottom-fermented brands: Hudson Lager, Woodstock Celebrated Maibock

Major seasonal brand: Ichabod Crane

## DG Yuengling & Son
5th & Manhantongo Streets
Pottsville, PA 17901

The oldest existing brewery in the United States, DG Yuengling & Son is alive and well, a family-owned and family-managed brewing company that is producing at capacity and brewing a wide variety of beer styles. Founded by David G Yuengling and his son in 1829, the brewery is, after Molson in Canada (1786), the second oldest in North America.

Annual production: 247,000 barrels

Flagship brand: Yuengling Premium

Major top-fermenting brands: Black & Tan, Lord Chesterfield Ale, Yuengling Porter

Major bottom-fermented brands: Yuengling Premium, Yuengling Premium Light, Yuengling Traditional Amber Lager

## Zip City Brewing
3 West 18th Street
New York, NY 10011

Manhattan's second brewpub was founded in 1991 in the building that once housed the National Temperance Society. The name 'Zip City' is derived from a term used by Sinclair Lewis in his novel *Babbit*.

Annual production: Under 1000 barrels

Major bottom-fermented brands: Dunkel, Helles, Märzen, Pilsener, Vienna

Major seasonal brands: Bock, Doppelbock, Maibock, Oktoberfest

# THE MIDDLE ATLANTIC AND SOUTH

**Samuel Adams:** See Boston Beer Company (Boston, MA) and Philadelphia Brewing (Philadelphia, PA)

## Abita Brewing
PO Box 762
Abita Springs, LA 70420

This brewery was founded by Jim Patton in 1986. It is reported that the Indians in the area believed that Abita Springs water protected them from yellow fever. Whether or not this is true, today, Abita Brewing uses that same spring water to brew their beers, which were designed to complement Louisiana cuisine.

Annual production: 20,000 barrels

Flagship brand: Abita Amber

Major top-fermented brand: Turbodog

Major bottom-fermented brands: Amber, Golden

Major seasonal brands: Bock, Fall Fest, Wheat, XXX-MAS

## Anheuser-Busch
3000 East Busch Boulevard
Tampa, FL 33612

This brewery was started by Anheuser-Busch in 1959.

Annual production: 2,600,000 barrels

Other breweries owned by the same company: See Anheuser-Busch, St Louis, MO for a list of Anheuser-Busch breweries.

Flagship brand: Budweiser

Major bottom-fermented brands: Budweiser, Bud Light, Busch, O'Doul's

See Anheuser-Busch, St Louis, MO for a list of medals awarded to Anheuser-Busch beers.

## Anheuser-Busch
775 Gellhorn Drive
Houston, TX 77029

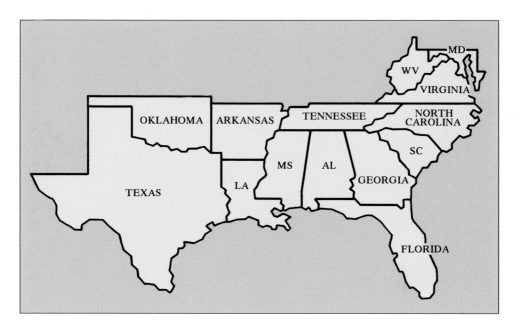

This brewery was started by Anheuser-Busch in 1966.

Annual production: 9,300,000 barrels

Other breweries owned by the same company: See Anheuser-Busch, St Louis, MO for a list of Anheuser-Busch breweries.

Flagship brand: Budweiser

Major bottom-fermented brands: Budweiser, Bud Light, Bud Dry, Michelob, Michelob Light, Michelob Dry, Natural Light, Busch, Busch Light Draft

See Anheuser-Busch, St Louis, MO for a list of medals awarded to Anheuser-Busch beers.

## Anheuser-Busch

111 Busch Drive
Jacksonville, FL 32229

This brewery was started by Anheuser-Busch in 1969.

Annual production: 7,200,000 barrels

Other breweries owned by the same company: See Anheuser-Busch, St Louis, MO for a list of Anheuser-Busch breweries.

Flagship brand: Budweiser

Major bottom-fermented brands: Budweiser, Bud Light, Michelob, Michelob Light, Michelob Dry, Natural Light, Busch

See Anheuser-Busch, St Louis, MO for a list of medals awarded to Anheuser-Busch beers.

## Anheuser-Busch

7801 Pocahontas Trail
Williamsburg, VA 23185

This brewery was started by Anheuser-Busch in 1972.

Annual production: 9,200,000 barrels

Other breweries owned by the same company: See Anheuser-Busch, St Louis, MO for a list of Anheuser-Busch breweries.

Flagship brand: Budweiser

Major bottom-fermented brands: Budweiser, Bud Light, Bud Dry, Michelob, Michelob Light, Michelob Dark, Natural Light, Busch, Busch Light

See Anheuser-Busch, St Louis, MO for a list of medals awarded to Anheuser-Busch beers.

## Anheuser-Busch

Cartersville, GA 30120

This brewery was started by Anheuser-Busch in 1993.

Annual production: 3,500,000 barrels

Other breweries owned by the same company: See Anheuser-Busch, St Louis, MO for a list of Anheuser-Busch breweries.

Flagship brand: Budweiser

See Anheuser-Busch, St Louis, MO for a list of medals awarded to Anheuser-Busch beers.

## Baltimore Brewing
104 Ablemarle Street
Baltimore, MD 21202

This brewery was founded in 1989. The president and master brewer is Theo DeGroen.

Annual production: 3000 barrels

Flagship brand: DeGroen's Lager

Major bottom-fermented brands: DeGroen's Dark, DeGroen's Lager, DeGroen's Pils

Major seasonal brand: DeGroen's Märzen

## Bardo Rodeo
2000 Wilson Boulevard
Arlington, VA 22201

This brewery was founded by Bill Stewart in 1993 in the old Olmstead Oldsmobile dealership and features the striking sight of a Plymouth Fury crashing through the plate glass front. The etimology of the name is intriguing. According to the *Tibetan Book of the Dead*, the Bardo is where the deceased spend 49 days before travelling to the underworld. A rodeo is a competition of cowboy skills that originated in the West.

Annual production: Under 1000 barrels

Flagship brand: To be announced

## Beach Brewing
Mill Bakery, Eatery & Brewery
5905 South Kirkman Road
Orlando, FL 32819

This brewery was founded in 1992.

Annual production: Under 1000 barrels

Major bottom-fermented brands: Beach Blonde, Knight Light, Magic Brew, Red Rock

## Birmingham Brewing
3118 3rd Avenue South
Birmingham, AL 35233

This brewery was founded by R Ben Hogan III in 1992 and is named for the original Birmingham Brewing Company, which existed prior to the county going dry in 1908.

Annual production: 6000 barrels

Flagship brand: Red Mountain Red Ale

Major top-fermented brand: Red Mountain Golden Ale

Major bottom-fermented brand: Red Mountain Golden Lager

Major seasonal brand: Red Mountain Wheat Beer

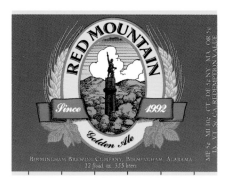

## Blue Ridge Brewing

709 West Main Street
Charlottesville, VA 22901

This brewery was founded by Paul Summers in 1988 and was Virginia's first restaurant/ brewery.

Annual production: 400 barrels

Flagship brands: Afton Ale, Hawksbill Lager, Humpback Stout, Piney River Lager

Major seasonal brands: Sugar Hollow Heller Bock, White Oak Weizen

## Bohannon Brewing

134 2nd Avenue North
Nashville, TN 37201

This brewery is the mid-South's first micro-brewery. It was founded by Lyndsay Bohannon in 1989 on the site of Crossman & Drucker Brewing (1859), Nashville's first brewery. Bohannon began distributing its Market Street Beer to local taverns and retail outlets in 1989.

Annual production: 5000 barrels

Flagship brand: Market Street

Major top-fermented brand: Market Street Golden Ale

Major bottom-fermented brands: Market Street Pilsner, Market Street Wheat

Major seasonal brands: Market Street Bock, Market Street Oktoberfest, Market Street Winter Lager

GABF Gold Medal: Market Street Oktoberfest, 1989

GABF Silver Medal: Market Street Oktoberfest, 1990

## Boscos Pizza Kitchen & Brewery

7615 West Farmington #30
Germantown, TN 38138

The brewpub was founded by Chuck Skypeck in 1992 with 18 styles of beer sold on the premises only.

Annual production: 700 barrels

Flagship brand: The Famous Flaming Stone Beer

Major top-fermented brands: Bluff City Amber, Germantown Alt, Tennessee Cream Ale

## Bricktown Brewery

One North Oklahoma Avenue
Oklahoma City, OK 73104-2413

This brewery was founded by Bryan Jester in 1992 in the Bricktown section of Oklahoma City.

Annual production: 1320 barrels

Major top-fermented brands: Bison Weisen, Copperhead Ale

Major bottom-fermented brand: Landrun Lager

Major seasonal brands: Bricktown, Stout

**Budweiser:** See Anheuser-Busch (St Louis, MO)

**Busch:** See Anheuser-Busch (St Louis, MO)

## Capitol City Brewing Company

1100 New York Avenue NW
Washington, DC 20005

Founded by Jack Keneily, William Foster and David von Storch in 1992, Capitol City operates a well-regarded brewery/restaurant in the heart of the nation's capital near the Mall. It is

the first brewery to operate in Washington, DC since Christian Heurich Brewing closed in 1956.

Annual production: 1400 barrels

Major top-fermented brands: Capitol City Brewing Company Alt, Capitol City Brewing Company Bräun Ale, Capitol City Brewing Company Kölsch

Major bottom-fermented brand: Capitol City Brewing Company Pilsener

Major seasonal brands: Fest Ale, Porter Stark Ale, Stout

## Celis Brewery
PO Box 141636
Austin, TX 78754

This brewery was founded in 1992 by Pierre Celis, the former owner of the De Kluis (The Cloister) Brewery in Hoegaarden, Belgium. He was responsible for the 1966 revival of Belgian witbier (white beer)—the cloudy ale made with almost 50% unmalted wheat. Celis is also brewing in Belgium for European distribution of Celis White and Celis Pale Bock.

Annual production: 10,000 barrels

Flagship brand: Celis White

Major top-fermented brands: Celis Pale Bock, Celis Grand Cru, Celis Raspberry

Major bottom-fermented brand: Celis Golden

GABF Gold Medals: Celis White (Herb-Spice), 1992, 1993

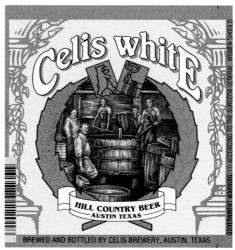

## Coors Brewing Company
Shenandoah Brewery
Route 340 South
Elkton, VA 22827

This brewery was established in 1987 as an expansion site by Coors Brewing Company of Golden, CO.

Annual production: 4,000,000 barrels

Other brewery owned by the same company: Coors Brewing Company (Golden, CO)

Flagship brand (at the Shennandoah Brewery): Coors Light

Major bottom-fermented brands: Coors, Coors Dry, Coors Cutter, Coors Extra Gold Draft, Coors Light, Keystone, Keystone Dry, Keystone Light, Turbo 1000

GABF Gold Medals: Coors Extra Gold Draft, 1989, 1990; Keystone Light, 1991; Coors Dry, 1991

GABF Silver Medals: Coors, 1989; Coors Light, 1990; Winterfest, 1990, 1993

## Crescent City Brewhouse
527 Decatur Street
New Orleans, LA 70130

This brewery/restaurant was founded by German brewmaster Wolfram Koehler in 1991.

Annual production: 1500 barrels

Flagship brand: Red Stallion Amber Lager (Märzen, German lager)

Major top-fermented brand: Weissbeer

Major bottom-fermented brands: Black Forest, Red Stallion Amber Lager, Pilsener

Major seasonal brands: Christmas Dark, Carnival, Spring Bock, Oktoberfest

## Dallas Brewing
West End Brewery
The Brewery Building
703 McKinney Avenue
Dallas, TX 75202

This brewery was founded about 1991 on the site of the original Dallas Brewing Company, founded in 1890.

Annual production: 3500 barrels

Major brands: Dallas Gold, Outback Lager, Texas Bluebonnet, Texas Cowboy, West End Lager

## Dilworth Brewing
1301 East Boulevard
Charlotte, NC 28203

This brewpub was founded about 1991.

Annual production: 1080 barrels

Major top-fermented brands: Albemarle Ale, Dilworth Porter

Major bottom-fermented brands: Latta Lite, Reed's Gold Pilsner

## Dixie Brewing
2401 Tulane Avenue
New Orleans, LA 70119

This brewery was founded in 1907, and until 1986 it was the only remaining brewery in the Louisiana city that once was the brewing capital of the entire South.

Annual production: 300,000 barrels

Flagship brand: Dixie

Major bottom-fermented brands: Dixie, Dixie Amber Light, Dixie Blackened Voodoo Lager, Fischer, Fischer Light, New Orleans Best, New Orleans Best Light

GABF Silver Medal: Dixie Amber Light, 1988

## Dock Street Brewing Brewery & Restaurant

Warner Theater Building
13th & Pennsylvania Avenue NW
Washington, DC 20005

The company was founded by Philadelphia chef Jeffrey Ware.

Annual production: Under 10,000 barrels

Other brewery owned by the same company: Dock Street Brewing Company (Philadelphia, PA)

Flagship brands: Dock Street Amber, Dock Street Bohemian Pilsner

Major top-fermented brands: Amber, IPA, Porter

Major bottom-fermented brands: Bock, Bohemian Pilsner, Dortmunder, Dunkel, Helles, Pils, Weiss

**Duncan:** See Florida Brewery (Auburndale, FL)

## Florida Brewery

202 Gandy Road
Auburndale, FL 33823

This brewery was founded as Duncan Brewing Company in 1973. It no longer brews its own brands, concentrating instead on contract

brewing. The principal brands brewed formerly were Dunk's Beer, Dunk's Ale, Fischer's Beer and Ale, Regal Beer, Master's Choice and ABC.

Annual production: 150,000 barrels

Major brands: ABC, America's Choice, Bayside, Bräun, Flying Aces, Gator Lager Beer, Hatney, Master's Choice, Old West Amber, Prince Gold Lager

GABF Gold Medal: Old West Amber, 1993

## Friends Brewing (Helenboch Brewing)

PO Box 29464
Atlanta, GA

This microbrewery was founded in 1989 by Don Scroggins, Rick Roberts, Frank Cronin and Phil Churchman. The brewery later closed but a new facility will open in Atlanta in 1995. In the meantime the beer is contract brewed by August Schell (New Ulm, MN).

Annual production: 1200 barrels

Flagship brand: Helenboch Beer

Major seasonal brands: Georgia Peach Wheat, Helenboch Oktoberfest

GABF Gold Medal: Helenboch Oktoberfest, 1991

GABF Silver Medal: Helenboch Beer, 1989

## Greenshields Pub & Brewery

214 East Martin Street
Raleigh, NC 27601

This brewpub was founded by Gary Greenshields in 1989.

Annual production: 1200 barrels

Major top-fermented brands: Amber Bitter, Oatmeal Stout, Porter

Major bottom-fermented brand: Pilsner Dark Lager

Major seasonal brands: Christmas Bitter, Dark Wheat, Nut Brown Ale, Wheat Beer

## G Heileman Brewing
4501 Hollins Ferry Road
Baltimore, MD 21227

This brewery was founded by Carling Brewing Company in 1961 and sold to G Heileman of La Crosse, WI in 1979.

Annual production: Over 10,000 barrels

Other breweries owned by same company: A division of G Heileman Brewing (La Crosse, WI), which also owns Blitz-Weinhard (Portland, OR), Lone Star (San Antonio, TX) and Rainier (Seattle, WA).

Flagship brand: Carling Black Label

Major top-fermented brands: Rainier Ale, Weinhard's Ale

Major bottom-fermented brands: Heileman's Old Style, Heileman's Old Style Light, Heileman's Special Export, Heileman's Special Export Light, Blatz, Carling Black Label, Colt 45, Colt 45 Dry, Lone Star, Lone Star Light, Lone Star Dry, Mickey's, Rainier, Rainier Light, Rainier Dry, Jacob Schmidt, Jacob Schmidt Light, Henry Weinhard's Private Reserve, Henry Weinhard's Private Reserve Dark

GABF Gold Medals: Rainier Beer (American Light Lager), 1987; Heileman's Old Style, 1988

GABF Silver Medals: Heileman's Special Export, 1991; Heileman's Special Export Light, 1993; Mickey's Malt Liquor, 1993

**Helenboch:** See Friends Brewing (Atlanta, GA)

## Hops Grill & Brewery
18825 US Highway 19 North
Clearwater, FL 34624

This brewpub was founded in 1989, the first in a chain of Hops pubs.

Annual production: Under 500 barrels

Other breweries owned by same company: Hops Grill & Bar (2 in Tampa, FL), Hops Grill & Bar (Palm Harbor, FL)

Flagship brand: Hops Extra Pale Ale

Major top-fermented brand: Hammerhead Red

Major bottom-fermented brands: Clearwater Light, Hops Golden Ale

Major seasonal brand: Anniversary Ale

## Hops Grill & Bar
14303 North Dale Mabry Highway
Tampa, FL 33618

This brewery was founded in 1991 as part of a chain of Hops brewpubs.

Annual production: Under 500 barrels

Other breweries owned by same company: Hops Grill & Brewery (Clearwater, FL), Hops Grill & Bar (Tampa, FL), Hops Grill & Bar (Palm Harbor, FL)

Flagship brand: Hops Extra Pale Ale

Major top-fermented brand: Hammerhead Red

Major bottom-fermented brands: Clearwater Light, Hops Golden Ale

## Hops Grill & Bar
327 North Dale Mabry Highway
Tampa, FL 33609

This brewery was founded in 1992, as part of a chain of Hops brewpubs.

Annual production: Under 500 barrels

Other breweries owned by same company: Hops Grill & Brewery (Clearwater, FL), Hops Grill & Bar (Tampa, FL), Hops Grill & Bar (Palm Harbor, FL)

Flagship brand: Hops Extra Pale Ale

Major top-fermented brand: Hammerhead Red

Major bottom-fermented brands: Clearwater Light, Hops Golden Ale

## Hops Grill & Bar
33086 US Highway 19 North
Palm Harbor, FL 34684

This brewery was founded in 1992, as part of a chain of Hops brewpubs.

Annual production: Under 500 barrels

Other breweries owned by same company: Hops Grill & Brewery (Clearwater, FL), Hops Grill & Bar (2 in Tampa, FL)

Annual production: Under 500 barrels

Flagship brand: Hops Extra Pale Ale

Major top-fermented brand: Hammerhead Red

Major bottom-fermented brands: Clearwater Light, Hops Golden Ale

## Irish Times Pub & Brewery
9920 Alt A1A, Suite 810
Palm Beach Gardens, FL 33410

This brewpub was founded in 1991.

Annual production: Under 500 barrels

Major top-fermented brands: Irish Lite, Irish Pale, Irish Red

Major seasonal brands: Dry Pale, Irish Red Raspberry, Octoberfest, Trappist Ale

## Kelly's Caribbean Bar, Grill, & Brewery
301 Whitehead Street
Key West, FL 33040

This brewpub was founded by film star Kelly McGillis and her husband, Fred Tillman, in 1993 in the former Pan American World Airways terminal.

Annual production: Under 500 barrels

Major top-fermented brands: Havana Red, Key West Golden, Paradiso Caribe, Southern Clipper (non-alcoholic)

## Loggerhead Brewpub & Restaurant
2006 West Vandalia Road
Greensboro, NC 27407

This brewpub was founded in 1990.

Annual production: Under 500 barrels

Flagship brand: Loggerhead

Major top-fermented brands: General Green, Gate City

Major bottom-fermented brands: Cherry Pilsner, Loggerhead Light, Loggerhead Pilsener

## Lone Star
## G Heileman Brewing
600 Lone Star Boulevard
San Antonio, TX 78204

Lone Star Brewing, which was independent until 1976 and owned by Olympia, was acquired by G Heileman in 1983. Despite its absentee ownership from Washington and Wisconsin since 1976, the Lone Star brand developed a strong cult following within its home state during the 1970s. Immortalized in the songs of Willie Nelson, Waylon Jennings and Jerry Jeff Walker, Lone Star is reverently known as 'the National Beer of Texas.'

Other brewery owned by same company: Lone Star is a subsidiary of G Heileman (La Crosse, WI)

Flagship brand: Lone Star

Major brands: Lone Star, Lone Star Light, Lone Star Dry

GABF Silver Medals: Lone Star, 1993; Lone Star Light, 1993

## Lone Star Cantina & Brewery
108 Campbell Avenue SE
Roanoke, VA 24011

This brewpub was founded as Blue Muse Brewing in 1991, closed in 1992 and reopened in 1993 as the Lone Star.

Annual production: Under 500 barrels

Major top-fermented brands: Estrella de Oro, Estrella Negra, Palona

Major seasonal brands: Esmoralda, Navidad

## McGuire's Irish Pub & Brewery
600 East Gregory Street
Pensacola, FL 32501

This brewpub was founded by McGuire Martin and brewmaster Steve Fried in 1988, although McGuire's pub and restaurant were established in 1974. Contract beer is also made by the Oldenburg Brewery in Kentucky.

Annual production: 800 barrels

Flagship brand: McGuire's Irish Red Ale

Major top-fermented brands: McGuire's Light, McGuire's Porter, McGuire's Stout

Major seasonal brands: Barleywine, Brown Ale, Christmas Ale, Lemon Shandy, Raspberry Wheat, Oktoberfest Amber

GABF Silver Medal: Christmas Ale, 1990

**Market Street:** See Bohannon (Nashville, TN)

## Market Street Pub
120 Southwest First Avenue
Gainesville, FL 32601

This brewpub was founded in 1989 in a 100-year-old grocery store.

Annual production: Under 500 barrels

Major top-fermented brands: Downtown Brown, Gainesville Gold, Kooka Brew

Major seasonal brands: Oktoberfest, Winter Special

**Michelob:** See Anheuser-Busch (St Louis, MO)

## Mill Bakery, Eatery & Brewery
11491 Cleveland Avenue
Fort Meyers, FL 33907

The Mill Bakery, Eatery & Brewery chain originated as a Huntsville, AL bakery and eatery. The first two brewpubs in the chain opened in 1989 in Gainesville and Tallahassee, FL, but these have since closed. This brewpub was founded as Kidder's Brewery in 1991, closed and reopened under Mill management in 1993.

Annual production: Under 500 barrels

Other breweries owned by same company:

Mill Bakery, Eatery & Brewery (Charlotte, NC), Mill Bakery, Eatery & Brewery (Orlando, FL), Mill Bakery, Eatery & Brewery (Winter Park, FL)

Major top-fermented brands: K Rock Red, Magic Brew, Scottish Ale, Seminole Light

GABF Silver Medals: Oktoberfest, 1990, 1991

## Mill Bakery, Eatery & Brewery
330 West Fairbanks
Winter Park, FL 32789

The Mill Bakery, Eatery & Brewery chain originated as a Huntsville, AL bakery and eatery. The first two brewpubs in the chain opened in 1989 in Gainseville and Tallahassee, FL, but these have since closed.

Annual production: 1000 barrels

Other breweries owned by same company: Mill Bakery, Eatery & Brewery (Fort Meyers, FL), Mill Bakery, Eatery & Brewery (Orlando, FL), Mill Bakery, Eatery & Brewery (Charlotte, NC)

Major top-fermented brands: Harvest Light, Knight Light, Magic Brew, Rolling Red

Major seasonal brands: Holiday Ale, Wheat Field Dry

GABF Silver Medals: Oktoberfest, 1990, 1991

## Mill Bakery, Eatery & Brewery
5905 South Kirkman Road
Orlando, FL 32819

The Mill chain originated as a Huntsville, AL bakery and eatery. The first two brewpubs opened in 1989 in Gainseville and Tallahassee, FL, but these have since closed. This brewpub was founded in 1992.

Annual production: Under 500 barrels

Other breweries owned by same company: Mill Bakery, Eatery & Brewery (Fort Meyers, FL), Mill Bakery, Eatery & Brewery (Charlotte, NC), Mill Bakery, Eatery & Brewery (Winter Park, FL)

Major top-fermented brands: Beach Blonde, Knight Light, Magic Brew, Red Rock

GABF Silver Medals: Oktoberfest, 1990, 1991

## Mill Bakery, Eatery & Brewery
122 West Woodland Road
Charlotte, NC 28217

The Mill Bakery, Eatery & Brewery chain originated as a Huntsville, AL bakery and eatery. The first two brewpubs in the chain opened in 1989 in Gainseville and Tallahassee, FL, but these have since closed.

Annual production: Under 500 barrels

Other breweries owned by same company: Mill Bakery, Eatery & Brewery (Fort Meyers, FL), Mill Bakery, Eatery & Brewery (Orlando, FL), Mill Bakery, Eatery & Brewery (Winter Park, FL)

Major top-fermented brands: Harvest Gold, Hornet Tail Ale, Wheat Field Dry

Major seasonal brands: Spiced Ale, Wooly's Winterfest

GABF Silver Medals: Oktoberfest, 1990, 1991

## Miller Brewing
405 Cordele Road
Albany, GA 31708-6601

This brewery was founded by Miller Brewing in 1980. See Miller Brewing, Milwaukee, WI, for details on the history of the company.

Annual production: 8,000,000 barrels

Other breweries owned by same company: See Miller Brewing, Milwaukee, WI, for a list of Miller breweries.

Major brands: See Miller Brewing, Milwaukee, WI, for a list of Miller brands.

GABF Medals: See Miller Brewing, Milwaukee, WI, for a list of GABF medals awarded to the company.

## Miller Brewing
PO Box 3327
Eden, NC 27288-2099

This brewery was founded by Miller Brewing in 1978. See Miller Brewing, Milwaukee, WI, for details on the history of the company.

Annual production: 8,000,000 barrels

Other breweries owned by same company: See Miller Brewing, Milwaukee WI, for a list of Miller breweries.

Major brands: See Miller Brewing, Milwaukee, WI, for a list of Miller brands.

GABF Medals: See Miller Brewing, Milwaukee, WI, for a list of GABF medals awarded to the company.

## Miller Brewing
7001 South Freeway
Fort Worth, TX 76134-4098

This brewery was founded by Carling Brewing in 1964, closed in 1966 and sold to Miller Brewing in 1979. See Miller Brewing, Milwaukee, WI, for details on the history of the Miller Brewing Company.

Annual production: 7,500,000 barrels

Other breweries owned by same company: See Miller Brewing, Milwaukee WI, for a list of Miller breweries.

Major brands: See Miller Brewing, Milwaukee, WI, for a list of Miller brands.

GABF Medals: See Miller Brewing, Mil-

waukee, WI, for a list of GABF medals awarded to the company.

**O'Doul's:** See Anheuser-Busch (St Louis, MO)

## Old Dominion Brewing
44633 Guilford Drive
Ashburn, VA 22011

This brewery was founded by Jerry Bailey in 1989. Today, Dominion beers are among the most widely available specialty beers in Virginia. Dominion Lager is, for example, served in the period restaurants of Colonial Williamsburg.

Annual production: 10,225 barrels

Flagship brand: Dominion Lager

Major top-fermented brands: Dominion Ale, Dominion Stout, Old Dubliner Irish Amber Ale

Major bottom-fermented brands: Aviator Amber, Hard Times, Virginia Native Brite

Major seasonal brands: Holiday Ale, Millennium, Octoberfest, Spring Bock, Summer Wheat

## The Olde Heurich Brewing Company
1111 34th Street NW
Washington, DC 20007

This brewery was founded by Gary Heurich in 1986. The original Heurich Brewing Company was founded by Gary's grandfather, Christian Heurich, in 1873. His Märzen beer won a medal for purity and excellence at the Paris Exposition of 1900. Heurich started a brewery in 1873 that overlooked the Potomac on the site now occupied by the Kennedy Center for the Performing Arts. Christian Heurich supervised the brewery until his death in 1945 at the age of 102. His son kept the brewery in business until 1965.

Annual production: 3600 barrels

Flagship brand: Olde Heurich Märzen

Major bottom-fermented brand: Olde Heurich Märzen

## Oliver Breweries (The Wharf Rat Camden Yards)
206 West Pratt Street
Baltimore, MD 21201

This brewery/restaurant was founded by William and Carole Oliver in 1993, featuring

hand-pumped, naturally conditioned English-style ales, including one regular, Oliver's Best Bitter, and several seasonals. Some seasonal ales are served both naturally conditioned and carbonated. Oliver's Ales in bottles are produced by the Wild Goose Brewery (Cambridge, MD).

Annual production: 820 barrels

Flagship brands: Oliver's Best Bitter, Oliver's Blackfriar Stout, Oliver's Irish Red Ale, Oliver's SW 1, Oliver's Summer Light Ale

Major top-fermented brands: Oliver's Best Bitter, Oliver's Blackfriar Stout, Oliver's Irish Red Ale, Oliver's SW 1, Oliver's Summer Ale

Major seasonal brands: Bock, Cherry Blossom Ale, ESB, Christmas Ale, Manchester Cream Ale, Pale Ale, Scottish Ale

## One Onion Brewery & Bistro
1291 University Avenue
Morgantown, WV 26505-5450

This brewery/restaurant was founded by Andrew Gongolla, David McClure and Jim Martin in 1992. One Onion is named for the Russian parable about a woman trying to get into heaven, who is required to recall a good deed she has done. She recalls having once given someone an onion, and a huge onion appears in the sky. She grabs it and floats upward, and the onion begins to peel layer by layer, and she falls into hell. The moral is that it takes more than one good deed (or one onion) to get into heaven.

Annual production: Under 500 barrels

Major top-fermented brands: AJ Ale, Cameron Scottish Stout, Fennen Celtic

## Oxford Brewing
611 #G Hammonds Ferry Road
Linthicum, MD 21090

Oxford Brewing was founded in January 1992 by Marianne O'Brien. The company purchased some assets of the now defunct British Brewing Company, including the rights to the

bled by Paul Kalmanovitz prior to his death in 1987.

Annual production: 1,900,000 barrels

Other breweries owned by same company: The Pabst Brewing Company also operates the Pabst Brewery (Milwaukee, WI) and the Olympia Brewery (Tumwater, WA).

GABF Gold Medals: Pearl Lager Beer, 1991; Olde English 800, 1991; Olympia Dry, 1993

GABF Silver Medals: Pabst Blue Ribbon, 1990; Olde English 800, 1990

name of their flagship brand, Oxford Class Amber Ale. Oxford Brewing's entire production line is focused on top-fermented British-style ales.

Flagship brand: Oxford Class Amber Ale

Major top-fermented brands: Oxford Class Amber Ale, Oxford Real Ale, Oxford Raspberry-Wheat Ale

Major seasonal brands: Piccadilly Porter English Style Porter, Santa Claus

## Pearl Brewing Company
312 Pearl Parkway
San Antonio, TX 78296

Pearl developed out of the brewery started by JB Behloradsky in 1881 and evolved into San Antonio Brewing in 1883. The company became Pearl Brewing in 1952, although the Pearl brand name had been used since 1886 by San Antonio Brewing. In 1961, Pearl acquired Goetz Brewing of St Joseph, MO, which was operated until 1976. Having become associated with General Brewing in 1978, Pearl, along with General, Falstaff and Pabst, became part of the group of breweries assem-

## Ragtime Tavern & Grill
207 Atlantic Boulevard
Atlantic Beach, FL 32233

This brewpub was founded in this Jacksonville suburb by Bill and Tom Morton as a tavern and restaurant in 1983. Ragtime began producing its own beer in 1991.

Annual production: Under 500 barrels

Major top-fermented brands: Redbrick Ale, Strange Stout

Major bottom-fermented brands: Dolphin's Breath Lager, Westburg Wheat

Major seasonal brands: Bock, Holiday Ale, Maddie's Märzen, Octoberfest

### Richland Beverages
7557 Rambler Road
Suite 1326
Dallas, TX 75231

Richland's Texas Select non-alcoholic beer is contract brewed off-site.

### River City Brewing
150 North Mosley
Wichita, KS 67202

This brewpub was founded in 1993.

River City Brewing received its name from the city of Wichita's nickname. It is not to be confused with River City Brewing in Sacramento, CA, which is also named for the city's nickname. River City is located in a 1905 paint store.

Annual production: Under 500 barrels

Other breweries owned by same company: Blue Cat Brew Pub (Rock Island, IL), Broadway Brewing Company (Denver, CO), CooperSmith's Pub & Brewing (Fort Collins, CO), Crane River Brew Pub & Cafe (Lincoln, NE), Firehouse Brewing Company (Rapid City, SD), Phantom Canyon Brewing Company (Colorado Springs, CO), Norman Brewing Company (Norman, OK), and Wynkoop Brewing (Denver, CO)

Major top-fermented brands: Four Horsemen Stout, Harvester Wheat, Hockaday Pale

Major bottom-fermented brand: Harvester Wheat

Major seasonal brands: Cherry, Fest

### Riverwalk Brewery
111 SW 2nd Avenue
Fort Lauderdale, FL 33301

This German-style, German-owned brewpub was founded in 1991.

Annual production: Under 500 barrels

Major top-fermented brands: Lauder Ale, Lauder Light

### Rolling Rock: See Latrobe Brewing (Latrobe, PA)

### Santa Rosa Bay Brewing
54 Miracle Strip Parkway
Fort Walton Beach, FL 32548

This brewpub was founded in 1992.

Annual production: Under 500 barrels

Major top-fermented brands: Golden Ale, Red Irish Ale, Wheat Ale

Major seasonal brands: Christmas Ale, Summer Dark Wheat

### Sarasota Brewing
5872 West 14th Street
Bradenton, FL 34207

This brewpub was founded in 1991 as an expansion site for the original Sarasota Brewing in the city of the same name.

Annual production: 1500 barrels

Other brewery owned by same company: Sarasota Brewery (Sarasota, FL)

Major top-fermented brand: Presidential Pale

Major bottom-fermented brands: Cobra Light, Sequoia Amber

Major seasonal brands: Andy's Maibock, Prince Albert Imperial Dark

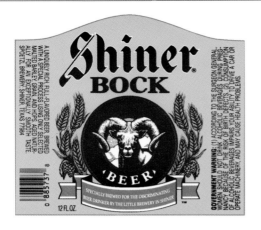

## Sarasota Brewing

6607 Gateway Avenue
Sarasota, FL 34231

This brewpub was founded in 1989.

Annual production: 1500 barrels

Other brewery owned by same company: Sarasota Brewing (Bradenton, FL)

Major top-fermented brand: Presidential Pale

Major bottom-fermented brands: Cobra Lite, Sequoia Amber

Major seasonal brands: Londonderry Porter, Weizen

**Schlitz:** See Stroh Brewing (Detroit, MI)

**Shiner:** See Spoetzl Brewery (Shiner, TX)

## Sisson's South Baltimore Brewing

36 East Cross Street
Baltimore, MD 21230

This Cajun/Creole-style brewpub was founded in 1990.

Annual production: 700 barrels

Major top-fermented brands: Cross Street Stout, Marble Golden, Stockade Amber

Major seasonal brand: Christmas Ale

## Spoetzl Brewery

603 East Brewery Street
Shiner, TX 77984

The Spoetzl Brewery evolved from the Shiner Brewing Association started by Kosmos Spoetzl in 1909 and was taken over by the Petzold and Spoetzl partnership in 1915. In 1989, the company was purchased by Gambinus Imports, the San Antonio-based importer of Modelo's Corona brand.

Annual production: 60,000 barrels

Flagship brand: Shiner

Major bottom-fermented brands: Shiner Premium, Shiner Premium Bock

## Spring Garden Brewing

714 Francis King Street
Greensboro, NC 27410

This establishment was founded in 1991 as the flagship brewpub for the Spring Garden Bar & Grill chain, which is based in North Carolina.

Annual production: Under 500 barrels

Major top-fermented brands: Hummin' Bird Light, Oak Ridge Amber

Major bottom-fermented brands: Black Rose Lager, Blackbeard Bock

Major seasonal brand: Oktoberfest

## Stroh Brewery

1400 West Cotton Street
Longview, TX 75604

This brewery was founded by the Joseph Schlitz Brewing Company of Milwaukee, WI in 1966, and it became a Stroh Brewery in 1982.

Annual production: 3,800,000 barrels

Other breweries owned by same company: Stroh, which is headquartered in Detroit, MI, also operates breweries in Fogelsville, PA; St Paul, MN; Tampa, FL; and Winston-Salem, NC.

Flagship brands: Schlitz, Stroh's

Major bottom-fermented brands: See Stroh Brewery (Detroit, MI) for a list of Stroh brands.

Major seasonal brands: See Stroh Brewery (Detroit, MI) for list of Stroh brands.

GABF Silver Medal: Signature, 1988

## Stroh Brewery

11111 North 30th Street
Tampa, FL 33612

This brewery was founded by the Joseph Schlitz Brewery Company of Milwaukee, WI in 1959, and it became a Stroh Brewery in 1982.

Annual production: 1,500,000 barrels

Other breweries owned by same company: Stroh, which is headquartered in Detroit, MI, also operates breweries in Fogelsville, PA; Longview, TX; St Paul, MN; and Winston-Salem, NC.

Flagship brands: Schlitz, Stroh's

Major bottom-fermented brands: See Stroh Brewery (Detroit, MI) for a list of Stroh brands.

Major seasonal brands: See Stroh Brewery (Detroit, MI) for a list of Stroh brands.

GABF Silver Medal: Signature, 1988

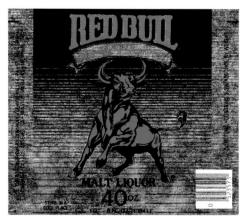

## Stroh Brewery
4791 Schlitz Avenue
Winston-Salem, NC 27107

This brewery was founded by the Joseph Schlitz Brewery Company of Milwaukee, WI in 1970, and it became a Stroh Brewery in 1982.

Other breweries owned by same company: Stroh, which is headquartered in Detroit, MI, also operates breweries in Fogelsville, PA; Longview, TX; St Paul, MN; and Tampa, FL.

Flagship brands: Schlitz, Stroh's

Major bottom-fermented brands: See Stroh Brewery (Detroit, MI) for a list of Stroh brands.

Major seasonal brands: See Stroh Brewery (Detroit, MI) for a list of Stroh brands.

GABF Silver Medal: Signature, 1988

## Tumbleweed Grill & Brewery
122 Blowing Rock Road
Boone, NC 28607

The Tumbleweed Grill was opened in 1989 and the brewery was added in 1992.

Annual production: Under 500 barrels

Flagship brands: Gold Rush Ale, Tumbleweed Amber

Major seasonal brand: Smoked Porter

## Weeping Radish Bavarian Restaurant and Brewery
Highway 64
Manteo, NC 27954

This Bavarian-style brewery/restaurant was founded in 1985 on Roanoke Island, the scene of Sir William Raleigh's lost colony of the same name which was the first English colony in North America. Weeping radishes have nothing to do with Sir Walter Raleigh but they are a Bavarian specialty. When sliced and salted, the German radishes sweat moisture, or 'weep.'

Annual production: 800 barrels

Major bottom-fermented brands: Black Radish Bier, Fest, Helles

GABF Silver Medal: Hopfen Helles Beer, 1990

## Weidman's Old Fort Brew Pub
422 North Third
Fort Smith, AR 72901

This brewery was founded by Bill Weidman and his brewer son Daniel in 1992.

Annual production: Under 500 barrels

Major top-fermented brands: Irish Red, Smoked Porter, Stout

Major bottom-fermented brands: Continental Pilsner, Weidman Light, Weizen

Major seasonal brands: Emerald Isle Ale, Oktoberfest, Ozark Lambic

## Wild Goose Brewery
20 Washington Street
Cambridge, MD 21613

The brewery was founded in 1989, and the Wild Goose brand is widely available in the Chesapeake Bay area.

Annual production: 7800 barrels

Flagship brand: Wild Goose Amber Beer

Major top-fermented brands: Samuel Middleton's Pale Ale, Thomas Point Light Golden Ale

# THE
# MIDWEST

**Samuel Adams:** See Boston Beer Company (Boston, MA) and Philadelphia Brewing (Philadelphia, PA)

## Anheuser-Busch
One Busch Place
St Louis, MO 63118-1852

The world's biggest brewing company traces its roots to a small brewery started in St Louis, Missouri in 1852 by George Schneider and taken over in 1860 by Eberhard Anheuser. Four years later, Anheuser's son-in-law Adolphus Busch joined the firm. A far-sighted marketing genius, Busch turned the small city brewery into a national giant. He launched the extraordinarily successful Budweiser brand as a mass-market beer in 1876, and in 1896 he introduced the still-popular Michelob brand as the company's premium beer. Originally a draft beer, Michelob was not marketed as a bottled beer until 1961.

Since 1980, the Anheuser-Busch brands have been brewed under license abroad as well. Budweiser is brewed in Canada by Labatt's; in South Korea by Oriental Brewery Co, Ltd; in Japan by Suntory; and in the United Kingdom by Grand Metropolitan Brewing Ltd.

Annual production (at the St Louis plant, which is also the headquarters for the other corporate brewing plants listed below): 13,200,000 barrels

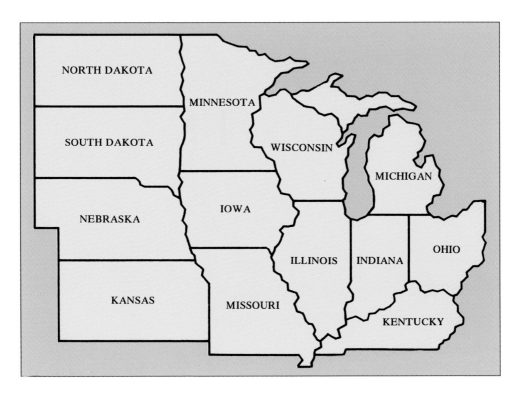

Other breweries owned by the same company: Today Anheuser-Busch's flagship brewery is still located in St Louis, MO, but beginning in 1951 other breweries were established at Newark, NJ (1951); Los Angeles, CA (1954); Tampa, FL (1959): Houston, TX (1966); Columbus, OH (1968); Jacksonville, FL (1969); Merrimack, NH (1970); Williamsburg, VA (1972); Fairfield, CA (1976); Baldswinville, NY (1983); Fort Collins, CO (1988); and Cartersville, GA (1993)

Flagship brand: Budweiser

Major bottom-fermented brands: Budweiser, Bud Light, Bud Dry, Bud Dry Draft, Michelob, Michelob Light, Michelob Dark, Michelob Dry, Natural Light, Busch, Busch Light, King Cobra, O'Doul's and LA (non-alcoholic). Elephant Malt Liquor, Carlsberg and Carlsberg Light are brewed under license from Carling in Copenhagen, Denmark.

GABF Gold Medals: Busch 1988, 1989; Michelob Dark, 1988; Bud Dry, 1989; Michelob Dry, 1990

GABF Silver Medals: Michelob Light, 1989; Michelob Classic Dark, 1989; Bud Dry, 1990; Michelob Dry, 1991; Budweiser, 1993; O'Doul's, 1993

## Anheuser-Busch

700 East Schrock Road
Columbus, OH 43229

This brewery was started by Anheuser-Busch in 1968.

Annual production: 6,800,000 barrels

Other breweries owned by the same company: See Anheuser-Busch, St Louis, MO for a list of Anheuser-Busch breweries.

Flagship brand: Budweiser

Major bottom-fermented brands: Budweiser, Bud Light, Bud Dry, Michelob, Michelob Light, Michelob Dry, Natural Light, Natural Pilsner, Busch, Busch Light, King Cobra, O'Doul's

See Anheuser-Busch, St Louis, MO for a list of medals awarded to Anheuser-Busch beers.

## Appleton Brewing-Adler Bräu

1004 South Olde Oneida Street
Appleton, WI 54915

This brewery was founded by John Jungers in 1989 and is located in the Between-the-Locks Mall in the 1858 Muench Brewery building. The brewery pipes beer directly to both Dos Bandidos and Johnny O's Pizzaria.

Annual production: 500 barrels

Major top-fermented brands: Oatmeal Stout, Pale Ale, Porter

Major bottom-fermented brands: Amber Lager, Golden Lager, Pilsner

Major seasonal brands: Bock, Dopplebock, Holiday Dark, Oktoberfest, Weiss

GABF Gold Medals: Adler Bräu Oktoberfest, 1990; Adler Bräu Amber Lager, 1991; Adler Bräu Lager, 1991

GABF Silver Medals: Adler Bräu Oatmeal Stout, 1991

## Barley's Brewpub

467 North High Street
Columbus, OH 43215

This brewery was founded in 1992.

Annual production: Under 500 barrels

Major top-fermented brands: Irish Rogue, Ivan Porter, Pale Ale

Major bottom-fermented brand: Pilsner

**Berghoff:** See Joseph Huber Brewing (Monroe, WI)

**Blatz:** See G Heileman Brewing (La Crosse, WI)

## Blue Cat Brew Pub

113 18th Street
Rock Island, IL 61202

This brewery was founded about 1993.

Annual production: Under 1000 barrels

Other breweries owned by same company: Broadway Brewing Company (Denver, CO), CooperSmith's Pub & Brewing (Fort Collins, CO), Crane River Brew Pub & Cafe (Lincoln, NE), Firehouse Brewing Company (Rapid City, SD), Norman Brewing (Norman, OK), Phantom Canyon Brewing Company (Colorado Springs, CO), River City Brewery (Wichita, KS), and Wynkoop Brewing (Denver, CO)

Flagship brand: Blue Cat

## Boulevard Brewing

2501 Southwest Boulevard
Kansas City, MO 64108

This brewery was founded in 1989, the first brewery in Kansas City since 1903. The president and master brewer is John McDonald.

Annual production: 8000 barrels

Major top-fermented brands: Boulevard Pale Ale, Bully Porter, Irish Ale

Major bottom-fermented brand: Wheat Beer

## Brewmasters Pub Restaurant & Brewery

4017 80th Street
Kenosha, WI 53142

This brewery was founded in 1987 in a former show horse stable.

Annual production: 9000 barrels

Major bottom-fermented brands: Gartenbräu Dark, Gartenbräu Lager, Gartenbräu Special

Major seasonal brands: Bock, Maibock, Oktoberfest, Wild Rice

## Broad Ripple Brewpub

840 East 65th Street
Indianapolis, IN 46220

The brewpub was founded in 1990. The president and master brewer is John Hill.

Annual production: Under 1000 barrels

Major top-fermented brands: ESB, Monon Porter, Pintail Pale, Red Bird Mild

Major seasonal brands: Bavarian Wheat, Copper Ale, Dry Stout, Kölsch, Wee Heavy

**Budweiser:** See Anheuser-Busch (St Louis, MO)

## Burkhardt Brewing

3700 Massilon Road
Uniontown, OH 44685

This brewery was founded by Thomas Burkhardt, Sr in 1991. Burkhardt represents the fifth generation of Burkhardt brewers.

Annual production: Under 1000 barrels

Major top-fermented brands: Eclipse, North Star, White Cliffs

**Busch:** See Anheuser-Busch (St Louis, MO)

## Capital Brewery

7734 Terrace Avenue
Middleton, WI 53562

This brewery was founded by Ed James in June 1986.

Annual production: 12,500 barrels

Flagship brand: Garten Bräu

Major top-fermented brand: Weizen

Major bottom-fermented brands: Bock, Dark, Doppelbock, Oktoberfest, Special Lager, Wild Rice, Winterfest, Wisconsin Amber

Major seasonal brands: Bock, Doppelbock, Maibock, Oktoberfest, Wild Rice, Winterfest

GABF Gold Medals: Gartenbräu Dark, 1988, 1990; Weizen, 1991

GABF Silver Medals: Gartenbräu Oktoberfest, 1989; Special, 1992

**Carling:** See G Heileman Brewing (La Crosse, WI) and Molson (Montreal, Canada)

## Cherryland Brewing
341 North Third Avenue
Sturgeon Bay, WI 54235

The brewpub was founded by Tom Alberts and Mark Feld in 1988.

Annual production: 1200 barrels

Flagship brands: Golden Rail, Silver Rail, Cherry Rail

Major bottom-fermented brands: Cherry Rail (fruit lager), Golden Rail (amber), Silver Rail (pilsner)

Major seasonal brands: Apple Bock, Winter Porter, Raspberry Light

GABF Silver Medals: Golden Rail, 1992; Cherry Rail, 1991

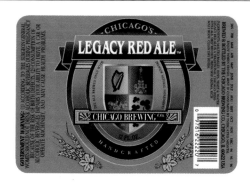

## Chicago Brewing
1830 North Besly Court
Chicago, IL 60622

This brewery was founded in 1990 by Stephen and Jennifer Dinehart, along with Stephen's brothers Craig and Keith.

Annual production: Under 500 barrels

Flagship brand: Legacy Lager

Major top-fermented brands: Legacy Red Ale, Heartland Weiss, Big Shoulders Porter

Major bottom-fermented brand: Legacy Lager

Major seasonal brand: Heartland Weiss

GABF Gold Medals: Legacy Lager, 1991, 1992

## The Chickery
453 Miamisburg-Centerville Road
Centerville, OH 45459

This brewery/restaurant was founded in 1991.

Annual production: Under 500 barrels

## Cold Spring Brewing
219 North Red River Avenue
Cold Spring, MN 56320

This brewery was founded by George Sargel in 1874 and evolved to its present name by 1898.

Annual production: 350,000 barrels

Flagship brand: Cold Spring

Major bottom-fermented brands: Cold Spring, Cold Spring Export, Cold Spring Light, Fox Deluxe, Kegle Bräu, North Star, White Label

## Columbus Brewing

476 South Front Street
Columbus, OH 43215

This brewery was founded in 1989 and is associated with two bars, Hagen's and Gibby's, although all three are separately owned by members of the same family. All three establishments are located in the old brewing district, near the former Hoster Brewery.

Annual production: Under 1000 barrels

## Crane River Brew Pub & Cafe

200 North 11th Street
Lincoln, NE 68508

This brewery was founded by Kristina Tiebel and Linda Vescio in 1992.

Crane River Brewpub & Cafe opened in October of 1992 in Lincoln's Commercial Club Building. Its large storefront windows make the pub bright during lunch and a good place to watch downtown crowds. An island bar of poured concrete, inlaid with rocks from Nebraska's Platte River, is overlooked by a massive quilt by a local artist which depicts the early morning dance of Sandhill Cranes. The ceramic tile floor in the bar area is original to the 1911 building, while the cafe floor is covered with carpet produced from fibers spun from recycled plastic soda pop bottles. The brewery, which backlights the cafe, regularly supplies the bar with seven brews at a time.

Five of these brews are served throughout the year and two are seasonal or speciality beers that allow the brewers to experiment and the customers to experience a multitude of beer styles.

Annual production: 700 barrels

Other breweries owned by same company: Broadway Brewing Company (Denver, CO), Blue Cat Brew Pub (Rock Island, IL), Cooper-Smith's Pub & Brewing (Fort Collins, CO), Crane River Brew Pub & Cafe (Lincoln, NE), Firehouse Brewing Company (Rapid City, SD), Norman Brewing (Norman, OK), Phantom Canyon Brewing Company (Colorado Springs, CO), River City Brewery (Wichita, KS), and Wynkoop Brewing (Denver, CO)

Major top-fermented brands: Good Life Stout, Homestead Pale Ale, Plato Pivo, Platte Valley ESB, Sod House Alt, Whooping Wheat

Major seasonal brands: Carhenge Wheat, Chili Beer, Cinco de Mayo, Festus (Oktoberfest), Solstice Spice

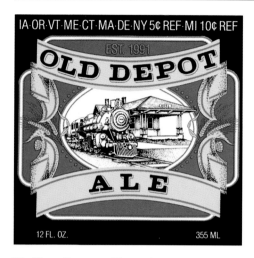

This brewery was founded in 1877 as the Ulmer & Hoedt Brewery, eventually becoming the Evansville Brewery in 1894. In 1934, it re-emerged from Prohibition as Sterling Brewers. It went through a number of name changes between 1966 and 1972, when it was bought by G Heileman of La Crosse, WI.

Annual production: 1,000,000 barrels

Major bottom-fermented brands: Cook's, Cook's Light, Drewrys, Drewrys Light 'N' Dry, Drummond Brothers, Drummond Brothers Light, Eagle Malt, Falls City, Falls City Light, Gerst Amber, Harley Davidson, Lemp, Lemp Light, Royal Amber, Sterling, Sterling Light, Wiedemann, Wiedemann Light

## Dallas County Brewing
Old Depot Restaurant
301 South 10th Street
Adel, IA 50003

The brewpub was founded by Kevin L Rice in 1991 in a former Milwaukee Road railroad station.

Annual production: 1500 barrels

Major top-fermented brands: Old Depot Ale, Old Depot Lager, Old Depot Light, Old Depot Porter

Major seasonal brands: Holiday Ale, May Bock, Oktoberfest, Old Depot Irish Style Red Ale

## Detroit & Mackinac Brewery
470 West Canfield
Detroit, MI 48201

This brewery was founded by Tom Burns in 1992.

Annual production: 1500 barrels

Major top-fermented brands: Irish Red Ale, Mackinac Black, Mackinac Gold

Major seasonal brand: Christmas Ale

## Falstaff Brewing
Fort Wayne, IN 46801

Falstaff Brewing traces its roots to the Forest Park Brewing Company of St Louis, MO that was established in 1910 and taken over by 'Papa Joe' Griesdieck in 1917. Renamed Falstaff (after the Shakespeare character) during Prohibition, the company expanded to become one of the Midwest's strongest multi-site regional brewers. After World War II, Falstaff became a leading national brewer, and by 1960 it was the nation's third largest brewer behind Anheuser-Busch and Schlitz.

Through its complicated association with General Brewing of Vancouver, WA, the Fal-

## Evansville Brewing
1301 Pennsylvania Street
Evansville, IN 47707

staff brand became prominent in the West. After the 1960s, however, Falstaff's market position gave way to other brands, such as Miller and Coors, and many of the company's breweries were sold or closed. By the early 1980s, when the company came under the control of the late Paul Kalmanovitz, who had acquired control of Pabst, only the Fort Wayne and Omaha, NE breweries, with respective capacities of 1.2 and 1.25 million barrels, remained. In 1990, both plants closed and production of the Falstaff and Ballantine brands was moved to the Pabst Milwaukee plant.

## Firehouse Brewing Company

610 Main Street
Rapid City, SD 57701

This brewpub was founded by Bob Fuchs, Pete Lien and Mark Polenz in 1991 in Rapid City's 1915 fire house.

Annual production: 800 barrels

Other breweries owned by same company: Blue Cat Brew Pub (Rock Island, IL), Broadway Brewing Company (Denver, CO), Cooper-Smith's Pub & Brewing (Fort Collins, CO), Crane River Brew Pub & Cafe (Lincoln, NE), Norman Brewing (Norman, OK), Phantom Canyon Brewing Company (Colorado Springs, CO), River City Brewery (Wichita, KS), and Wynkoop Brewing (Denver, CO)

Major top-fermented brands: Wilderness Wheat, Chukkar Ale, Rushmore Stout

Major seasonal brand: Rough Rider Barley Wine

## Fitzpatrick's Alehouse

525 South Gilbert
Iowa City, IA 52240

This brewpub was founded by Gary Fitzpatrick in 1990 as an expansion of a tavern that opened in 1983.

Annual production: Under 500 barrels

Major top-fermented brands: Celtic Ale, Mighty Stout

Major bottom-fermented brands: Golden Lager, Wheat

Major seasonal brands: Bock, Christmas Ale

## Frankenmuth Brewery

425 South Main Street
Frankenmuth, MI 48734

This brewery was founded by Ferdinand M Schumacher in 1988 to renovate and operate the former Geyer Brothers Brewery in the town of Frankenmuth, near Detroit, MI. The Geyer Brothers Brewery grew out of the Heubisch & Knaust Cass River Brewery, established on Main Street in 1862. Taken over by John G

Geyer in 1874, the brewery operated under his name until 1908, at which time it became the Geyer Brothers Brewery. The first beer produced by the Frankenmuth Brewery appeared in 1988, although the Frankenmuth name had been used as a brand name by Geyer Brothers.

Annual production: 12,000 barrels

Flagship brand: Frankenmuth

Major top-fermented brand: Old Detroit Amber Ale

Major bottom-fermented brands: Frankenmuth Pilsener, Frankenmuth Dark, Frankenmuth Bock, Frankenmuth Light, Old Detroit Red Lager

Major seasonal brands: Bock, Weisse

GABF Gold Medals: Frankenmuth Old German Dark, 1989, 1992; Frankenmuth German Style Bock, 1991

GABF Silver Medals: Frankenmuth Bock (Old German-style Bock), 1989; Frankenmuth Old German Dark, 1990

## Free State Brewing
636 Massachusetts
Lawrence, KS 66044

This brewpub was founded in 1989 in an old trolley depot.

Annual production: 2100 barrels

Major top-fermented brand: Ad Astra Ale

Major bottom-fermented brands: Hefeweizen, Wheat State Golden

Major seasonal brands: Holiday Porter, Maibock, Octoberfest

## Front Street Brewing
208 East River Drive
Davenport, IA 52801

This brewpub was founded by Randy Junis and Steve Zuidema in 1992.

Annual production: Under 500 barrels

Major top-fermented brands: Biddy McGee's Irish Red, Bucktown Stout, Burton Ale, Wheat Ale

## Golden Prairie Brewing
1820 West Webster Avenue
Chicago, IL 60614

This brewery was founded by Ted Furman, his wife, Laura Elliot, and David Bouhl in 1992. Furman was a former brewer with the now-defunct Sieben's River North Brewery (1987-1990) in Chicago.

Annual production: Under 1000 barrels

Flagship brand: Golden Prairie Ale

## Goose Island Brewing
1800 North Clybourn
Chicago, IL 60614

This brewpub was founded by John Hall in 1988 in the former Turtle Wax Factory.

Annual production: 2500 barrels

Flagship brand: Honkers Ale

Major top-fermented brands: Honkers Ale, Blonde Ale

Major bottom-fermented brand: Golden Goose Pilsner

Major seasonal brands: Old Aberration (January), India Pale Ale (January), Lincoln Park Lager (February), Russian Imperial Stout (February), Märzen (March), Irish Red Ale (March),

Porter (April), Nelson Algren Alt (April), Maibock (May), Hopscotch Ale (May), Weizen (June), Dunkel Munich (June), Dunkel Weizenbock (August), Raf Best Bitter (August), Oatmeal Stout (September), Oktoberfest (September), PMD Mild Ale (October), Special Brown Ale (October), Extra Special Bitter (November), Doppelbock (December), and Christmas Ale (December)

GABF Gold Medal: PMD Mild Ale, 1992

GABF Silver Medal: Chicago Vice Weizen, 1989

**Grain Belt:** See Minnesota Brewing (St Paul, MN)

## Great Lakes Brewing
2516 Market Street
Cleveland, OH 44113

This brewpub was founded by Patrick F Conway and Daniel J Conway in 1988 in a tavern that is alleged to be famous crimefighter Eliot Ness' favorite drinking place in the 1930s.

Annual production: 4000 barrels

Flagship brands: Dortmunder Gold, Eliot Ness, Edmund Fitzgerald Porter, Burning River Pale Ale

Major top-fermented brands: Edmund Fitzgerald Porter, Burning River Pale Ale, Commodore Perry IPA, Moon Dog Ale (English bitter)

Major bottom-fermented brands: Eliot Ness, Dortmunder Gold

Major seasonal brands: Oktoberfest, Christmas Ale, Rockefeller Bock, Market Street Wheat

GABF Gold Medals: Dortmunder Gold, 1990; Edmund Fitzgerald Porter, 1991, 1993; Moon Dog Ale, 1992

GABF Silver Medal: Burning River Pale Ale, 1993

**Hamm's:** See Pabst (Milwaukee, WI)

## G Heileman Brewing
La Crosse Brewery
100 Harborview Plaza
La Crosse, WI 54601

The company was founded by Gottlieb Heileman and John Gund in 1858. Heileman remained a small regional brewer until the early 1960s, when it began to acquire other smaller regional breweries, notably the Associated Breweries in 1963 and Blatz in 1969. In 1960, Heileman was the thirty-first largest brewer in the United States, but by 1982 it ranked fourth. Other key regional breweries it acquired included Falls City, Grain Belt, Schmidt and Wiedemann.

The most important additions to the Heileman portfolio occurred in the early 1980s. These were Blitz-Weinhard (Portland, OR), Lone Star (San Antonio, TX) and Rainier (Seattle, WA). All three of these breweries had been,

Light, Henry Weinhard's Private Reserve, Henry Weinhard's Private Reserve Dark

GABF Gold Medals: Rainier Beer (American Light Lager), 1987; Heileman's Old Style, 1988

GABF Silver Medals: Heileman's Special Export, 1991; Heileman's Special Export Light, 1993; Mickey's Malt Liquor, 1993

## Hoster Brewing
550 South High Street
Columbus, OH 43065

This brewpub was founded in about 1992 in a former streetcar shop.

Annual production: 1500 barrels

Major bottom-fermented brands: Eagle Light, Eagle Top Dark, Hoster Amber Lager, Hoster Gold

Major seasonal brands: Independence English Ale, Maibock, Oktoberfest

## Joseph Huber Brewing
1208 14th Street
Monroe, WI 53566

This major regional brewery was founded as the Bissinger Brewery in 1845. Between 1848 and 1906, it operated successively under the names John Knipschilt, Ed Ruegger, Jacob Hefty, Fred Hefty and Adam Blumer. It survived as Blumer Brewing until 1947, when it became Joseph Huber Brewing. In 1985, when

and continue to be, just as important in their own regional markets as Heileman itself had once been in the upper Midwest.

Annual production: 12,000 barrels

Other breweries owned by same company: Also brewed in Baltimore, MD, as well as Blitz-Weinhard (Portland, OR), Lone Star (San Antonio, TX) and Rainier (Seattle, WA)

Flagship brand: Heileman's Old Style

Major top-fermented brands: Rainier Ale, Weinhard's Ale

Major bottom-fermented brands: Heileman's Old Style, Heileman's Old Style Light, Heileman's Special Export, Heileman's Special Export Light, Blatz, Carling Black Label, Colt 45, Colt 45 Dry, Lone Star, Lone Star Light, Lone Star Dry, Mickey's, Rainier, Rainier Light, Rainier Dry, Jacob Schmidt, Jacob Schmidt

Paul Kalmanovitz took over Pabst, the latter's president and vice president purchased Huber. In 1989, Huber was in turn purchased by the Berghoff in Chicago, a restaurant for whom it had long brewed a house brand beer. The resulting company is now known officially as Berghoff-Huber Brewing.

Annual production: 450,000 barrels

Flagship brands: Berghoff, Huber

Major top-fermented brand: Dempsey's Ale

Major bottom-fermented brands: Alpine, Bavarian Club, Berghoff Bock, Berghoff Dark, Berghoff Light, Bohemian Club, Boxer Malt Liquor, Bräumeister Light, Hi-Bräu, Holiday, Huber Bock, Old Chicago, Regal Bräu, Rhinelander, Rhinelander Bock, Van Merritt Light, Wisconsin Club, Wisconsin Gold Label

GABF Gold Medal: Berghoff Dark, 1993

## Hudepohl-Schoenling Brewing
1625 Central Parkway
Cincinnati, OH 45214

The breweries which form the core of this major regional brewing company were founded by Hudepohl Brewing by Gottfried

Koehler in 1852, and Schoenling Brewing and Malting by the family of the same name in 1934.

Known locally as 'Cincinnati's Brewery,' Hudepohl-Schoenling Brewing was created in December 1986 by the merger of Hudepohl Brewing and Schoenling Brewing. Hudepohl originated with Gottfried Koehler in 1852 and was taken over as the Buckeye Brewery of Ludwig 'Louis' Hudepohl and George Kotte in 1885. The company became Hudepohl Brewing in 1899. In 1982, the company introduced Christian Moerlein, a superpremium brand named for one of Cincinnati's first great brewers, whose famous brewery was started on Elm Street in 1853 but did not survive Prohibition.

Annual production: 650,000 barrels

Major top-fermented brand: Little Kings Cream Ale

Major bottom-fermented brands: Banks, Big Jug, Burger, Christian Moerlein, Hudepohl, Hudy Delight, Mt Everest, Prestige, Top Hat

GABF Gold Medals: Little Kings Cream Ale (American Cream Ales), 1987; Hudepohl 14-K, 1989

GABF Silver Medals: Midnight Dragon Malt Liquor, 1989; Little Kings Cream Ale, 1990; Big Jug Xtra Malt Liquor, 1991

## Indianapolis Brewing

3250 North Post Road #285
Indianapolis, IN 46226

This brewery was founded in 1989.

Annual production: 2000 barrels

Flagship brand: Duesseldorfer

Major top-fermented brands: Duesseldorfer Amber, Duesseldorfer Dark, Duesseldorfer Pale

Major seasonal brands: Brickyard Bock, Oktoberfest

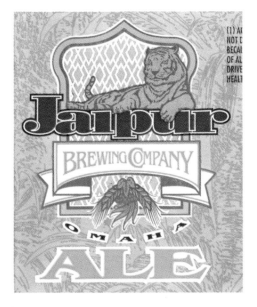

## Jaipur Brewing

10922 Elm Street
Omaha, NE 68144

This brewery/restaurant was founded by Mark Herse in 1992 and specializes in northern Indian and tandoori cooking.

Annual production: 100 barrels

Flagship brand: Jaipur Omaha Ale

## Joe's Brewery

706 South 5th Street
Champaign, IL 61820

This brewpub was founded by in 1992 on the campus of the University of Illinois.

Annual production: Under 500 barrels

Flagship brand: Young Williams' Pale Ale

Major seasonal brands: Aviator Porter, Brownstone Porter, Harvest Moon Oatmeal Stout

## Jones Street Brewery

1316 Jones Street
Omaha, NE 68102

This brewpub was founded by in 1992.

Annual production: 250 barrels

Major top-fermented brands: Bolt Nut & Screw Golden, Patch Pale, Ryan's Irish Stout

Major bottom-fermented brand: Harvester Wheat

Major seasonal brands: Holiday Ale, Slap Shot Winter Ale

GABF Silver Medal: Esquire Extra Dry, 1993

## Kalamazoo Brewing

315 East Kalamazoo Avenue
Kalamazoo, MI 49007

This brewery was founded by Larry Bell in 1985.

Annual production: 3000 barrels

Flagship brand: Bell's

Major bottom-fermented brands: Bell's Amber Ale, Bell's Best Brown Ale, Bell's Cherry Stout, Bell's Kalamazoo Stout, Bell's Porter, Bell's Special Double Cream Stout

Major seasonal brands: Bell's Eccentric Ale, Bell's Expedition Stout, Bell's Harvest Ale, Debs' Red Ale, Third Coast Beer, Third Coast Old Ale

## Lafayette Brewing
622 Main Street
Lafayette, IN 47901

This brewery/restaurant was founded in 1993 by Greg and Joe Emig.

Annual production: 750 barrels

Major top-fermented brands: Oatmeal Stout, Pale Ale

Major bottom-fermented brand: Kölsch

## Lakefront Brewery
818A East Chambers Street
Milwaukee, WI 53212

Founded by Russ and Jim Klisch in 1987, Lakefront Brewery is a tiny microbrewery located in Milwaukee, WI, one of a growing trend of such establishments in the city that was once the center of American brewing. With brewing under the direction of Jim Klisch, Lakefront is noted for its distinctive Klisch Cherry Beer, a cherry lager which differs from the familiar kreiks of Belgium by being a lager rather than a spontaneously fermented beer.

Annual production: 1424 barrels

Flagship brand: Riverfront Steam Beer

Major top-fermented brand: Cream City Pale Ale

Major bottom-fermented brands: Amber Lager, East Side Dark, Golden Lager, Klisch Pilsner, Riverfront Steam Beer

Major seasonal brands: Christmas Dark, Lakefront Bock, Lakefront Holiday Spice, Lakefront Weiss, Lakefront Pumpkin, Lakefront Cherry, Mardi Gras Bock, Oktoberfest

## Lazlo's Brewery & Grill
710 P Street
Lincoln, NE 68508

This brewpub was founded by Jay Jarvis, Scott Boles and Brian Boles in 1991.

Annual production: 1100 barrels

Major top-fermented brands: Black Jack Stout, Lougales Gold, Reckless Red's Special Amber

## Jacob Leinenkugel Brewing
1-3 Jefferson Avenue
Chippewa Falls, WI 54729

This major regional brewing company was founded by Jacob Leinenkugel and John Miller as the Spring Brewery in 1867. Leinenkugel and Miller remained partners for the next 16 years. Located on top of Big Eddy Springs, the brewery was known as the Spring Brewery until 1898. In 1987, the company was purchased by Miller Brewing (no relation) of Milwaukee, but it remains autonomous as a separate operating unit. Every Leinenkugel's label carries the distinctive Indian maiden head ('Leinie') motif. This reflects the brewery's location in 'Indian Head Country,' so named because of the Indian profile created on maps by the meanderings of the Mississippi River along the Wisconsin-Minnesota border near Chippewa Falls.

Annual production: 175,000 barrels

Other brewery owned by same company: Jacob Leinenkugel Brewing is a subsidiary of Miller Brewing (Milwaukee, WI)

Flagship brand: Leinenkugel's

Major bottom-fermented brands: Leinenkugel's, Leinenkugel's Genuine Bock, Leinenkugel's Light, Leinenkugel's Limited, Leinenkugel's Red

Major seasonal brands: Leinenkugel's Lager

GABF Gold Medals: Leinenkugel's (American Light Lager), 1987; Leinenkugel's Limited, 1993

GABF Silver Medals: Leinenkugel's Limited, 1991

## Melbourne's Brewing
12492 Prospect Road
Strongsville, OH 44136

This brewpub was founded by William I Lersich and Edgar Ross in 1989.

Annual production: 600 barrels

Flagship brands: Wombat Wheat, Bondi Beach Blonde, Down Under

Major bottom-fermented brands: Amber Lager, Golden Lager

Major seasonal brands: Christmas Red, Oktoberfest, Porter, Stout

**Michelob:** See Anheuser-Busch (St Louis, MO)

## Mid-Coast Brewing
35 Wisconsin Street
Oshkosh, WI 54901

This contract brewing company was founded in 1991 by Jeff Fulbright. The Chief Oshkosh brand name was previously in use from 1865 to 1970.

Annual production: None. The beer is contract brewed by the Stevens Point Brewery (Stevens Point, WI).

Major bottom-fermented brands: Chief Oshkosh Munich Gold, Chief Oshkosh Red Lager

## Miller Brewing
4000 West State Street
Milwaukee, WI 53201

The second largest brewing company in North America for the past two decades, Miller Brewing evolved from the Plank Road Brewery started in the Milwaukee suburb of Waqwatosa (now inside the Milwaukee city limits) by Frederick Charles Best in 1850. It was purchased by Frederick Edward John Miller in 1855, and was the eleventh biggest United States brewer when the Philip Morris Com-

Miller also operates plants under its own name in Albany, GA; Eden, NC; Fort Worth, TX; Irwindale, CA; and Trenton, OH, as well as Leinenkugel Brewing in Chippewa Falls, WI.

Flagship brand: Miller

Major top-fermented brand: Miller Reserve Amber Ale

Major bottom-fermented brands: Lite, Löwenbräu (produced under license from the Löwenbräu Brewery in Munich, Germany), Magnum, Meister Bräu, Miller Genuine Draft, Miller Genuine Draft Light, Miller High Life, Miller Reserve, Miller Reserve Light, Milwaukee's Best, Sharp's

GABF Gold Medals: Lowenbräu Dark Special, 1989, 1990; Lowenbräu Light, 1990; Löwenbräu Dark, 1993

GABF Silver Medals: Miller High Life, 1989; Lowenbräu, 1990; Magnum (Malt Liquor), 1993

## Miller Brewing
2525 Wayne Madison Road
Trenton, OH 45067

This brewery was founded by Miller Brewing in 1982. See Miller Brewing, Milwaukee, WI for details on the history of the company.

Annual production: 8,000,000 barrels

Other breweries owned by same company: See Miller Brewing, Milwaukee WI, for a list of Miller breweries.

Major brands: See Miller Brewing, Milwaukee, WI for a list of Miller brands.

See Miller Brewing, Milwaukee, WI for a list of medals awarded to the company.

## Mill Rose Brewing
45 South Barrington Road
South Barrington, IL 60010

This brewpub was founded by the Rose Meat Packing Company in 1991, with the pub menu focusing on meat dishes.

pany purchased a controlling interest in 1969. Lite beer, introduced in 1975, was North America's first mass-market, reduced-caloric beer. It is now Miller's leading brand and the second biggest selling in North America after Anheuser-Busch's Budweiser.

Annual production: 8,500,000 barrels

Other breweries owned by same company:

Annual production: 175 barrels

Major top-fermented brands: Country Inn, Downtown Brown, General's Ale, Wheat 'n' Honey

Major bottom-fermented brands: Dark Star, Prairie Pilsner, Weiss

## Millstream Brewing
Lower Brewery Road
Amana, IA 52203

This brewpub was founded by Joe Pickett, Sr in December 1985.

Annual production: 2000 barrels

Major bottom-fermented brands: Millstream Lager, Millstream Wheat, Schild Bräu

Major seasonal brand: Oktoberfest

GABF Gold Medals: Schild Bräu (European Amber), 1989; Millstream Wheat, 1990

GABF Silver Medals: Schild Bräu (Vienna Style Lager), 1987, 1991

## Minnesota Brewing Company
882 West 7th Street
St Paul, MN 55102

Originally founded by Christian Stahlmann in 1854, this facility became the Jacob Schmidt Brewing Company in 1990, which produced the well-known Schmidt brand for over half a century. G Heileman of La Crosse, WI acquired the brewery in 1972 but continued brewing Schmidt beer. The present company was founded in 1991 by Karen Carels.

Minnesota Brewing now produces beer under its own brand names and also produces 74,000 barrels annually under contract for Pete's Brewing of Palo Alto, CA.

Annual production: 2,200,000 barrels (including production for Pete's Brewing)

Major top-fermented brands: McMahon's Irish Style, Potato Ale

Major bottom-fermented brands: Grain Belt, Grain Belt Premium, Grain Belt Light, Grain Belt Non-alcoholic, Pig's Eye Lean, Pig's Eye Pilsner, Pig's Eye non-alcoholic

Major seasonal brands: Landmark Bock, Landmark Octoberfest

## Miracle Brewing Company
311 South Emporia
Wichita, KS 67202

This, the first brewery in Kansas since Prohibition, was founded in 1992 by Dennis and Joe Boone.

Annual production: 750 barrels

Flagship brand: Red Devil Ale

Major top-fermented brands: Miracle Mild, Puragtory Porter

## Mishawaka Brewing
3703 North Main Street
Mishawaka, IN 46545

This English-style brewpub was founded by John Foster and Tom Schmidt in 1992. It is the first brewery to operate in Mishawaka since the Kamm & Schellinger Brewery closed in 1951.

Annual production: 1000-1200 barrels

Flagship brands: Ankenbrock, Founder's Stout, Lake Effect Pale Ale, Mishawaka Gold Lager, South Shore Amber Ale, Weizen

Major bottom-fermented brands: Mishawaka Gold, Silver Hawks Pilsner

Major seasonal brands: Christmas Ale, Four

Horsemen Irish Ale, JS Bock, Pumpkin Beer, Raspberry Wheat, Resolution Ale, 7 Heisman Weizen, Silver Hawks Pilsner

**O'Doul's:** See Anheuser-Busch (St Louis, MO)

## Oldenberg Brewing

I-75 at Buttermilk Pike
Fort Mitchell, KY 41017

The Oldenberg complex was founded by Jerry Deters and David Heidrich in 1988. More than just a brewery or a brewpub, Oldenberg includes a brewpub, bakery, beer garden, gift shop, brewery and the American Museum of Brewing History & Arts, with the Western Hemisphere's biggest collection of brewing memorabilia. Displayed throughout the complex is the largest collection of breweriana in the world, which includes over 125,000 labels, 45,000 coasters, 27,000 bottles, 12,500 cans, 2000 tap knobs, 600 books and magazines and a beer delivery truck.

Annual production: 13,000 barrels

Flagship brand: Oldenberg Premium Verum

Major top-fermented brand: Oldenberg Vail Ale

Major bottom-fermented brands: Oldenberg Blonde, Oldenberg Premium Verum, Oldenberg Weiss

Major seasonal brands: Oldenberg Oktoberfest Lager, Oldenberg Outrageous Bock, Oldenberg Winter Ale

GABF Silver Medal: Oldenberg Blonde, 1989

## Pabst Brewing Company

917 West Juneau
Milwaukee, WI 53201

The Pabst Brewing Company was the largest brewery in the United States at the turn of the century and has remained in the top six ever since. In 1988, Pabst brewed just over 6,000,000 barrels of beer at four plants, with an aggregate capacity of 14,700,000 barrels. The original brewery was started in 1844 by

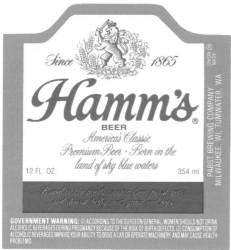

Other breweries owned by same company: Pabst Brewing also operates the Olympia Brewery (Tumwater, WA) and Pearl Brewing (San Antonio, TX).

Flagship brand: Pabst Blue Ribbon

Major bottom-fermented brands: Andecker, Ballantine, Buckhorn, Falstaff, Hamm's, Hamm's Draft, Hamm's Special Light, Jacob Best Premium Light, Low Alcohol Gold, Olde English 800, Olympia, Pabst Blue Ribbon, Pabst Extra Light, Pabst Light

GABF Gold Medals: Pearl Lager Beer, 1991; Olde English 800, 1991; Olympia Dry, 1993

GABF Silver Medals: Pabst Blue Ribbon, 1990; Olde English 800, 1990

## James Page Brewing
1300 Quincy Street NE
Minneapolis, MN 55413

This brewery was founded by James Page in 1987.

Jacob Best and later run by Philip Best in partnership with Captain Frederick Pabst. The captain essentially ran the brewery himself after Philip retired in 1866. Pabst acquired Olympia Brewing in 1983 (which had recently acquired the Theodore Hamm Brewery in St Paul, MN) and was itself taken over in February 1985 by the reclusive California millionaire Paul Kalmanovitz, who already owned the Falstaff, General and Pearl breweries. After Kalmanovitz died in 1987, all four companies passed to the S&P holding company.

Annual production: 6,000,000 barrels

Annual production: 5000 barrels

Flagship brand: Boundary Waters

Major brand: James Page Private Stock

Major seasonal brand: Boundary Waters Bock

## Pavichevich Brewing

383 Romans Road
Elmhurst, IL 60126

This brewery was founded by Ken Pavichevich in 1989.

Annual production: 6200 barrels

Flagship brand: Baderbraü

Major bottom-fermented brands: Baderbraü, Baderbraü Bock, Pilsener

## RJ's Ginseng

Chicago, IL 60610

This contract beer company was founded in 1993 to market a unique beer developed by RJ Corr, which exploits the invigorating qualities of the Asian Ginseng root.

Annual production: None. Beer is produced under contract by Stevens Point Brewery (Stevens Point, WI).

Flagship brand: RJ's Ginseng Beer

**Rolling Rock:** See Latrobe Brewing (Latrobe, PA)

## Rowland's Calumet Brewing

25 North Madison Street
Chilton, WI 53014

The Roll Inn bar opened in 1983, with the brewery being added in 1990 by Robert Row-

land. The establishment is located in Chilton's original firehouse.

Annual production: 200 barrels

Major bottom-fermented brands: Calumet Amber, Calumet Dark, Calumet Pilsner, Calumetic Heat

Major seasonal brands: Calumet Bock, Calumet Oktoberfest, Calumet Rye

## Saint Louis Brewery

2100 Locust Street
St Louis, MO 63103

This brewpub, voted the best new bar in St Louis in 1992, was founded by Tom Schlafly and Dan Kopman in 1991.

Annual production: 1253 barrels

Flagship brands: Schlafly Brand Beers

Major top-fermented brands: Schlafly Hefeweizen, Schlafly Pale Ale, Schlafly Stout, Schlafly Wheat

Major bottom-fermented brand: Schlafly Pils

Major seasonal brands: Burn's Scotch Ale, Independence Ale, Maibock, Oktoberfest-Märzen

## August Schell Brewing
Schell's Park
New Ulm, MN 56073

This brewery was founded by August Schell in 1860. The brewery survived the 1862 Sioux uprising because of August Schell's good relations with the Indians, and has existed as a small regional brewery ever since.

Annual production: 40,000 barrels

Flagship brand: August Schell Pils

Major top-fermented brands: August Schell Weizen, Schmaltz's Alt

Major bottom-fermented brand: August Schell Pils

Major seasonal brands: August Schell Bock, August Schell Octoberfest

GABF Gold Medals: August Schell Pils, 1988; August Schell Weizen, 1988

GABF Silver Medals: Octoberfest, 1991; August Schell Weizen, 1993

**Schlitz:** See Stroh Brewing (Detroit, MI)

**Jacob Schmidt:** See G Heileman Brewing (La Crosse, WI) and Minnesota Brewing (St Paul, MN)

**Schoenling:** See Hudepohl-Schoenling (Cincinnati, OH)

## Sharkey's Brewery
7777 Cass Street
Omaha, NE 68114

This brewpub was founded by the Simonson family in 1992 in an old train depot, and it features a 400-gallon aquarium with live sharks.

Annual production: 1000 barrels

Flagship brands: Great White Pale Ale, Red Shark Amber Ale

Major seasonal brand: The Great Pumpkin Ale

**Sharp's:** See Miller Brewing (Milwaukee, WI)

## Sherlock's Home
11000 Red Circle Drive
Minnetonka, MN 55343

This brewpub was founded about 1992.

Annual production: 2000 barrels

Major top-fermented brands: Bishop's Bitter, Palace Porter, Stag's Head Stout, Star of India IPA

Major bottom-fermented brands: Gold Crown Lager, Queen Anne Light

Major seasonal brands: Alt Bier, Wheat Beer, Winter Ale

## Silo Brewpub
630 Barret Avenue
Louisville, KY 40204

This brewpub was founded in 1992 in a renovated warehouse that once belonged to the Ballard Biscuit Company, which eventually evolved into Pillsbury.

Annual production: Under 500 barrels

Major top-fermented brands: Silo Premium Light, Red Rock Ale, River City Raspberry

Major seasonal brands: Hercules, Wheat, Winter Warmer, Yuletide Light

GABF Silver Medal: Yuletide Ale, 1993

## Sprecher Brewing
730 West Oregon Street
Milwaukee, WI 53204

This brewery was founded by master brewer Randy Sprecher in 1985. The brewery plans to move to a new location in 1995.

Annual production: 9000 barrels of beer and 10,000 barrels of root beer soda

Flagship brand: Special Amber

Major top-fermented brand: Hefe Weiss

Major bottom-fermented brands: Black Bavarian, Special Amber

Major seasonal brands: Maibock, Oktoberfest, Winter Brew

**Sterling:** See Evansville Brewing (Evansville, IN)

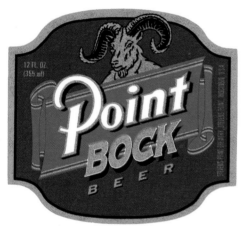

## Stevens Point Brewery
2617 Water Street
Stevens Point, WI 54481

The brewery was originally founded by Frank Wahle and George Ruder before 1857, and by 1902 it had taken its present name. The success enjoyed by the Stevens Point Brewery and its Point Special Beer since the 1970s is seen as being due, at least in part, to its decision to limit distribution to a very narrow geographical area, permitting demand to exceed supply.

Annual production: 60,000 barrels

Flagship brand: Point Special Beer

Major bottom-fermented brands: Eagle Premium Pilsner, Point Classic Amber, Point Light, Point Special

Major seasonal brands: Point Bock, Spud Premier

GABF Gold Medal: Spud Premier, 1991

## Stroh Brewery
100 River Place
Detroit, MI 48207

The company was founded by Bernhard Stroh in 1850 and has been headquartered in Detroit ever since, although the aging Stroh Detroit brewing plant was closed and demolished in 1985. A major regional brewer for over a century, Stroh became one of the big four American brewing companies in 1982 when it

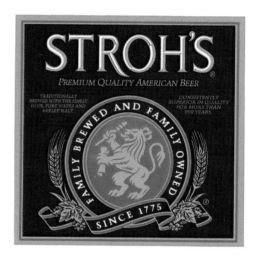

acquired the larger, but financially troubled, Joseph Schlitz Brewing Company of Milwaukee, WI, which had brewed one of America's top two national brands for as long as there had been national brands.

Schlitz evolved from the August Krug Brewery, founded in 1849. In 1856, when Krug died, his bookkeeper, Joseph Schlitz, married Krug's widow and renamed the brewery after himself. Although Schlitz and his wife died in a boating mishap in 1875, the company became the most powerful company in Milwaukee, which was the de facto 'capital city' of American brewing. Indeed, the Schlitz flagship lager was known simply as 'the Beer that Made Milwaukee Famous.'

Today, Stroh still includes the Schlitz brand as a major part of its portfolio and continues to brew at former Schlitz facilities.

Annual production: No production in Detroit. A total of 18,400,000 barrels is brewed at its operating breweries.

Other breweries owned by same company: Stroh operates breweries in Fogelsville, PA; Longview, TX; St Paul, MN; Tampa, FL; and Winston-Salem, NC.

Flagship brands: Schlitz, Stroh's

Major bottom-fermented brands: Augsburger, Augsburger Bock, Augsburger Dark, Augsburger Golden, Bull Ice, Goebel, Goebel Light, Old Milwaukee, Old Milwaukee Genuine Draft, Old Milwaukee Genuine Draft Light, Old Milwaukee Light, Old Milwaukee NA, Piels, Piels Light, Primo, Red Bull Malt Liquor, Schaefer, Schaefer Genuine Draft, Schaefer Light, Schaefer Light Draft, Schaefer Premium Light, Schlitz, Schlitz Genuine Draft, Schlitz Ice, Schlitz Light, Schlitz Malt Liquor, Signature, Stroh's, Stroh's Light, Stroh's NA, Thunder Malt Liquor

Major seasonal brands: Augsburger Doppelbock, Augsburger Oktoberfest, Augsburger Weiss

GABF Gold Medal: Signature, 1988

## Stroh Brewery
707 East Minnehaha
St Paul, MN 55164

This brewery was founded in 1860 by Andrew Keller as the Pittsburgh Brewery. In 1864, it was

**Summit Brewing**
2264 University Avenue
St Paul, MN 55114

This brewery was founded in 1986 and is operated by Mark Stutrud.

Annual production: 15,000 barrels

Flagship brand: Summit Extra Pale Ale

Major top-fermented brand: Great Northern Porter

purchased by Theodore Hamm and it became the flagship of his empire in 'The Land of Sky Blue Waters.' In 1975, Hamm Brewing was sold to Olympia Brewing of Tumwater WA, which was in turn sold to Pabst Brewing of Milwaukee, WI in 1983. Later in 1983, the St Paul plant became a Stroh Brewery.

Annual production: 3,500,000 barrels

Other breweries owned by same company: Stroh, which is headquartered in Detroit, MI, also operates breweries in Fogelsville, PA; Longview, TX; Tampa, FL; and Winston-Salem, NC.

Flagship brands: Schlitz, Stroh's

Major bottom-fermented brands: See Stroh Brewery (Detroit, MI) for list of Stroh brands.

Major seasonal brands: See Stroh Brewery (Detroit, MI) for list of Stroh brands.

GABF Silver Medal: Signature, 1988

Major bottom-fermented brand: Heimertingen Maibock

Major seasonal brand: Summit Winter Ale

GABF Gold Medal: Great Northern Porter, 1987

## Water Street Brewery
1101 North Water Street
Milwaukee, WI 53202

This brewery/restaurant was founded in 1987 and features an antique bottle collection and brewery lithographs.

Annual production: 1500 barrels

Flagship brand: Water Street

Major top-fermented brands: Cream City Porter, Felix Callan's Irish Red, Water Street Amber, Water Street Weiss

Major bottom-fermented brands: Kilburn's Special Bock, Sporten European Lager, Water Street Pils

Major seasonal brand: Old World Oktoberfest

GABF Gold Medal: Oktoberfest, 1988

## Weinkeller Brewery
6417 West Roosevelt Road
Berwyn, IL 60402

This German-style brewpub was founded by Udo Harttung in 1992.

Annual production: 900 barrels

Other brewery owned by the same company: Weinkeller Brewery (Westmont, IL)

Flagship brands: Amber Lager, Berwyn Brew Pilsner, Düsseldorfer Doppelbock, Golden Lager

Major top-fermented brands: Aberdeen Amber Ale, Bavarian Weiss

Major bottom-fermented brands: Amber Lager, Berwyn Brew Pilsner, Golden Lager

Major seasonal brands: Alt, Christmas Dark, Mardi Gras Bock, Maibock, Oktoberfest

GABF Silver Medal: Düsseldorfer Doppelbock, 1990

## Weinkeller Brewery
651 Westmont Drive
Westmont, IL 60559

The brewery was founded by Udo Harttung in 1992.

Annual production: 900 barrels

Other brewery owned by the same company: Weinkeller Brewery (Berwyn, IL)

Flagship brands: Amber Lager, Berwyn Brew Pilsner, Düsseldorfer Doppelbock, Golden Lager

Major top-fermented brands: Aberdeen Amber Ale, Bavarian Weiss

Major bottom-fermented brands: Amber Lager, Berwyn Brew Pilsner, Golden Lager

Major seasonal brands: Alt, Christmas Dark, Mardi Gras Bock, Maibock, Oktoberfest

GABF Silver Medal: Düsseldorfer Doppelbock, 1990

## White River Mining
1027 East Walnut
Springfield, MO 65806

This brewpub was founded in 1992 in a former Southern Missouri State University fraternity house.

Annual production: Under 500 barrels

Major top-fermented brands: Black River Stout, Copperhead, Golden Nougat, Raspberry Ale

Major seasonal brand: Winterblast Ale

**Wiedemann:** See Evansville Brewing (Evansville, IN)

# THE MOUNTAIN WEST

## Albuquerque Brewing & Bottling
637½ Broadway SE
Albuquerque, NM 87102

Founded by Michael Buckner in 1986, Albuquerque Brewing & Bottling is a brewpub.

Annual production: over 1200 barrels

Flagship brand: Michael's Golden Ale

## Anheuser-Busch
3500 East County Road 52
Fort Collins, CO 80524

This brewery was started by Anheuser-Busch in 1988.

Annual production: 6,100,000 barrels

Other breweries owned by the same company: See Anheuser-Busch, St Louis, MO for a list of Anheuser-Busch breweries.

Flagship brand: Budweiser

See Anheuser-Busch, St Louis, MO for a list of medals awarded to Anheuser-Busch beers.

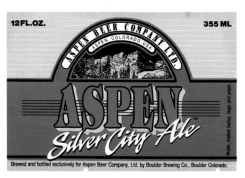

## Aspen Brewing Company
Aspen, CO 81612

The company was founded in 1988.

Annual production: None. This beer is brewed under contract by Rockies Brewing (Boulder, CO).

Flagship brand: Aspen Silver City Ale

## Assets Grille & Brewing
6910 Montgomery NE
Albuquerque, NM 87110

This establishment was founded as a grill in 1977 and the brewery was added by Russ Zeigler, Doug Smith and Don Goodenough in 1993.

Annual production: 1500 barrels

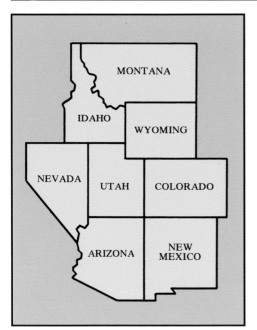

This brewery was founded by Jürgen Knöller in August 1987 and is located in the former Northern Pacific Railway station. The brewery and restaurant are separately owned and operated.

Annual production: 1500 barrels

Flagship brand: Bayern Amber

Major bottom-fermented brands: Amber, Wheat Dark, Wheat Light, Pils

Major seasonal brands: Doppelbock, Maibock, Oktoberfest

Major top-fermented brands: Albuquerque Pale, Cactus Kölsch, Duke City Amber, Old Avalanche Barleywine, Pablo's Porter, Rio Grande Copper, Rio Grande Wheat, Roadrunner Ale, Sandia Stout

Major seasonal brands: St Paddy's Red Eye Red, Negra Linda

## MJ Barleyhoppers Brewery & Public House
507 South Main
Moscow, ID 83843

This brewpub was founded in 1991.

Annual production: 1040 barrels

Major bottom-fermented brands: Barleyhopper Brown Ale, McGinty's Old Irish Stout, Palouse Weizen, Paradise Pale Ale

**Bandersnatch:** See Christopher Joseph (Tempe, AZ)

## Bayern Brewing
Missoula Northern Pacific
100 Railroad Street
Missoula, MT 59807-8043

## Beaver Street Brewery & Whistle Stop Cafe
11 South Beaver Street
Flagstaff, AZ 86001

This brewery was founded by Evan and Winnie Hanseth and Dick and Jean Wilson in 1994.

Annual production: 1200 barrels

Flagship brand: Red Ale

Major top-fermented brands: Bitter, Oatmeal Stout, Pale Ale

Major bottom-fermented brand: Bohemian Pilsner

Major seasonal brands: Christmas Ale, Raspberry Ale

1 PINT 6 FL. OZ.
Brewed & Bottled by the
H.C. Berger Brewing Co. Ft. Collins, Colorado

## HC Berger Brewing

1900 East Lincoln Avenue
Fort Collins, CO 80524

This brewery was founded by Sandy and Karen Jones in 1992.

Annual production: 6800 barrels

Flagship brand: Indego Pale Ale

Major top-fermented brands: Red Ass Ale, Red Banshee, Whistlepin Wheat

Major seasonal brands: Chestnut Ale, Katcher's Rye

GABF Silver Medal: Whistlepin Wheat, 1993

**Black Dog:** See Spanish Peaks Brewing (Bozeman, MT)

**Boulder Brewing:** See Rockies Brewing (Boulder, CO)

## Breckenridge Brewery & Pub

600 South Main Street
Breckenridge, CO 80424

This brewery was founded by Richard Squire in 1990.

Annual production: 3000 barrels

Other brewery owned by the same company: Breckenridge Brewery & Pub, Denver, CO

Flagship brands: Avalanche Ale, India Pale Ale, Mountain Wheat, Oatmeal Stout

Major top-fermented brands: All ales with the exception of Specials

Major bottom-fermented brands: Blue River Bock, Christmas Ale

Major seasonal brands: Blue River Bock, Christmas Ale, Irish Red

GABF Silver Medal: India Pale Ale, 1991

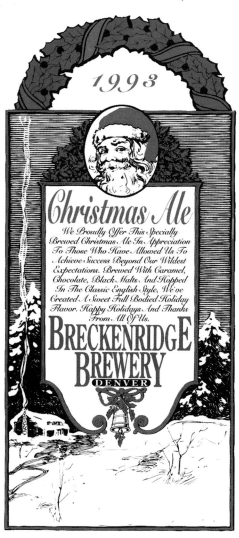

## Breckenridge Brewery & Pub
2220 Blake Street
Denver, CO 80205

This brewery was founded by Richard Squire in December 1992. The brewpub offers rides via a red London double-decker bus to Mile High Stadium.

Annual production: 15,000 barrels

Other brewery owned by the same company: Breckenridge Brewery & Pub, Breckenridge, CO

Flagship brand: Avalanche Ale

Major top-fermented brands: India Pale Ale, Mountain Wheat, Oatmeal Stout

Major seasonal brands: Christmas Ale, Brectoberfest, Hefe-Weizen, spring and summer ales

GABF Silver Medal: India Pale Ale, 1991

## Brewed & Baked in Telluride
127 South Fir Street
Telluride, CO 81435

This brewery was founded by Jerry Greene in 1991 in a Jewish bakery and pizza restaurant which opened in 1976.

Annual production: 62.75 barrels

Flagship brand: Redcloud Wheat

Major bottom-fermented brand: Runners High Oktoberfest

## Broadway Brewing Company
2441 Broadway Street
Denver, CO 80205

This brewery was founded in about 1993.

Annual production: Under 500 barrels

Other breweries owned by same company: Blue Cat Brew Pub (Rock Island, IL), Cooper-Smith's Pub & Brewing (Fort Collins, CO), Crane River Brew Pub & Cafe (Lincoln, NE), Firehouse Brewing Company (Rapid City, SD),

Norman Brewing (Norman, OK), Phantom Canyon Brewing Company (Colorado Springs, CO), River City Brewery (Wichita, KS), Wynkoop Brewing (Denver, CO)

**Budweiser:** See Anheuser-Busch (St Louis, MO)

**Busch:** See Anheuser-Busch (St Louis, MO)

## Carver Brewing
Carver's Bakery Cafe & Brewery
1022 Main Street
Durango, CO 81301

This brewery was founded by Jim and Bill Carver in 1988, two years after the Bakery Cafe opened in 1986.

Annual production: 600 barrels

Major top-fermented brands: Carver IPA, Golden Wheat & Honey, Iron Horse Stout, Old Oak Amber Ale

Major bottom-fermented brand: Purgatory Honey Pilsner

Major seasonal brands: Barley Wine, Raspberry Wheat Ale

## Champion Brewing

1442 Larimer Square
Denver, CO 80202

The brewpub was founded in 1991.

Annual production: Under 500 barrels

Major top-fermented brands: Coal Porter, Home Run Ale, Stout Street Stout

Major bottom-fermented brands: Buck Wheat, Larimer Lager

Major seasonal brands: Octoberfest, St Patrick's Day

GABF Gold Medal: Home Run Ale, 1993

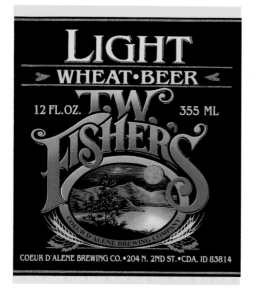

## Coeur d'Alene Brewing

'TW Fisher's, A Brewpub'
204 North Second Street
Coeur D'Alene, ID 83814

Tom Fisher opened 'TW Fisher's, A Brewpub' in July 1987, just three weeks after brewpubs officially became legal in Idaho.

Annual production: 8000 barrels

Flagship brand: TW Fisher's

Major top-fermented brands: Centennial Pale Ale, Festival Dark, Full Moon Stout

Major bottom-fermented brand: Weizen Light

Major seasonal brands: Red Oktober, Winter Warmer

GABF Gold Medal: TW Fisher's Centennial Pale Ale, 1988

## CooperSmith's Pub & Brewing

#5 Old Town Square
Fort Collins, CO 80524

This brewpub was founded in 1989.

CooperSmith's is located in what was originally two separate buildings, built around 1901, in Old Town Fort Collins. The brewery is the first opened in Fort Collins since 1900.

Annual production: Less than 1000 barrels

Other breweries owned by same company: Broadway Brewing Company (Denver, CO), Blue Cat Brew Pub (Rock Island, IL), Crane River Brew Pub & Cafe (Lincoln, NE), Firehouse Brewing Company (Rapid City, SD), Norman Brewing (Norman, OK), Phantom Canyon Brewing Company (Colorado Springs, CO), River City Brewery (Wichita, KS), Wynkoop Brewing (Denver, CO)

Major top-fermented brands: Albert Damn Bitter, Dunraven Ale, Horsetooth Stout, Not

Brown Ale, Pedestrian Ale, Poudre Pale Ale, Punjabi Pale Ale, Scooter's Scottish Ale

Major bottom-fermented brands: Havel Lager, Mountain Avenue Wheat, Sigda's Green Chili Beer

Major seasonal brands: Black Powder Barley Wine, Bock Beer, CooperSmith's Christmas Ale, Oktoberfest Beer

GABF Silver Medal: Sigda's Green Chili Beer, 1991

## Coors Brewing Company
12th & Ford Streets
Golden, CO 80401

Coors Brewing operates at the same site high in the Rocky Mountains that was selected by Adolph Coors himself in 1873. Today, Coors is operated by third and fourth generation Coors family members.

The Coors brewing plant in Golden is one of the largest single-site breweries in the world. In 1987, the company celebrated the grand opening of its second brewery in Virginia's Shennandoah Valley, near the town of Elkton.

This facility was part of a successful drive, begun in the 1980s, to expand the company from a regional to a national brewer.

Annual production: 9,000,000 barrels

Other brewery owned by the same company: Coors Shennandoah Brewery (Elkton, VA)

Flagship brand: Coors

Major top-fermented brand: Killian's Red

Major bottom-fermented brands: Coors, Coors Dry, Coors Cutter, Coors Extra Gold, Coors Light, Keystone, Keystone Dry, Keystone Light, Turbo 1000

Major seasonal brand: Winterfest

GABF Gold Medals: Coors Extra Gold, 1989, 1990; Keystone Light, 1991; Coors Dry, 1991

GABF Silver Medals: Coors, 1989; Coors Light, 1990; Winterfest, 1990, 1993

## Coyote Spring Brewing & Cafe
4883 North 20th Street
Phoenix, AZ 85016

This establishment was founded around 1992 as Barley's Brewpub.

Annual production: 1200 barrels

Major top-fermented brands: Brown Ale, Fair Dinkun Ale, Nuts-to-You Nut Toby Stout, Trick Pale Ale

Major bottom-fermented brand: Koyote Kölsch

## Crazy Ed's Black Mountain Brewing
6245 East Cave Creek Road
Cave Creek, AZ 85331

This brewery was founded in 1989 by Ed Chilleen, whose wife, Maria, owns The Satisfied Frog restaurant next door.

Annual production: 18,000 barrels

Flagship brand: Cave Creek Chili Beer

Major bottom-fermented brand: Arizona Pilsner

Major seasonal brand: Crazy Ed's Bock

## Crested Butte Brewing (The Idlespur)
226 Elk Avenue
Crested Butte, CO 81224

This brewery/restaurant was founded in 1991.

Annual production: 1000 barrels

Major top-fermented brands: Bucks Wheat, Raspberry Stout, Red Lady Ale, Rodeo Stout, 3-Pin Grin Porter, White Buffalo Peace Ale

## Durango Brewing
3000 Main Street
Durango, CO 81301

This brewery was founded by Steve and Linda McClaren in 1990.

Annual production: 400 barrels

Flagship brand: Anasazi Wheat, Durango Dark Lager

Major seasonal brands: Durango Colorfest, Durango Winter Ale

## Electric Dave Brewing
1A DD Street
South Bisbee, AZ 85603

This brewery was founded by Dave Harvan in 1988.

Annual production: 490 barrels

Major brands: Electric Light, Electric Dark, Electric Wheat

**TW Fisher:** See Coeur d'Alene Brewing (Coeur d'Alene, ID)

## Flying Dog Brewpub & Grille
424 East Cooper
Aspen, CO 81611

Founded by George Stranahan in 1991, Flying Dog is the first brewery in Aspen since the 1890s silver boom.

Annual production: 1500 barrels

Flagship brand: Doggie Style Amber Ale

Major top-fermented brands: Doggie Style Amber Ale, Flying McDog Scotch Ale, Greyhound Golden Honey Ale

Major seasonal brands: Doghouse Wheat, Gnarley Barley Wine, Raspberry Wheat

GABF Gold Medals: Flying McDog Scotch Ale, 1991; Greyhound Golden Honey Ale, 1992

## Gentle Ben's Brewing

841 North Tyndall
Tucson, AZ 85719

This brewpub was founded near the University of Arizona campus in 1991.

Annual production: Under 500 barrels

Major top-fermented brands: Arizona Gold, Pusch Ridge Pale, Red Cat Amber, Tucson Blond

Major seasonal brands: Bear Down Brown, Cinnamon Christmas Beer, Copperhead, McKale's Ale, Taylor's Raspberry Ale

## Golden City Brewing

920 12th Street
Golden, CO 80401

This brewery was founded by Charlie Sturdavant in 1993.

Annual production: 200 barrels

Flagship brand: Golden City Red (a Düsseldorf-style Altbier)

Major top-fermented brand: Golden Cream Ale

## Harrison Hollow Brewhouse

2455 Harrison Hollow Boulevard
Boise, ID 83702

This brewpub was founded in 1992.

Annual production: 750 barrels

Flagship brand: Figewirth

Major top-fermented brand: Western Ale

Major bottom-fermented brand: Ginger Wheat

## Holy Cow! Casino Cafe Brewery

2423 Las Vegas Boulevard South
Las Vegas, NV 89104

This brewpub was founded as the Las Vegas Strip in 1993, six months after the casino and cafe of the same name.

Annual production: Under 500 barrels

Major top-fermented brands: Holy Cow! Dark Ale, Holy Cow! Pale Ale

GABF Gold Medal: Holy Cow! Pale Ale, 1993

## Hops! Bistro & Brewery

7000 East Camelback Road
Scottsdale, AZ 85251

This brewpub was founded by Lessing Stern in 1990, the first in his chain of brewpubs.

Annual production: 1350 barrels

Other breweries owned by the same company: Hops! Bistro & Brewery (Phoenix, AZ), Hops! Bistro & Brewery (San Diego, CA)

Flagship brand: Hops! Hefe-Weizen

Major top-fermented brands: Amber Ale, Hefe-Weizen, Oatmeal Stout, Raspberry Ale

Major bottom-fermented brands: Bock, Doppelbock, Export Lager, Maibock, Pilsner

Major seasonal brand: Barley Wine

GABF Gold Medal: Hops! Hefe-Weizen, 1992

GABF Silver Medals: Hops! Wheat Beer, 1991; Hops! Barley Wine, 1991

## Hops! Bistro & Brewery

Biltmore Fashion Park
24th & Camelback Road
Phoenix, AZ 85015

This brewpub was founded by Lessing Stern in 1992, the third in his chain of brewpubs.

Other breweries owned by the same company: Hops! Bistro & Brewery (Scottsdale, AZ), Hops! Bistro & Brewery (San Diego, CA)

Flagship brand: Hops! Hefe-Weizen

GABF Gold Medal: Hops! Hefe-Weizen, 1992

GABF Silver Medals: Hops! Wheat Beer, 1991; Hops! Barley Wine, 1991

### Hubcap Brewery & Kitchen
143 East Meadow Drive
Vail, CO 81657

This brewpub was founded by Dean L Liotta in 1991 near the Vail ski slopes.

Annual production: 1750 barrels

Other brewery owned by the same company: Equity position in Hubcap Brewery/West End, Dallas, TX

Flagship brands: Beaver Tail Brown Ale, Rainbow Trout Stout, Vail Pale Ale

Major top-fermented brands: Beaver Tail Brown Ale, Rainbow Trout Stout, Vail Pale Ale

Major seasonal brands: Killer Bee Honey Ale, Ozone Ale

GABF Gold Medal: Vail Pale Ale, 1992

GABF Silver Medals: Beaver Tail Brown Ale, 1991; Rainbow Trout Stout, 1992

### Irons Brewing
12354 West Alameda Parkway, Unit E
Lakewood, CO 80228

This brewery was founded by Larry Irons in 1992.

Annual production: 33 barrels

Major top-fermented brands: Irons Green Mountain, Irons High Plains Porter

Major bottom-fermented brands: Irons Alpine Pilsner, Irons Europa Lager

## Christopher Joseph Brewing
Bandersnatch Brewpub
125 East 5th Avenue
Tempe, AZ 85281

This brewpub was founded by Joseph Mocca and Joseph Risi in 1988.

Annual production: 500 barrels

Flagship brand: Big Horn Premium Ale

## Judge Baldwin's Brewing
4 South Cascade
Colorado Springs, CO 80903

This brewpub was founded in 1991 at Antler's Doubletree Hotel and named for Judge WH Baldwin, known as a memorable orator and beer lover.

Annual production: Under 500 barrels

Major top-fermented brands: Amber Ale, Nut Brown Ale, Pale Ale

Major bottom-fermented brand: Wheat

## Lovetree Brewing
375 East 55th Avenue
Denver, CO 80216

This brewery was founded in 1993 by James Dallarosa and Ken Piel.

Annual production: 1500 barrels

Major top-fermented brands: Country Cream Ale, Iron Horse Dark Ale, Sunset Red Ale

GABF Gold Medal: Country Cream Ale, 1993

**Kessler:** See Montana Beverages (Helena, MT)

## Eddie McStiff's Brewpub
57 South Main
Moab, UT 84532

This brewpub was founded as Moab's oldest legal brewery by Mike McTeague, Steve Patterson and Ed Snyder in 1991, an amalgam of whose names became 'Eddie McStiff.'

Annual production: 1000 barrels

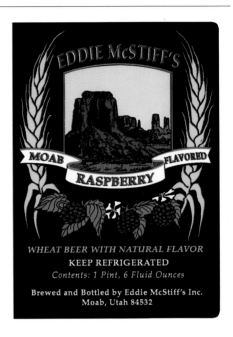

WHEAT BEER WITH NATURAL FLAVOR
KEEP REFRIGERATED
Contents: 1 Pint, 6 Fluid Ounces

Brewed and Bottled by Eddie McStiff's Inc.
Moab, Utah 84532

Flagship brand: Raspberry Wheat

Major top-fermented brands: Raspberry Wheat, Wheat Beer, Cream Ale, Amber Ale, Chestnut Brown, Stout, Ginger, Blueberry Wheat, Jalapeño, Spruce Beer, Passion Fruit Pale, Cherry Stout

Southwest Brewmeister's Festival '92-'93: Best Beer

Breckenridge Brewski Tasting: First Place, 1992

## Milestown Brewing
1014 South Haynes
Miles City, MT 59301

The brewery was founded by Sonny Butts and Larry Grant in 1992 with the beer available at the adjacent Golden Spur bar.

Annual production: 648 barrels

Flagship brand: Old Milestown

Major top-fermented brands: Coal Porter, Le Mongrass Wheat, Old Milestown

Major bottom-fermented brands: Buckinghorse Bock, Lemongrass Wheat, Prof Bach Festbier

## Montana Beverages
## Kessler Brewery
1439 Harris Street
Helena, MT 59601

Montana's first microbrewery was founded by Dick Burke and Bruce DeRoster in 1982. The original Kessler Brewery was founded in 1865 in Last Chance Gulch by Luxembourg native Nick Kessler and later grew into one of Montana's most important breweries. The town was renamed Helena. The Kessler trademark was bought by Bruce DeRoster and is currently used by Montana Beverages. By 1957, the market for small breweries in Montana, as in most of the rest of the United States, had been reduced to the point where it was no longer economically viable. Kessler Brewing closed, and its copper kettles were shipped to South America.

When Montana Beverages revived the Kessler brand 27 years later, it was an entirely new beer and an entirely new market. Under the direction of master brewer Julius Hummer, the brewery produces the Kessler brand beers, as well as having brewed under contract for companies in Eugene, OR; Santa Barbara, CA; and Jackson Hole, WY.

Annual production: 5000 barrels

Flagship brand: Kessler

Major bottom-fermented brands: Extra Pale, Kessler Bock, Kessler Centennial Lager, Kessler Wheat, Lorelei

Major seasonal brands: Oktoberfest, Winter Beer

GABF Gold Medal: Kessler Grand Teton Dopplebock, 1989

GABF Silver Medal: Kessler Bock (Bocks/Doppelbocks), 1987

## New Belgium Brewing Company
350 Linden Street
Fort Collins, CO 80524

This brewery was founded by Kim Jordan and her husband, Jeffrey Lebesch, in 1991 with the express purpose of brewing Belgian-style beers in the United States. Jordan and Lebesch had studied beer making techniques at breweries in Belgium.

Annual production: 19,000 barrels

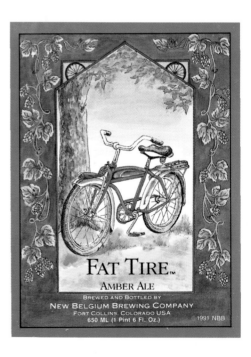

Flagship brand: Fat Tire Amber Ale

Major top-fermented brands: Abbey Trappist Style Ale, Fat Tire Amber Ale, Old Cheny Ale, Sunshine Wheat Beer, Trippel Trappist Style Ale

Major seasonal brand: Frambozen Raspberry Brown Ale

GABF Gold Medal: Abbey Trappist Style Ale, 1993

## Oasis Brewery & Restaurant

1095 Canyon Boulevard
Boulder, CO 80302

This brewery/restaurant, with its overriding Egyptian ambience and all-American menu, was founded in 1991.

Annual production: 1500 barrels

Flagship brand: Oasis Pale Ale

Major top-fermented brands: Scarab Red, Tut Brown, Zosar Oatmeal Stout

Major seasonal brands: Christmas Spiced Ale, Terminator Doppelbock

GABF Silver Medal: Zosar Oatmeal Stout, 1993

**O'Doul's:** See Anheuser-Busch (St Louis, MO)

## Odell Brewing

119 Lincoln Avenue
Fort Collins, CO 80524

The brewery was founded by Doug Odell in 1989.

Annual production: 5627 barrels

Flagship brand: 90 Shilling

Major top-fermented brands: Easy Street Wheat, Cutthroat Porter, 90 Shilling

Major seasonal brands: Christmas Shilling, Festival Ale, Riley's Red

GABF Gold Medal: Easy Street Wheat, 1993

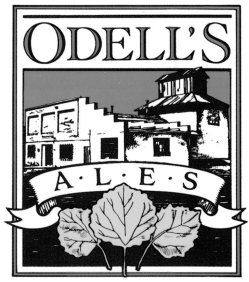

**Organ Mountain:** See O'Ryan's (Las Cruces, NM)

## O'Ryan's Tavern & Brewery

700 South Telshor Boulevard
Las Cruces, NM 88001

This brewpub was founded in 1993 as a micro-brewery, Organ Mountain Brewing, but in 1994 took the name of the existing adjacent tavern with which it is associated.

Annual production: 584 barrels

Major top-fermented brand: Brown Dog Ale, Dog Spit Stout, Red Dog Pale Ale

Major bottom-fermented brand: Organ Mountain Weizen

Major seasonal brands: Bock, Christmas, Golden Wheat, Oktoberfest

## Otto Brothers' Brewing

1295 West Street
Wilson, WY 83014

This brewery was founded by Charlie and Ernie Otto in 1989. Their Old Faithful Ale is served at the Old Faithful Lodge in Yellowstone National Park, almost within sight of the famous geyser of the same name.

Annual production: 625 barrels

Flagship brand: Teton Ale

Major top-fermented brands: Moose Juice Stout, Old Faithful Ale, Teton Ale

Major seasonal brand: Huckleberry Wheat

## Phantom Canyon Brewing Company

2 East Pikes Peak Avenue
Colorado Springs, CO 80903

This brewpub was founded by John Hickenlooper in 1993.

Annual production: Under 500 barrels

Other breweries owned by same company: Blue Cat Brew Pub (Rock Island, IL), Broadway Brewing Company (Denver, CO), Cooper-Smith's Pub & Brewing (Fort Collins, CO), Crane River Brew Pub & Cafe (Lincoln, NE), Firehouse Brewing Company (Rapid City, SD), River City Brewery (Wichita, KS), Norman Brewing Company (Norman, OK), and Wynkoop Brewing (Denver, CO)

Major top-fermented brands: Cascade Amber, Queen's Blonde, Phantom IPA, Zebulon's Peated Porter

## Preston Brewery

PO Box 154
Embudo, NM 87531

The brewery and the Embudo Station Restaurant were founded in 1992 in the 'Chili Line' train station, located on Route 68 between Santa Fe and Taos.

Annual production: Under 500 barrels

Major top-fermented brands: Narrow Gauge Ale, Railroader's Stout, Rio Grande Rista-Red Chili Ale

## Rock Bottom Brewery
1001 16th Street
Denver, CO 80265

This brewpub was founded in 1991.

Annual production: 3000 barrels

Other breweries owned by same company: Rockies Brewing (Boulder, CO), Walnut Brewery (Boulder, CO)

Flagship brand: Rockies Premium

Major top-fermented brands: Arapaho Amber, Black Diamond Stout, Falcon Pale Ale, Molly's Brown, Red Rocks Red

Major seasonal brands: Jazzberry, Jingle Bells Rock, Old Thumper

## Rockies Brewing
2880 Wilderness Place
Boulder, CO 80301

The company was founded by David Hummer and 'Stick' Ware as Boulder Beer Company in a goat shed near Longmont in 1979, and as such it is the oldest existing microbrewery in

the United States. The present facility opened in 1984 and changed the company name in 1992.

Annual production: 14,000 barrels

Other breweries owned by same company: Rock Bottom (Denver, CO), Walnut Brewery (Boulder, CO)

Major bottom-fermented brands: Boulder Extra Pale Ale, Boulder Porter, Boulder Stout, Buffalo Gold, Rockies Premium Draft, Wrigley Red

GABF Gold Medal: Wrigley Red, 1993

GABF Silver Medal: Boulder Amber, 1993

**Rolling Rock:** See Latrobe Brewing (Latrobe, PA)

## Russell Brewery
1242 Siler Road
Santa Fe, NM 87501

This brewery was founded by Robert Russell in 1992.

Annual production: Under 500 barrels

Major top-fermented brands: Light Ale, Pale Ale, Porter

## Salt Lake Brewing
## Squatter's Pub Brewery
147 West Broadway
Salt Lake City, UT 84101

This brewpub was founded in 1989 in the former Boston Hotel.

Annual production: 1600 barrels

Major top-fermented brands: City Creek Pale, Emigration Amber, Millcreek Cream Stout

Major seasonal brands: Dark Winter Wheat, Holiday Nut Brown Ale, Squatter's Anniversary Pilsner

## San Francisco Bar & Grill
3922 North Oracle Road
Tucson, AZ 85705

This brewpub was founded in 1993.

Annual production: Under 500 barrels

Major top-fermented brands: Mesquite Ale, Pale Ale, Wildcat Ale

Major bottom-fermented brands: Amber Light, Cactus Lager, Old Mission

## San Juan Brewing
300 South Townsend
Telluride, CO 81435

This brewpub was founded by James Loo in 1991 in a restored Victorian station once served by the Rio Grande Southern Railroad.

Annual production: 700 barrels

Flagship brand: Little Rose Amber Ale

Major hybrid yeast brands: Boomerang Brown Ale, India Pale Ale

Major seasonal brands: Temptation Stout, Willie's Wheat

## Sangre De Cristo Brewing
106 Des Georges Lane
Taos, NM 87571

This brewpub was founded by Steve Eskeback in 1992.

Annual production: Under 500 barrels

Major top-fermented brands: Brown Ale, Mesa Pale, Scottish Ale, Taos Mountain Gold

Major seasonal brand: Weizen

## Santa Fe Brewing
Flying M Ranch
Galisteo, NM 87540

This brewery was founded in 1987 by Mike Levis on his Flying M Ranch in Galisteo, NM, about a half hour south of Santa Fe.

Annual production: 1000 barrels

Major top-fermented brands: Fiesta Ale, Old Pojoaque Porter, Santa Fe Pale Ale

Major seasonal brands: Galisteo Weiss, Sangre de Frambuesa

## Schirf Brewing
250 Main Street
Park City, UT 84060

The brewery, and the adjacent Wasatch Brewpub, were founded by Greg Schirf in 1986. Schirf was the first brewery to operate in Utah since the 1965 closure of the Becker Brewery in Ogden. In 1989, Greg Schirf was able to convince the state legislature to pass a law legalizing brewpubs and added the Wasatch to his brewery in July of the same year.

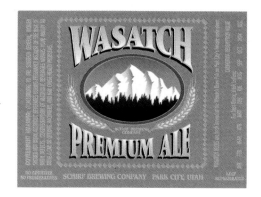

Annual production: 7300 barrels

Flagship brand: Wasatch Premium Ale

Major top-fermenting brands: Wasatch Irish Stout, Wasatch Premium Ale, Wasatch Stout

Major bottom-fermenting brands: Wasatch Light Beer, Wasatch Slickrock Lager, Wasatch Wheat Beer

Major seasonal brands: Wasatch Bock, Wasatch Christmas Ale

**Schlitz:** See Stroh Brewing (Detroit, MI)

## Spanish Peaks Brewing
120 North 19th Avenue
Bozeman, MT 59715

The brewery was founded by Mark Taverniti in 1991 near the foot of the Spanish Peaks Mountain Range.

Black Dog Ale, an English style amber beer first introduced in 1991, was awarded a Gold medal at the Great International Beer Tasting Competition in Denver, CO. Yellowstone Pale Ale, a golden, traditional style ale, has had a strong local following since its 1991 premiere. Chugwater Charlie Hill is the name of the Labrador Retriever shown on the Spanish Peaks label. 'Chug,' a title-winning black Labrador, was selected to represent the fine breed that the company honors with these great Rocky Mountain ales. In keeping with 'Montana tradition,' the ales are all natural, brewed from malted barley, Pacific Northwest hops and spring water.

Annual production: 950 barrels

Flagship brand: Black Dog Ale

Major top-fermented brands: Black Dog Bitter, Eye of the Rockies Wheat, Spanish Peaks Porter, Yellowstone Pale

Major seasonal brands: Autumn Harvest Fest, Holiday Wheat, Irish Red, Oatmeal Stout, Raspberry Honey Ale, Spring Rye Ale

## Spring Brewing
Heavenly Daze Brewery & Grill
1860 Ski Time Square Drive
Steamboat Springs, CO 80479

The first brewpub in this popular ski resort was Spring Brewing's Heavenly Daze Brewery & Grill.

Annual production: Under 500 barrels

Major top-fermented brands: Cow Creek Cream, Dog's Breath Brown, Heavenly Hefe Weizen, Iggy's Indian Pale, Wapiti Wheat, Woodchuck Porter

GABF Gold Medal: Heavenly Hefe Weizen, 1993

## Steamboat Brewery & Tavern
435 Lincoln Avenue
Steamboat Springs, CO 80477

This brewpub was founded in 1993 by Joel Kinkel, Joe Walker and David Breaton.

Annual production: 750 barrels

Major top-fermented brands: Hahn's Peak Gold, Jane's Brown Ale, Pinnacle Pale, Powder Keg Porter, Raspberry Wheat, Whitewater Wheat

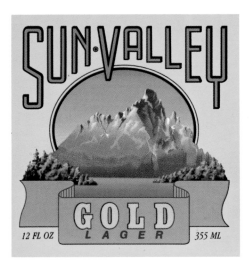

## Sun Valley Brewing
103 Garnet
Sun Valley, ID 83353

This brewery was founded by Michael J Kraynick and Gordon Gammell in November 1986 near the Sun Valley Ski Resort.

Annual production: 3000 barrels

Flagship brand: Sun Valley White Cloud Ale

Major top-fermented brands: Sun Valley White Cloud Ale, Sun Valley Our Holiday Ale

Major bottom-fermented brands: Sun Valley Blonde Pilsner, Sun Valley Gold Lager

Major seasonal brands: Sun Valley Mai Bock, Sun Valley Our Holiday Ale

GABF Gold Medals: Sun Valley Our Holiday Ale, 1989, 1990

GABF Silver Medals: Sun Valley White Cloud Ale, 1989; Sun Valley Cream Ale, 1989; Sun Valley Sawtooth Gold Lager, 1991

## TableRock Brewpub & Grill
705 Fulton
Boise, ID 83702

This brewpub was founded in 1991.

Annual production: 1500 barrels

Major top-fermented brands: Dept Gold, TableRock Red, TD's Nut Brown

## Union Brewery
28 North C Street
Virginia City, NV 89440

Beer was first brewed at the original Union Brewery in 1866. The saloon at this address opened in 1859 and the present brewery opened in 1987. It is still a saloon but no food is served. However, it is now the only brewery in Nevada. The Union Brewery also features a beer museum and a 1978 Indianapolis 500 race car.

Annual production: Under 500 barrels

Flagship brand: Union Beer

Major bottom-fermented brand: Union Beer

## Vail Brewing Company
100 South Frontage Road West
Vail, CO 81658

This contract beer company was founded in 1988 by Andy Norris, Jerry Jones, Vince Cook and John Lohre.

Annual production: None. The beer is brewed under contract by Oldenberg (Ft Mitchell, KY).

Flagship brand: Vail Ale

## Walnut Brewery
1123 Walnut Street
Boulder, CO 80303

This brewery/restaurant was founded by Gina Day and Dianne Greenlee in 1990.

Annual production: 2200 barrels

Major top-fermented brands: Big Horn Bitter, Buffalo Gold Premium Ale, Devil's Thumb

Stout, Indian Peaks Pale Ale, The James Irish Red Ale, Old Elk Brown Ale

Major seasonal brands: Jazzberry, Old Thumper Barleywine, Red Rooster, Subzero, White Pelican Pilsner

GABF Gold Medal: Old Elk Brown Ale, 1993

GABF Silver Medal: Big Horn Bitter, 1991

**Wasatch:** See Schirf Brewing (Park City, UT)

## Whitefish Brewing
Whitefish, MT 59937

This brewery was founded by Gary Hutchinson in 1991 after several years as a contract brewer. Whitefish beers are available, bottled or on draft, throughout northwestern Montana.

Annual production: Under 500 barrels

Major top-fermented brands: Melikian Ale, Melikian Pale, Melikian Porter

## Wild Wild West Gambling Hall & Brewery
443 East Bennett Avenue
Cripple Creek, CO 80813

This brewpub with a Tex-Mex slant was founded by Nick Aliberti in 1992 in the former Eagle's Dance Hall.

Annual production: Under 500 barrels

Major top-fermented brands: Cripple Creek, Full Moon, Mine Shaft Stout, Vindicator Pale

Major seasonal brands: West Fest, Womach Loheat

## Wynkoop Brewing
1634 18th Street
Denver, CO 80202

Named for Major Edward Wansheer 'Ned' Wynkoop, the founder and first sheriff of Denver, this brewpub was founded by John Hickenlooper, Jerry Williams and Russell Schehrer in October 1988. It was the first brewpub in Colorado and the Rocky Mountain region, and is the only brewery in the world founded by two ex-geologists and a computer programmer. Brewmaster Russell Schehrer is a professional beer judge and a member of the GABF Professional Panel Blind Tasting.

Annual production: 4300 barrels

Other breweries owned by the same company: Blue Cat Brew Pub (Rock Island, IL), Broadway Brewing Company (Denver, CO), CooperSmith's Pub & Brewing (Fort Collins, CO), Crane River Brew Pub & Cafe (Lincoln, NE), Firehouse Brewing Company (Rapid City, SD), Norman Brewing Company (Norman, OK), Phantom Canyon Brewing Company (Colorado Springs, CO), River City Brewery (Wichita, KS)

Flagship brands: Patty's Chile Beer, Railyard Ale, St Charles Extra Special Bitter (ESB), Wilderness Wheat

Major top-fermented brands: Patty's Chile Beer, Railyard Ale, St Charles Extra Special Bitter (ESB), Wilderness Wheat

Major bottom-fermented brands: Monday's Märzen, Pinhead Pils, Welcome Bock

Major seasonal brands: Cherry Ale, Cranberry Ale, Holiday Ale, Honeymooner's Mead, Oktoberfest, Wassail, Welcome Bock, Western Slope Cider

# SOUTHERN CALIFORNIA

**Samuel Adams:** See Boston Beer Company (Boston, MA) and Philadelphia Brewing (Philadelphia, PA)

**Alpine Village:** See Southern California Brewing (Torrance, CA)

## Anheuser-Busch

15800 Roscoe Boulevard
Los Angeles, CA 91406

This brewery was started by Anheuser-Busch in 1954.

Annual production: 11,600,000 barrels

Other breweries owned by the same company: See Anheuser-Busch, St Louis, MO for a list of Anheuser-Busch breweries.

Flagship brand: Budweiser

Major bottom-fermented brands: Budweiser, Bud Dry, Bud Light, Michelob, Michelob Dry, Michelob Golden Draft, Michelob Light, Michelob Classic Dark, Natural Light, King Cobra

See Anheuser-Busch, St Louis, MO for a list of medals awarded to Anheuser-Busch beers.

## Belmont Brewing

25 39th Street
Long Beach, CA 90803

This brewery was founded by David Hansen and David Lott in 1990.

Annual production: 1000 barrels

Major brands: Long Beach Crude, Marathon, Top Sail

**Biersch:** See Gordon Biersch (Palo Alto, CA; Pasadena, CA; San Francisco CA; and San Jose, CA)

## Biersch Brewery & Restaurant

41 Hugus Alley
Pasadena, CA 91105

Founded by Dean Biersch and Dan Gordon in 1994, this was the fourth of the Gordon Biersch brewery/restaurants.

Annual production: 2054 barrels

Other breweries owned by the same company: Gordon Biersch Brewery (Palo Alto,

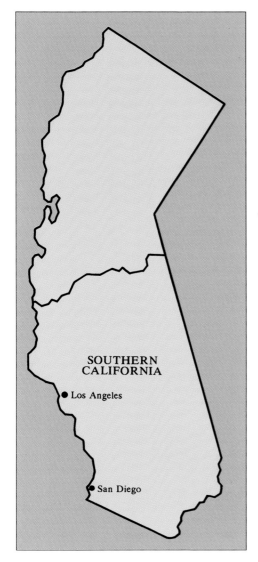

**SOUTHERN CALIFORNIA**

● Los Angeles

● San Diego

1992 in the Gaslamp Quarter of downtown San Diego.

Annual production: Under 1000 barrels

Major top-fermented brands: Aztec Amber, Red Sails Ale, Pioneer Porter, Raspberry Ale, Stingaree Stout, Whale's Tale Pale, Welsh Beer

**Buckhorn:** See Anderson Valley (Boonville, CA)

**Budweiser:** See Anheuser-Busch (St Louis, MO)

**Busch:** See Anheuser-Busch (St Louis, MO)

## Butterfield's Brewing Company
777 East Olive Street
Fresno, CA 93726

This brewery and restaurant were founded by Jeff Wolpert in March 1989 and named for the Butterfield Overland Express Company, the operators of the famous stagecoach company. Wolpert is a distant relative of the founder of Butterfield Overland.

Annual production: Under 1000 barrels

Major bottom-fermented brands: Bridal Veil Ale, Golden Ale, San Joaquin, Tower Dark Ale

Major seasonal brands: Mt Whitney Ale, Oktoberfest, Raspberry, Sierra Spring Ale, Wheat Ale

GABF Gold Medals: Tower Dark Ale (Porter), 1989; Bridal Veil Ale (Amber Ale), 1990

GABF Silver Medal: Brown Ale, 1993

CA); Gordon Biersch Brewery (San Francisco, CA); Gordon Biersch Brewery (San Jose, CA)

Major bottom-fermented brands: Dunkles, Export, Märzen, Weiss

## Brewski's GasLamp Pub, Bistro & Brewery
310 5th Avenue
San Diego, CA 92101

This brewery was founded by Dennis and Mary Lou Moore and RJ and Mary Sibler in

**Calistoga:** See Napa Valley Brewing (Calistoga, CA)

## Callahan's Pub & Brewery
8280-A Mira Mesa Boulevard
San Diego, CA 92126

This brewery was founded by Lee Doxtader and Scott Stamp in 1989.

Annual production: Under 500 barrels

Other brewery owned by the same company: San Diego Brewing (San Diego, CA)

Major top-fermented brands: Bernard Bitter, Black Mountain Porter, Callahan Red, Mesa Pale, Secret Stout, Shamrock Gold

Major seasonal brands: Anniversary Ale, Christmas Ale

## Crown City Brewing
300 South Raymond Avenue
Pasadena, CA 91105

This brewpub was founded by Dennis Hartman, Mike Lanzarotta, Jack Robinson and Bob Talbot in July 1988 and serves 170 beers from around the world.

Annual production: 400 barrels

Flagship brands: Arroyo Amber Ale, Mt Wilson Wheat

Major top-fermented brands: Black Bear Stout, Father Christmas Wassail, Midsummer Night Stout

Major seasonal brands: Father Christmas Wassail, Midsummer Night Stout, Oom Pah Pah Oktoberfest

**Front Street Pub:** See Santa Cruz Brewing (Santa Cruz, CA)

## Fullerton Hofbräu Brewery
323 North State College Boulevard
Fullerton, CA 92631

This brewery was founded by Russell Brent and Gunther Buerk in 1990.

Annual production: 1800 barrels

Major top-fermented brand: Earl's Ale

Major bottom-fermented brands: Duke's Bock, King's Lager, Prince's Pilsner

Major seasonal brands: Märzen, Oktoberfest, Weizen

**Hopland Brewery Restaurant:** See Mendocino Brewing (Hopland, CA)

## Hops! Bistro & Brewery
University Towne Center
4353 La Jolla Village Drive
San Diego, CA 92122-1212

This brewpub was founded by Lessing Stern in 1992, the second in his chain of brewpubs.

Annual production: 1250 barrels

Flagship brand: Hops! Hefe-Weizen

Other breweries owned by the same company: Hops! Bistro & Brewery (Scottsdale, AZ), Hops! Bistro & Brewery (Phoenix, AZ)

Major top-fermented brands: Barley Wine, ESB, Hefe-Weizen, IPA, Oatmeal Stout, Russian Imperial Stout, Scottish Ale

Major bottom-fermented brands: Bock, Eis-Bock, Export Lager, Märzen, Oktoberfest, Raspberry Lager, Pilsner

Major seasonal brands: Bock, Eis-Bock, Oktoberfest, Russian Imperial Stout

GABF Gold Medal: Hops! Hefe-Weizen, 1992

GABF Silver Medals: Hops! Wheat Beer, 1991; Hops! Barley Wine, 1991

**Hübsch:** See Sudwerk (Davis, CA)

## Huntington Beach Beer Company
201 Main Street, Suite E
Huntington Beach, CA 92648

This brewpub was founded by Peter Andriet in 1992.

Annual production: 1500 barrels

Flagship brands: Brickshot Red, Huntington Beach Blonde

Major top-fermented brands: Amber Destras Ale, Black Gold Porter, Bolsa Chica Bitter, Brickshot Red, Main Street Wheat, Pier Pale Ale

Major bottom-fermented brand: Huntington Beach Blonde

Major seasonal brands: Huntington Peach, Pumpkinhead Ale

## La Jolla Brewing
7536 Fay Avenue
San Diego, CA 92037

This brewpub was founded by Jon Atwater and Mike Green in La Jolla 1990.

Annual production: 1000 barrels

Major top-fermented brands: Little Point, Pumphouse Porter, Red Roost, Sea Lane Amber

Major seasonal brands: Blitzen Ale, Red Irish Ale, Windsea Wheat

**Lighthouse:** See Santa Cruz Brewing (Santa Cruz, CA)

## Manhattan Beach Brewhouse Grill
1300 North Highland Avenue
Manhattan Beach, CA 90266

This brewpub was founded by Bob Cano and Fred Kukulus in 1992.

Annual production: Under 500 barrels

Major top-fermented brands: Headlight Ale, Highland Amber, London Porter, Past Stout

Major bottom-fermented brands: Imperial Stout, Irish Mild Brown, Oatmeal Stout, Rye Beer, Wheat Beer

## Manhattan Beach Brewing Company
124 Manhattan Beach Boulevard
Manhattan Beach, CA 90266

This brewpub was founded by David and Mike Zislis and John Waters in 1991.

Annual production: 1400 barrels

Other brewery owned by the same company: Redondo Beach Brewing (Redondo Beach, CA)

Flagship brand: Rat Beach Red

Major top-fermented brands: Manhattan Beach Blond, Rat Beach Red

Major bottom-fermented brand: Dominator Wheat Beer

Major seasonal brands: Bayview Bock, Beach Octoberfest Lager, Bohemian Pilsner, Buccaneer Pilsner, Dominator Dunkle Weisse, Halloween Pumpkin Ale, India Pale Ale, James Brown Ale, Pacifica Pale Ale, Pier Pale Ale, Riptime Raspberry (Ale), South Bay Bitter, Stoney Stout, Strand Amber

**Michelob:** See Anheuser-Busch (St Louis, MO)

## Miller Brewing
15801 East First Street
Irwindale, CA 91706-2036

This brewery was founded by Miller Brewing in 1980. See Miller Brewing, Milwaukee, WI for details on the history of the company.

Annual production: 5,000,000 barrels

Other breweries owned by the same company: See Miller Brewing, Milwaukee WI, for a list of Miller breweries.

Major brands: See Miller Brewing, Milwaukee, WI for a list of Miller brands.

GABF Medals: See Miller Brewing, Milwaukee, WI for a list of GABF medals awarded to the company.

**O'Doul's:** See Anheuser-Busch (St Louis, MO)

## Karl Strauss' Old Columbia Brewery & Grill
1157 Columbia Street
San Diego, CA 92101

This brewpub was founded by Chris Cramer and Matthew Rattner in 1989, and is owned by Associated Microbrewers, Ltd. It is named for Karl Strauss, the master brewer, who is also a distant cousin of Cramer.

Annual production: 7000 barrels

Major top-fermented brands: Berliner Weiss, Black's Beach Extra Dark, Downtown After Dark Ale, Dry Hopped Brown Ale, Gaslamp Gold Ale, Hefeweiss, Ice 'Koll' Weissbier, Karl's Cream Ale, Red Trolley Ale, Strauss Stout, Waterfront Weiss

Major bottom-fermented brands: America's Finest Pilsner, First National Bock, Karl Strauss Amber Lager, Point Loma Lighthouse Light

Major seasonal brands: Blond Bavarian, Cabot Christmas Ale, Oktoberfest Beer

## Pacific Beach Brewhouse
4475 Mission Boulevard #H
San Diego, CA 92109

This brewpub was founded by Rick Schoenberg, Tony Brooke and Phil Faraci in 1991.

Annual production: Under 500 barrels

Major top-fermented brands: Crystal Pale Ale, Over the Line Stout, Sunset Red

Major bottom-fermented brand: Pacific Beach Blonde

Major seasonal brands: Christmas Ale, Coaster Lager, October Fest, Raspberry Ale

**Pacifica:** See Sanktgallen (San Francisco, CA)

## Paso Robles Brewing

7320 Union Road
Paso Robles, CA 93446

This brewery was founded in 1994.

Annual production: Under 500 barrels

**Red Tail:** See Mendocino Brewing (Mendocino, CA)

## Redondo Beach Brewing

1814 Catalina Avenue
Redondo Beach, CA 90274

This brewery was founded by David and Mike Zislis in 1993.

Annual production: 1800 barrels

Other brewery owned by the same company: Manhattan Beach Brewing Company (Manhattan Beach, CA)

Flagship brand: Rat Beach Red

**Rhino Chasers:** See William & Scott (Culver City, CA)

## Riverside Brewing

Orange Empire Brewing
3397 Seventh Street
Riverside, CA 92507

This brewpub was founded in 1993.

Annual production: Under 500 barrels

**Rolling Rock:** See Latrobe Brewing (Latrobe, PA)

## San Diego Brewing Company

10450 Friars Road
San Diego, CA 92126

This brewpub was founded by Lee Doxtader and Scott Stamp in 1993. The original manufacturing facility, known as the San Diego Brewing Company, opened in 1896 with much fanfare. AE Horton, the father of San Diego,

referred to the brewery as 'the most important industrial enterprise since I founded the town.' It was the largest manufacturing enterprise in the county.

The brewery delivered its products to all parts of the city and county in bottles or in barrels. Its beers were said to 'sparkle like nectar.' Sadly, the company was removed from 32nd Street by the Navy in 1942 and replaced by a base for the Pacific fleet.

Annual production: 1200 barrels

Other brewery owned by the same company: Callahan's Pub & Brewery (San Diego, CA)

Major top-fermented brands: Grantville Gold, Mission Gorge Porter, San Diego Amber

Major seasonal brands: Montgomery Mild, Old 395, Old Town Nut Brown

## San Marcos Brewery & Grill

1080 West San Marcos Boulevard
San Marcos, CA 92069

The brewery was founded in 1994.

Annual production: Under 500 barrels

## Santa Clarita Brewing

20655 Soledad Canyon Road
Santa Clarita, CA 91351

This brewery was founded by Mark and Sheila Van Leeuwen in January 1994.

Annual production: 1000 barrels

Flagship brand: Golden Oak Ale

Major top-fermented brands: Beale's Bitter, Railroad Porter, Tumbleweed Wheat

Major seasonal brand: Spring Bock

**Schlitz:** See Stroh Brewing (Detroit, MI)

## Shields Brewing
24 East Santa Clara Street
Ventura, CA 93001

This brewery, and its adjacent pub and grill, were founded by Bob and Trudy Shields in 1990.

Located in a 1920s blacksmith shop, Shields Brewing is the first brewery in Ventura County since before Prohibition. Its Channel Islands Ale, Gold Coast Beer, Channel Islands Wheat Beer and Shields Stout are available in 22-ounce bottles and are distributed statewide. All seasonal brands are available in-house only.

Annual production: 275 barrels

Other brewery owned by the same company: Trademark licensing agreement for production of Gold Coast Beer in Sichuan Province, PRC (China)

Flagship brand: Channel Islands Ale

Major bottom-fermented brands: Channel Islands Ale, Channel Islands Wheat Beer, Gold Coast Beer, Shields Stout

Major seasonal brands: Bobby's Bock Beer, Oktoberfresh Ale, Winter Storm Ale

## SLO Brewing
1119 Garden Street
San Luis Obispo, CA 93401

This brewpub was founded by Michael and Becky Hoffman in September 1988 in the historic Hanna Hardware Building, built in 1906. During reconstruction in 1988, an old brewery bottle and tankard from the McCaffrey Brothers Brewery—one of the town's original breweries—were found, and they are now displayed in the brewery's entrance.

Annual production: 1200 barrels

Flagship brand: Garden Valley Amber

Major seasonal brand: ESB Nut Brown Ale

## Solana Beach Brewery
135 North Highway 101
Solana Beach, CA 92075

The Pizza Port was opened by Vince and Gina Marsaglia in 1987 as a pizza restaurant, and the brewery was added in 1992.

Annual production: Under 500 barrels

Major top-fermented brands: Clean Ocean Pale, Hefeweizen, Pilbox Pale Ale, Port's Porter, Rivermouth Raspberry, Sharkbite Red Ale

Major seasonal brands: Chocolate Cherry, Jalapeño Chili, Octoberfest, Summer Wheat

## Southern California Brewing

833 West Torrance Boulevard
Torrance, CA 90502

This establishment was founded in 1988 as the Village Hofbräu, a German-style brewpub. In 1992, the brewery changed owners. Today, the separately owned and operated Southern California Brewing is a microbrewery which is visible through a window from the Alpine Inn restaurant. This gives it the atmosphere of a brewpub.

Annual production: 10,500 barrels

Flagship brand: Alpine Pilsner

Major top-fermented brands: Old Red Eye Ale, Alpine Wheat

Major bottom-fermented brands: Alpine Lager, Alpine Pilsner, Alpine Premium Light

Major seasonal brands: Alpine Bock, Alpine Märzen

## State Street Brewpub

209 State Street
Santa Barbara, CA 93101

This brewpub, and the adjacent Brewhouse Grill, were founded by Fred Kukules in 1990.

Annual production: 500 barrels

Major top-fermented brands: Anacapa Ale, Mission Creek Porter

Major bottom-fermented brand: City Lager

**Karl Strauss:** See Old Columbia (San Diego, CA)

**Tied House:** See Redwood Coast Brewing (Alameda, CA; Mountain View, CA; and San Jose, CA)

## William & Scott Brewing Company

8460 Higuera Street
Culver City, CA 90232

This contract beer company was founded in 1991, with sales increasing to 20,000 cases monthly in the first two years. A portion of the profits is shared with the African Wildlife Foundation for the preservation of endangered species.

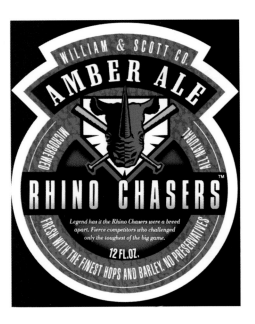

Annual production: None. The beer is contract brewed by Minnesota Brewing (St Paul, MN), Lone Star Brewing (San Antonio, TX) and FX Matt (Utica, NY)

Flagship brand: Rhino Chasers

Major top-fermented brands: Rhino Chasers Lager, Rhino Chasers Dark Lager

Major bottom-fermented brands: Rhino Chasers Amber Ale, Rhino Chasers American Ale

Major seasonal brand: Rhino Chasers Winterful

GABF Silver Medal: Rhino Chasers, 1993

# NORTHERN CALIFORNIA

## Anchor Brewing

1705 Mariposa Street
San Francisco, CA 94107

The brewery was founded in 1896. Appliance heir Fritz Maytag bought the company in 1965 when it was on the verge of collapse and turned it into the very model of an efficient, smaller regional brewery. Despite Maytag's relentless quality control and insistence on high-quality ingredients, such as expensive, pure malted, two-row barley instead of a mix of cheaper cereal grains, the brewery turned a profit by 1975.

The company's flagship product is Anchor Steam Beer, one of the West's most prized premium beers, which was developed by master brewer Maytag himself, and is loosely based on what is known of the legendary 'steam' beers produced in Gold Rush days. Anchor is renowned locally for its annual Christmas beer, which has been specially brewed since 1975, using a different recipe each year, and is available from the day after Thanksgiving until early January. Liberty Ale had its start as the original Christmas beer.

In August 1989, Anchor amazed and delighted its many fans by brewing a beer which was based on a 4000-year-old recipe which Fritz Maytag and his consulting histo-

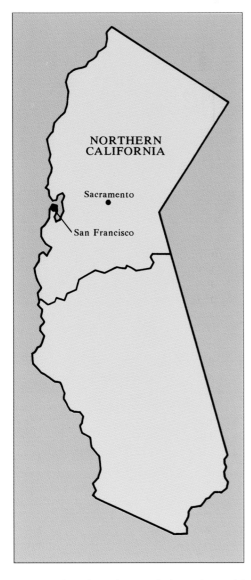

NORTHERN
CALIFORNIA

Sacramento

San Francisco

Annual production: 50,000 barrels

Flagship brand: Anchor Steam Beer

Major top-fermented brands: Liberty Ale, Old Foghorn Barley Wine

Major bottom-fermented brand: Anchor Wheat

Major seasonal brand: Anchor Christmas Beer (brewed annually since 1975)

GABF Gold Medals: Anchor Porter, 1988; Christmas Ale, 1989; Old Foghorn Barley Wine, 1989, 1991

GABF Silver Medals: Anchor Steam Beer (Continental Amber Lager), 1987; Anchor Wheat Beer, 1988; Anchor Liberty Ale, 1988, 1989, 1990, 1993; Anchor Porter, 1990

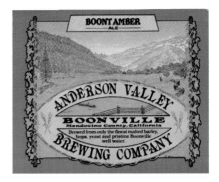

## Anderson Valley Brewing
The Buckhorn Saloon
14081 Highway 128
Boonville, CA 95415

rians and archaeologists believed would 'duplicate mankind's earliest professionally brewed beer.' Named Ninkasi after the Sumerian goddess of brewing, the beer was produced from an ancient recipe for barley bread called *bappir*, which is flavored with dates and honey. It was baked by Anchor's brewing team in a bakery hired for the day. It was unveiled at the 1989 National Microbrewers Conference and released privately in 11 ounce bottles for a short time thereafter.

This brewery was founded by Dr Kenneth Allen in 1987. The present Buckhorn Saloon, named for the original built in 1873, was the first building in California to be designed specifically as a brewpub. Large glass windows frame views of the valley's hillsides, as pictured on the beer bottle's label. Light, airy music 'wafts to high, open ceilings over intimate dining tables, while micro bubbles overflow heads of brew poured at the long, polished wooden bar.' Patrons lunch and dine on country cuisine in the company of a friendly local crowd.

Annual production: 4000 barrels

Flagship brand: Boont Amber Ale

Major top-fermented brands (each of which are named for a region of the Anderson Valley): Barney Flats Oatmeal Stout, Belk's Extra Special Bitter Ale, Boont Amber Ale, High Rollers Wheat Beer, Deependers Dark Porter

Major seasonal brands: High Rollers Wheat Beer, Winter Solstice Select Ale

GABF Gold Medal: Barney Flats Oatmeal Stout, 1990

## Anheuser-Busch
3101 Busch Drive
Fairfield, CA 94533

This brewery was started by Anheuser-Busch in 1976.

Annual production: 4,100,000 barrels

Other breweries owned by the same company: See Anheuser-Busch, St Louis, MO for a list of Anheuser-Busch breweries.

Flagship brand: Budweiser

Major bottom-fermented brands: Budweiser, Bud Light, Bud Dry, Michelob, Michelob Classic Dark

See Anheuser-Busch, St Louis, MO for a list of medals awarded to Anheuser-Busch beers.

## Benchmark Brewing
## Stoddard's Brewhouse
## & Eatery
111 South Murphy Avenue
Sunnyvale, CA 94086

This brewery was founded by Bob Stoddard in 1993.

Annual production: 2000 barrels

Flagship brand: Stoddard's

Major top-fermented brands: Kölsch, Pale Ale, Porter

Major seasonal brands: American Wheat, ESB

**Biersch:** See Gordon Biersch (Palo Alto, CA; Pasadena, CA; San Francisco CA; and San Jose, CA)

## Bison Brewing
2598 Telegraph Avenue
Berkeley, CA 94704

This brewery was founded by Buffalo Bill Owens in 1988, but as of 1989 he was no longer associated with Bison. The principals are Eric Freitag, president; Scott Meyer, head alchemist; and Daniel Rogers, publican. The brewpub has a local distribution of bottle-conditioned ales and uses 'a perpetual variety of recipes based on innovation, culinary principles and modern, as well as archaic, brewing practices.'

Annual production: 960 barrels

Major top-fermenting brands: Cardamon Ale, Chocolate Porter, Coffee Stout, Honey-Basil Ale, India Pale Ale, Nut Brown Ale

## Boulder Creek Brewing
Boulder Creek Grill
13040 Highway 9
Boulder Creek, CA 95006

This brewery was founded by Nancy Long and Steve Wyman in 1989 in a former grocery store/post office that later became the Boulder Creek Grill.

Annual production: 350 barrels

Major top-fermented brands: St Severin's Kölsch, Pilsner Vaclar

Major bottom-fermented brands: Ghost Rail Pale, Old MacLunk's Scottish Ale, O'Meal Stout, Pound of Flesh ESB, Redwood Ale

Major seasonal brand: Danish Holiday Cheer

## The Brewery at Lake Tahoe
3542 Lake Tahoe Boulevard
South Lake Tahoe, CA 96150

The brewpub was founded by Greg Cook, Cory McGuire, Rick Myers and Russell Penn in 1992 near the Heavenly Valley Ski Resort.

Annual production: Under 500 barrels

Major top-fermented brands: Alpine Amber, Needle Park Ale, Paramont Porter, Washoe Amber

**Budweiser:** See Anheuser-Busch (St Louis, MO)

## Buffalo Bill's Brewpub
1082 B Street
Hayward, CA 94541

This brewery was founded by Bill Owens in 1983, becoming the second brewpub to open in California since Prohibition. In 1988, Owens opened another brewpub, Bison Brewing Company, in nearby Berkeley, CA, which has since been sold.

Annual production: 330 barrels

Flagship brand: Buffalo Brew

Major top-fermented brands: Alimony Ale, Amber, Stout

Major bottom-fermented brand: Rausch

Major seasonal brand: Pumpkin Ale

**Busch:** See Anheuser-Busch (St Louis, MO)

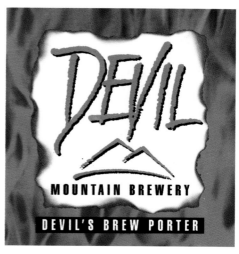

**Calistoga:** See Napa Valley Brewing (Calistoga, CA)

## Devil Mountain Brewery
2283 Camel Road
Benicia, CA 94510

This brewery was founded as a brewpub in Walnut Creek, CA in 1987, but brewing operations at Devil Mountain Brewery and Restaurant in Walnut Creek ended in 1988 and were moved to Benicia, so Devil Mountain is no longer a brewpub.

Annual production: 4000 barrels

Flagship brands: Devil's Brew Porter, Diablo Golden Ale, Railroad Ale

Major seasonal brands: Oktoberfest, Winter Warmer

GABF Gold Medal: Railroad Ale, 1988

GABF Silver Medal: Iron Horse Alt, 1988

## Downtown Joe's Brewery & Restaurant
902 Main Street
Napa, CA 94559

This brewpub was founded by Joe Peatman, Brian Hunt and Joe Ruffino. Brewer Brian Hunt also owns Moonlight Brewing.

Annual production: 1000 barrels

Major top-fermented brands: Ace High Cream Ale, Tail Waggin' Ale, Past Due Dark Ale, Golden Thistle Bitter Ale

Major bottom-fermented brands: Foundation Lager, Black Beer

Major seasonal brands: Peaceful Night Holiday Ale, Worthy's Leprechaun Stout, Specter of Worthy Stout

## Etna Brewery
131 Callahan Street
Etna, CA 96027

This brewery was founded by Andrew Hurlimann in 1990 on the site of the pre-Prohibition Etna Brewery.

Annual production: 300 barrels

Flagship brand: Etna Ale

Major bottom-fermented brands: Etna Dark, Etna Lager, Etna Weizen

## Fremont Brewing
Brewery and Sports Cafe
3350 Stevenson Boulevard
Fremont, CA 94538

This brewpub was founded by John Rennels in 1988 as Brewpub on the Green, the first brewpub located on a golf course. It was owned for a time by Buffalo Bill Owens.

Annual production: 600 barrels

Major top-fermented brand: California Mission Peak Porter

Major bottom-fermented brands: California Amber, Gold Coast Lager

Major seasonal brands: Spring Wheat, Summer Blond, Pumpkin Lager

**Front Street Pub:** See Santa Cruz Brewing (Santa Cruz, CA)

## Golden Pacific Brewing
5515 Doyle Street #4
Emeryville, CA 94608

This brewery was founded in 1985, and in 1989, Golden Pacific signed an agreement with Thousand Oaks Brewing of Berkeley—then the world's smallest brewing company—to begin producing their Golden Bear and Cable Car products in Emeryville.

Annual production: 3000 barrels

Major top-fermented brands: Golden Pacific Bittersweet Ale

Major bottom-fermented brands: Black Bear Dark Lager, Cable Car Lager, Cable Car Classic Lager, Golden Bear Lager, Golden Gate Amber Lager, Golden Gate Malt Liquor

GABF Silver Medal: Golden Gate Red Ale, 1993

## Gordon Biersch Brewery
625 Emerson Street
Palo Alto, CA 94301

This establishment was founded by Dean Biersch and Dan Gordon in 1988, the first of four Gordon Biersch brewery/restaurants.

Annual production: 4500 barrels

Other breweries owned by the same company: Gordon Biersch Brewery (Pasadena, CA); Gordon Biersch Brewery (San Francisco, CA); Gordon Biersch Brewery (San Jose, CA)

Major bottom-fermented brands: Dunkles, Export, Märzen, Weiss

## Gordon Biersch Brewery & Restaurant
33 East San Fernando Street
San Jose, CA 95113

This brewery was founded as the Biers Brasserie Brewery. It was acquired by Dean Biersch and Dan Gordon and completely remodeled as the second of their chain of brewery/restaurants in 1989.

Annual production: 2000 barrels

Other breweries owned by the same company: Gordon Biersch Brewery (Palo Alto, CA); Gordon Biersch Brewery (Pasadena, CA); Gordon Biersch Brewery (San Francisco, CA)

Major bottom-fermented brands: Dunkles, Export, Märzen

## Gordon Biersch Brewery & Restaurant
2 Harrison Street
San Francisco, CA 94105

Founded in 1992, Dean Biersch and Dan Gordon's third brewery/restaurant is located in the renovated Hills Brothers Coffee Building in the Embarcadero Center.

Annual production: 5000 barrels

Other breweries owned by the same company: Gordon Biersch Brewery (Palo Alto,

CA); Gordon Biersch Brewery (Pasadena, CA); Gordon Biersch Brewery (San Jose, CA)

Major bottom-fermented brands: Dunkles, Export, Märzen

## Heckler Brewing
Tahoe City, CA 96145

This brewery was founded by Keith Hilken, Jr in 1993.

Annual production: 4800 barrels

Flagship brands: Heckler Bräu, Hell Lager

Major bottom-fermented brands: Fest Märzen, Doppel Bock, Hell Lager

## Heritage Brewing
24921 Dana Point Harbor Drive
Dana Point, CA 92629

This brewpub was founded by Mark Merick and John Stoner in 1989.

Annual production: 1250 barrels

Major top-fermented brands: Dana Porter, Lantern Bay Blonde, Sail Ale

Major seasonal brands: Christmas Ale, High Seas Oatmeal Stout, No Doubt Stout

GABF Gold Medal: Lantern Bay Blonde, 1991

## Hogshead Brewing
114 J Street
Sacramento, CA 95814

This brewpub was founded by Jim Schlueter in 1986 in an old saloon built during the Gold Rush era.

Annual production: 500 barrels

Flagship brand: Hogshead Lager

Major top-fermented brand: Hogshead Pale

Major bottom-fermented brand: McSchlueter

**Hopland Brewery Restaurant:** See Mendocino Brewing (Hopland, CA)

**Hübsch:** See Sudwerk (Davis, CA)

## Humboldt Brewing
856 Tenth Street
Arcata, CA 95521

This brewpub was founded in 1988 by Mario Celotto, a former defensive linebacker for the Oakland Raiders. The brewpub features classic Raiders memorabilia.

Annual production: 1500 barrels

Major top-fermented brands: Gold Rush Ale, Humboldt Oatmeal Stout, Red Nectar Ale, Storm Cellar Porter

Major seasonal brands: Cheshire Cat Barley Wine, Holidaze Ale, Humboldt Honey, Wheat

GABF Gold Medal: Humbolt Oatmeal Stout, 1988

GABF Silver Medal: Red Nectar, 1993

**Lighthouse:** See Santa Cruz Brewing (Santa Cruz, CA)

## Lind Brewing
1933 Davis Street
Westgate Mall #177
San Leandro, CA 94577

This brewery was founded by Roger Lind in 1989.

Annual production: 850 barrels

Flagship brand: Drake's Ale

Major top-fermented brands: Drake's Ale, Drake's Brown Ale, Drake's Extra Pale Ale, Drake's Gold, Drake's IPA, Sir Francis Stout. Lind also produces the house ale for the Lucky 13 Pub in San Francisco, CA.

Major bottom-fermented brands: Drake's Amber Lager, Drake's Pilsener

Major seasonal brands: Drake's Autumn-Fest, Drake's Dunkel-Weizen, Drake's Maibock, Drake's Midsummer's Wheat Beer, Jolly Roger's Holiday Ale

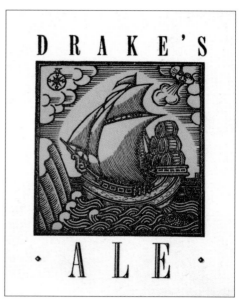

## Live Soup Brewery & Cafe
1602 Ocean Street
Santa Cruz, CA 95010

This brewpub was founded by Michael Fischer, David Perie and Hugh Weiler in 1993.

Annual production: Under 500 barrels

## Los Gatos Brewing
130-G North Santa Cruz Avenue
Los Gatos, CA 95030

This brewpub was founded by Andrew Pavicich in 1992.

Annual production: 2000 barrels

Major bottom-fermented brands: Dunkel Poppel Bock, Hefe-Weizen, Lager, Pilsner

Major seasonal brands: Mai Bock, Oktoberfest

GABF Silver Medal: Los Gatos Lager, 1993

## Lost Coast Brewery and Cafe
617 4th Street
Eureka, CA 95501

This brewpub was founded by Barbara Groom and Wendy Pound in 1990 in the former Knights of Pythias Lodge—a Victorian storefront built in 1892—and remodeled it to simulate a turn-of-the-century saloon.

Annual production: 1700 barrels

Flagship brand: Downtown Brown Ale

Major top-fermented brands: Downtown Brown Ale, Harvest Ale, Pale Ale, Stout, Amber

Major seasonal brands: Black Irish Stout, Raspberry Wheat, Winterbräun Ale

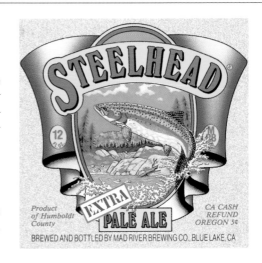

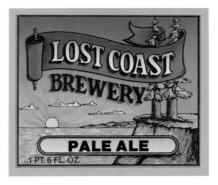

## Mad River Brewing
195 Taylor Way
Blue Lake, CA 95525

This brewery was founded by Bob Smith in 1989 and operated solely as a microbrewery. However, tours are welcome by appointment or on Saturdays between 10:00 am and 4:00 pm.

Annual production: 7000 barrels

Flagship brands: Steelhead Extra Pale Ale, Jamaica Red, John Barleycorn Barleywine, Steelhead Extra Stout

Major top-fermented brands: Jamaica Red, John Barleycorn Barleywine, Steelhead Extra Pale Ale, Steelhead Extra Stout

Major seasonal brand: John Barleycorn Barleywine Style Ale

## Marin Brewing
1809 Larkspur Landing Circle
Larkspur, CA 94939

This brewpub was founded by Grant Johnston and Brendan Moylan in April 1989.

Annual production: 3000 barrels

Flagship brand: Mt Tam Pale Ale

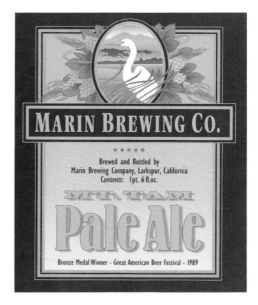

Major top-fermented brands: Albion Amber Ale, Blueberry Ale, Bodega Bay Bitter, Holy Smoke Harvest Ale, Marin Doppel Weizen, Marin Hefe Weiss, Marin Weiss, Miwok Weizen Bock, Mt Tam Pale Ale, San Quentin Breakout Stout, Old Dipsea Barleywine, Pt Reyes Porter, St Brendan's Irish Red Ale, Star Brew VI, Stinson Beach Peach Raspberry Trail Ale

Major seasonal brand: Hoppy Holidaze Ale

GABF Gold Medals: San Quentin's Breakout Stout, 1989; Hoppy Holidaze Ale, 1990, 1991; Marin Weiss, 1991; Marin Hefe Weiss, 1992; Blueberry Ale, 1990, 1991, 1993

GABF Silver Medals: Old Dipsea Barleywine, 1989, 1990; Pt Reyes Porter, 1991, 1993

## Mendocino Brewing

13351 Highway 101 South
Hopland, CA 95449

Founded by Norman Franks, Michael Leybourn, and John Scahill in 1982, Hopland was California's first brewpub since Prohibition. Mendocino operates as a brewpub but also bottles for regional distribution. The brewpub is located in a 100-year-old building which served as a post office and later as the Hop Vine Saloon. The original brew kettle from New Albion Brewing can be seen in the beer garden.

Annual production: 13,000 barrels

Flagship brand: Red Tail Ale

Major top-fermented brands: Black Hawk Stout, Blue Heron Pale Ale, Peregrine Pale Ale, Red Tail Ale

Major seasonal brands: Eye of the Hawk Ale, Springtime Celebration, Yuletide Porter

GABF Gold Medal: Eye of the Hawk Special Ale, 1991

GABF Silver Medal: Eye of the Hawk Special Ale, 1990

**Michelob:** See Anheuser-Busch (St Louis, MO)

## Moonlight Brewing

Fulton, CA 95439

This brewery was founded in 1992 by Brian Hunt, the master brewer at Downtown Joe's Brewing in Napa. The name 'Moonlight Brewing' is derived from the fact that he brews his own beer in his off hours.

Annual production: 550 barrels

Major top-fermented brands: Full Moon Light Ale, Twist of Fate Bitter Ale

Major bottom-fermented brands: Death and Taxes Black Beer, Moonlight Pale Lager, Rising Tide Amber Lager

Major seasonal brand: Santa's Tipple Stout

## Murphy's Creek Brewing Company
4667 French Gulch Road
Angel's Camp, CA 95222

This brewery was founded in 1993 by Dan Ayal and Micah Millspaw.

Annual production: 1200 barrels

Flagship brand: Murphy's Red

Major top-fermented brands: Black Gold, Golden Wheat, Raspberry Wheat

## Napa Valley Brewing
1250 Lincoln Avenue
Calistoga, CA 94515

Flagship brand: Calistoga Ale

Major top-fermented brands: Calistoga Red, Calistoga Wheat Ale

Major bottom-fermented brand: Calistoga Golden Lager

Major seasonal brands: Calistoga Barley Wine, Calistoga Oktoberfest, Calistoga Porter, Calistoga Stout

The historic Calistoga Inn (1882) was a hotel and restaurant for many years and Phil Rogers added the brewery in 1987. The brewery is in the old water tower on the patio of the turn-of-the-century inn. A brewery located in the heart of North America's premier wine-producing region may seem to be out of place, but Napa Valley Brewing's beers are just as world class as the wines being produced from the adjacent fields.

Annual production: 330 barrels

## Nevada City Brewing
75 Bost Avenue
Nevada City, CA 95959

This brewery was founded by Gene Downing in 1986 and is a sister brewery to Truckee Brewing.

Annual production: 988 barrels

Flagship brand: Nevada City Brew

Major bottom-fermented brands: Nevada City Brew Dark Lager, Nevada City Brew Gold Lager

## North Coast Brewing
444 North Main Street
Fort Bragg, CA 95437

This brewery/restaurant was founded by Tom Allen, Joe Rosenthal and Mark Ruedrich in 1988, with the back bar being from an old Eureka saloon.

Annual production: 15,000 barrels

Flagship brand: Red Seal Ale

Major top-fermented brands: Alt Nouveau, Blue Star Wheat Beer, Old #38 Stout, Red Seal Ale, Scrimshaw

Major seasonal brands: Centennial, Christmas Ale, Oktoberfest, Traditional Bock

GABF Gold Medal: Scrimshaw, 1992

GABF Silver Medals: Red Seal Ale, 1992; Oktoberfest, 1992; Old #38 Stout, 1993

**O'Doul's:** See Anheuser-Busch (St Louis, MO)

## Pacific Coast Brewing
## Pub & Restaurant
906 Washington Street
Oakland, CA 94607

The brewery was founded by Don Gortemiller and Steve Wolff in 1988. Part of historic downtown Oakland, the brewpub incorporates an elaborate antique stained glass window, bar and beer cooler from the historic Cox Saloon. The brewing equipment was the first turn key brewery imported into this country for use as a microbrewery and was used at the Palo Alto Brewing Company from 1984 to 1986.

Annual production: 500 barrels

Flagship brand: Blue Whale Ale

Major top-fermented brands: Blue Whale Ale, Gray Whale Ale, Imperial Stout

Major seasonal brands: Amethyst Ale (blackberry), Amber Alt, Killer Whale Stout, Harpoon ESB, Emerald Ale (Irish Red), Orca Porter, Pilgrim's Pride (Maple Brown), Traditional India Pale Ale

GABF Silver Medals: Blue Whale Ale, 1989; Killer Whale Stout, 1990; Imperial Stout, 1992, 1993

## Pacific Hop Exchange Brewing
158 Hamilton Drive, #A1
Novato, CA 94949

One of the smallest microbreweries in the United States, this brewery was founded in 1993 by Warren Stief.

Annual production: Under 500 barrels

Major top-fermented brands: Gaslight Pale Ale, Graintoader Wheat Ale, '06 Stout

Major seasonal brand: Holly Hops

## Pacific Tap & Grill

812 Fourth Street
San Rafael, CA 94901

The brewery was founded by Keith Borrall and Keith Borral II in 1993.

Annual production: 1000 barrels

Flagship brand: Bootjack Amber

Major top-fermented brands: Bootjack Amber, Mission Gold, Noah's Dark, Riley's Wheat

Major seasonal brands: High Time Barleywine, Santa's Vengeance

**Pacifica:** See Sanktgallen (San Francisco, CA)

## Pete's Brewing Company

514 High Street
Palo Alto, CA 94301

This contract beer company was founded in 1986 by Pete Slosberg. The beer was originally produced by the now-defunct Palo Alto Brewing Company, but it is now produced by Minnesota Brewing (St Paul, MN), formerly Jacob Schmidt Brewing.

Annual production: None. Beer is produced under contract by Minnesota Brewing (St Paul, MN).

Major top-fermented brands: Lager, Pete's Wicked Ale, Winter Brew

**Red Tail:** See Mendocino Brewing (Hopland, CA)

## Red, White 'n' Brew

2181 Hilltop
Redding, CA 96002

This brewery was founded by Bill Ward in 1993.

Annual production: Under 500 barrels

## Redwood Coast Brewing
## Tied House Restaurant
## & Brewery

954 Villa Street
Mountain View, CA 94041

The brewery/restaurant was founded by Andreas Heller, PS Hung, Lou Jemison and Cheuck Tom in 1987. The first of three Tied Houses, the pub is operated by Redwood

Coast Brewing Company. The term 'tied house' originated in 18th century England. A tied house is a pub which is contracted to a single brewery and sells only that brewery's beer. Each of the pubs brews its own beer on the premises. The beers and the menus are the same at all three pubs. Brewing is under the direction of Dr Andreas Heller, and the three breweries have a combined capacity in excess of 8000 barrels a year.

Annual production: 8000 barrels (three sites combined)

Other breweries owned by the same company: Redwood Coast Brewing (Alameda, CA), Redwood Coast Brewing (San Jose, CA)

Flagship brand: Cascade Amber Tied House Gold (Pale)

Major top-fermented brands: Alpine Pearl Pale, Amber Light, Blueberry Pale, Cascade Amber, Ironwood Dark, New World Wheat, Passion Pale, Strawberry-Blonde, Tied House Dry, Tied House Stout

Major seasonal brands: Alameda Mai-Bock, Bavaria Weizen-Bock, Berliner Weisse (aka Raspberry Wheat), Munich Oktoberfest, Yule-Tied (Christmas Ale)

GABF Gold Medals: Ironwood Dark (Brown Ale), 1991; Passion Pale (Fruit Beer), 1991

GABF Silver Medals: Cascade Amber (Brown Ale), 1990; Tied House Dry (Blonde Ale), 1991; Pearl Pale (Blonde Ale), 1993; Passion Pale (Fruit Beer), 1993

## Redwood Coast Brewing
## Tied House Cafe & Brewery
Pacific Marina, #8
Alameda, CA 94501

This brewery was founded by Lou Jemison and Cheuck Tom in 1991. It is the third Tied House established by Redwood Coast Brewing. The first was established in 1987 in Mountain View, CA. It is also the only American beer hall at the waterfront on an island in the continental

United States. Brewing is under the direction of Dr Andreas Heller, and the three breweries have a combined capacity in excess of 8000 barrels a year, with immediate plans of expansion for this brewery.

Annual production: 8000 barrels (three sites combined)

Other breweries owned by the same company: Redwood Coast Brewing (Mountain View, CA), Redwood Coast Brewing (San Jose, CA)

Flagship brand: Cascade Amber Tied House Gold (Pale)

Major top-fermented brands: Alpine Pearl Pale, Cascade Amber, Ironwood Dark, New World Wheat, Amber Light, Tied House Stout, Tied House Dry, Passion Pale, Blueberry Pale, Strawberry-Blonde

Major seasonal brands: Bavaria Weizen-Bock, Munich Oktoberfest, Alameda Mai-Bock, Yule-Tied (Christmas Ale), Berliner Weisse (aka Raspberry Wheat)

GABF Gold Medals: Passion Pale (Fruit Beer), Ironwood Dark (Brown Ale)

GABF Silver Medals: Tied House Dry (Blonde Ale), Pearl Pale (Blonde Ale), Passion Pale (Fruit Beer), Cascade Amber (Brown Ale)

## Redwood Coast Brewing
## Tied House Cafe & Brewery
65 North San Pedro
San Jose, CA 95110

The brewery was founded by Lou Jemison and Cheuck Tom in 1991, as the second Tied House since the original was established in Mountain View, CA in 1987. Also in 1991, a third location was opened in Alameda. Brewing is under the direction of Dr Andreas Heller, and the three breweries have a combined capacity in excess of 8000 barrels a year.

Annual production: 8000 barrels (three sites combined)

Other breweries owned by the same company: Redwood Coast Brewing (Mountain View, CA), Redwood Coast Brewing (Alameda, CA)

Flagship brand: Cascade Amber Tied House Gold (Pale)

Major top-fermented brands: Alpine Pearl Pale, Cascade Amber, Ironwood Dark, New World Wheat, Amber Light, Tied House Stout, Tied House Dry, Passion Pale, Blueberry Pale, Strawberry-Blonde

Major seasonal brands: Bavaria Weizen-Bock, Munich Oktoberfest, Alameda Mai-Bock, Yule-Tied (Christmas Ale), Berliner Weisse (aka Raspberry Wheat)

GABF Gold Medals: Passion Pale (Fruit Beer), Ironwood Dark (Brown Ale)

GABF Silver Medals: Tied House Dry (Blonde Ale), Pearl Pale (Blonde Ale), Passion Pale (Fruit Beer), Cascade Amber (Brown Ale)

**Rhino Chasers:** See William & Scott (Culver City, CA)

## River City Brewing
545 Downtown Plaza
Sacramento, CA 95814

Sacramento's original River City Brewing was started in 1980 as one of America's original microbreweries, but it was also one of the first to close. The present River City brewery/restaurant was founded by Manuel Pereira more than a decade later, in 1993. Brewmaster Luke DiMichele was previously at Bricktown Brewery (Oklahoma City, OK).

Annual production: Under 500 barrels

Major top-fermented brand: River City Ale

Major bottom-fermented brand: River City Lager

Major seasonal brands: Dunkel, Hefeweizen, Maibock

**Rolling Rock:** See Latrobe Brewing (Latrobe, PA)

## Rubicon Brewing
2004 Capitol Avenue
Sacramento, CA 95814

This brewpub was founded by Ed Brown in 1989.

Annual production: 2160 barrels

Major bottom-fermented brands: Rubicon Amber Ale, Rubicon IPA, Rubicon Stout

Major seasonal brands: Rubicon Porter, Rubicon Summer Wheat, Rubicon Winter Wheat Wine

GABF Gold Medals: Rubicon India Pale Ale, 1989, 1990

## San Andreas Brewing Company
737 San Benito Street
Hollister, CA 95023

The brewery was founded in September 1988 and named for California's famed San Andreas earthquake fault. Located in California's 'earthquake capital,' the pub has a policy of serving nickel drafts during earthquakes and its brews are named on an earthquake theme. The locals had a chance to fill up cheaply after the Loma Prieta earthquake on 17 October 1989. The brewery suffered only minor damage but had to dump a 1000-gallon batch of wort. Amazingly, their Oktoberquake Ale was first put on the market only one month before this quake.

Annual production: 500 barrels

Major top-fermented brands: Apricot Ale, Cranberry Ale, Earthquake Pale, Earthquake Porter, Kit Fox Amber, Oktoberquake, Seismic Ale, Woodruff Ale

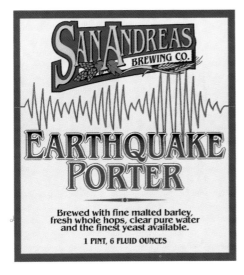

## San Francisco Brewing

155 Columbus Avenue
San Francisco, CA 94133

America's fourth brewpub, its brewing began here in November 1986 under the direction of owner and master brewer Allen Paul. Originally opened in 1907 as the Andromeda Saloon, the building is located in what was known as the Barbary Coast district. It later became the Albatross Saloon. The future heavyweight champion, Jack Dempsey, was the bouncer, polishing his skills on the sailors and miners who frequented the area. Babyface Nelson was captured here in 1929.

Annual production: 800 barrels

Major top-fermented brands: Alcatraz Stout, Gripman's Porter, Pony Express Ale

Major bottom-fermented brands: Albatross Lager, Andromeda Wheat Beer, Emperor Norton Lager, Grace Darling Bock

## Sanktgallen Brewery

Cafe Pacifica
333 Bush Street
San Francisco, CA 94104

This brewpub, a small Japanese restaurant producing beer named for Switzerland's patron saint of brewing, was founded in 1993.

Annual production: Under 500 barrels

Flagship brand: Sanktgallen Lager

## San Rafael Brewing

7110 Redwood Boulevard
Novato, CA 94949

This brewery, adjacent to TJ's Bar & Grill, was founded by Jim Hyde and Lee Strauss in 1990.

Annual production: 3000 barrels

Major top-fermented brands: San Rafael Amber, San Rafael Diamond Ale, San Rafael Golden Ale

## Santa Cruz Brewing

516 Front Street
Santa Cruz, CA 95060

The brewery, and the adjacent Front Street Pub, were founded by Scotty Morgan & Bernie and Gerry Turgeon in 1985. Santa Cruz Brew-

ing brews bottled beer for the local Northern California market.

Annual production: 2000 barrels

Flagship brands: Lighthouse Lager, Lighthouse Amber, Pacific Porter

Major seasonal brands: Pacific Stout, Beacon Bock, Pacific Pils, Hoppy Holidays, Pacific Beacon Barley Wine

## Santa Rosa Brewing

458 B Street
Santa Rosa, CA 95401

This brewpub was founded by Bruce Kelm as Kelmer's Brewpub in 1987. Frank, Kevin and Diana McCullough renamed and reopened the brewpub in April 1993. The new owners retained brewmaster Timothy O'Day, who had previously won two GABF medals in 1990 for his Golden Ale (Silver) and Strong Ale (Bronze). In 1994, the brewpub began local distribution of Two Rock Amber, named after a small local berg. Prior to this time, their beer had been available only on draft and at a limited number of other tap houses in the San Francisco Bay area.

Annual production: 900 barrels

Flagship brand: Two Rock Amber

Major top-fermented brands: Bodega Bitter, Cascades IPA, Chocolate Stout, Golden Pale, Timothy's Tipple

Major seasonal brands: Amber Weizen, Cotati Cream Ale, Goat Rock Bock, Padraic's Wit, Raspberry Wheat

GABF Silver Medal: (Kelmer's) Burbank Bitter, 1990

**Schlitz:** See Stroh Brewing (Detroit, MI)

## Seabright Brewery

519 Seabright, Suite 107
Santa Cruz, CA 95062

This brewpub was founded by Keith Cranmer and Charlie Meehan in 1988.

Annual production: 1200 barrels

Flagship brand: Pelican Pale

Major seasonal brands: Banty Rooster, Red-nose Ale

GABF Gold Medals: India Pale Ale, 1991; Banty Rooster, 1992; Oatmeal Stout, 1992, 1993

GABF Silver Medals: Seabright Amber, 1991; Pleasure Point Porter, 1992

## Sierra Nevada Brewing

1075 East 20th Street
Chico, CA 95928

One of the first microbreweries in the United States and the oldest surviving microbrewery in California, Sierra Nevada was founded by Paul Camusi and Ken Grossman in 1980. The taproom and restaurant were opened in 1990. Its annual production now places Sierra Nevada well beyond the microbrewery level, such that it can be considered to be one of the nation's major regional brewing companies.

Annual production: 115,000 barrels

Flagship brand: Sierra Nevada Pale Ale

Major top-fermented brands: Sierra Nevada Pale Ale, Porter, Stout, Celebration, Bigfoot Barleywine

Major bottom-fermented brands: Sierra Nevada Summerfest Beer, Sierra Nevada Pale Bock

Major seasonal brands: Sierra Nevada Bigfoot Barleywine, Sierra Nevada Pale Bock, Sierra

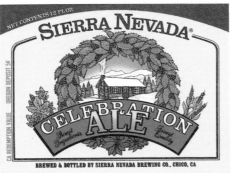

Nevada Summerfest Beer, Sierra Nevada Celebration Ale

GABF Gold Medals: Sierra Nevada Bigfoot Barleywine Style Ale, 1987, 1988, 1992; Sierra Nevada Pale Ale, 1989, 1990; Sierra Nevada Classic English Pale Ale, 1992; Sierra Nevada Amber Pale Ale, 1993

GABF Silver Medals: Sierra Nevada Stout, 1988, 1989; Sierra Nevada Summerfest, 1991

## St Stan's Brewing
821 L Street
Modesto, CA 95354

This brewery was founded by Garith Helm and Romy Angle in 1984 and was known originally as Stanislaus Brewing. A microbrewery, it was named for St Stanilaus and brewed St Stan's brand altbiers. The 'patron saint' of St Stan's Brewing is 'St Stan,' a public relations man who assumes the character of a brewer named Brother Stanislaus who is said to have brewed for Frederick the Great. St Stan's produces only altbier, a German-style, top-fermented brew similar to ale. The brewery, along with St Stan's Restaurant & Pub, opened at its present location in 1990.

Annual production: 9000 barrels

Flagship brands: Red Sky Ale, St Stan's Amber, St Stan Dark

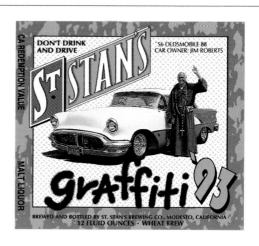

Major top-fermenting brands: Fest, Graffiti Wheat, Red Sky Ale, St Stan's Amber, St Stan Dark

Major seasonal brands: Fest (winter), Graffiti (summer)

**Karl Strauss:** See Old Columbia (San Diego, CA)

## Sudwerk Privatbraüerei Hubsch
2001 Second Street
Davis, CA 95616

This German-style brewery/restaurant was founded by Ron Broward and Dean Unger in 1990.

Annual production: 4261 barrels

Flagship brand: Hübsch Märzen

Major top-fermented brands: Hübsch Hefeweizen

Major bottom-fermented brands: Hübsch Lager, Hübsch Märzen, Hübsch Pilsner

Major seasonal brands: Hübsch Doppelbock, Hübsch Märzen

GABF Silver Medals: Hübsch Pilsner, 1991, 1993

**Tied House:** See Redwood Coast Brewing (Alameda, CA; Mountain View, CA; and San Jose, CA)

## Triple Rock Brewing

1920 Shattuck Avenue
Berkeley, CA 94704

The brewery was founded by David, John and Reid Martin in 1986. One of the first of California's brewpubs, Triple Rock originally opened as Roaring Rock, but was renamed to avoid confusion with Latrobe Brewing's Rolling Rock brand.

Annual production: 1300 barrels

Other breweries owned by the same company: Reid Martin also founded Big Time Brewing in Seattle, WA (1988) and John Martin founded the Twenty Tank Brewery in San Francisco, CA (1990).

Flagship brand: Red Rock Ale

Major top-fermented brands: Black Rock Porter, Pinnacle Pale Ale, Stonehenge Stout

Major seasonal brands: Hop of the Rock IPA, Resolution Ale, Springtime Wheat Wine, Reindeer Ale, Tree Frog

## Truckee Brewing Company

11401 Donner Pass Road
Truckee, CA 95734

Steve Downing originally opened a restaurant, the Pizza Junction, and he founded the brewery with Peggy Downing in 1985. The brewer and co-owner is Jean-Luc Gibassier. Bottling is carried out in the box car in the back of the building.
Annual production: 800 barrels

Other brewery owned by the same company: Boca Brewing Company [Nevada City Brewing (Nevada City, CA)]

Flagship brands: Boca Bock, Truckee Amber, Truckee Dark

Major seasonal brand: Boxcar Bock

## Twenty Tank Brewery

316 11th Street
San Francisco, CA 94103

The brewery was founded in 1990 by John Martin in the heart of San Francisco's South of Market (SOMA) district, an area known for its nightclubs and night life.

Annual production: 1600 barrels

Other breweries owned by the same company: John, with brothers David and Reid, founded Triple Rock Brewing in Berkeley, CA (1986). Reid Martin also founded Big Time Brewing in Seattle, WA (1988).

Flagship brand: Kinnikinick Club Standard Ale

Major top-fermented brands: Bowser's Brown, Holstein 'Heifer'-Weizen, King Tut Golden, Kinnikinick Old Scout Stout, Kinnikinick Standard, Mellow-glow Pale, Red Top, Moody's Hi-Top, Nyack Barley Wine, Pollywanna Porter

Major seasonal brands: ESB, Dunkelweizen Oatmeal Stout, Holstein 'Heifer'-Weizen, India Pale Ale, Nyack Barleywine

# OREGON

**Samuel Adams:** See Boston Beer Company (Boston, MA) and Philadelphia Brewing (Philadelphia, PA)

## Bayfront Brewery & Public House
748 SW Bay Boulevard
Newport, OR 97365

This brewpub was founded in 1989 in the coastside town of Newport, OR by Jack Joyce, an early investor in Oregon Brewing, which owns the Rogue Brewery & Public House in Ashland, OR. In 1992, brewing operations moved to larger quarters in South Beach, about one mile south across the mouth of the Yaquina River. The new facility is known as the Rogue Brewery & Tasting Room.

Annual production: Under 500 barrels

Other breweries owned by same company: Rogue Brewery & Public House (Ashland, OR), Rogue Brewery & Tasting Room (Newport/South Beach, OR)

Major top-fermented brands: Golden Ale, Maierbock, Mexicali Rogue, Mogul Madness, Newporter, Rogue Rauchbier, Rogue Saint Red, Rogue-n-Berry Ale

Major bottom-fermented brand: Waterfront Lager

GABF Gold Medals: Rauchbier, 1990; Old Crustacean, 1993

GABF Silver Medals: Rogue Welkommen, 1991, 1993

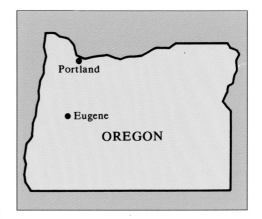

## Blitz-Weinhard Brewing
1133 West Burnside Street
Portland, OR 97209

This brewery evolved from the City Brewery, started by Henry Saxer in 1852, which was bought by Muench Brewery in 1862. The owner of the Muench Brewery at this time was a young German named Henry Weinhard, who had been a brewer in Portland since 1857. The brewery became the Henry Weinhard Brewery in 1904 and Blitz-Weinhard in 1928. It was purchased by Pabst in 1979 and sold to Heileman in 1983, but the Blitz-Weinhard name is still used and the company's premium brand is named for Henry Weinhard.

Annual production: Over 100,000 barrels

Other breweries owned by the same company: Division of G Heileman Brewing of La Crosse, WI, operating breweries in that city and Baltimore, MD and Rainier Brewing (Seattle, WA)

Flagship brand: Henry Weinhard's Private Reserve

Major top-fermented brand: Weinhard's Ale

Major bottom-fermented brands: Henry Weinhard's Private Reserve, Henry Weinhard's Private Reserve Dark

GABF Silver Medal: Henry Weinhard's Dark, 1990

## Brewing Northwest
Oregon Trail Brewery
Corvallis, OR 97339

This brewery was founded by Jerry Shadomy in 1987 and purchased by Dave Wills in July 1993.

Annual production: 400-480 barrels

Major top-fermented brands: Oregon Trail Ale, Oregon Trail Brown Ale, Oregon Trail White Ale

Major seasonal brand: Oregon Trail Stout

## BridgePort Brewing & Public House
1313 NW Marshall
Portland, OR 97209

This brewery was founded as Columbia River Brewing in 1984 and is the oldest surviving microbrewery in Oregon. The brewpub was added in 1986.

Annual production: 14,000 barrels

Major brands: Blue Heron, BridgePort Ale, BridgePort Stout, Coho Pacific, Old Knucklehead

**Budweiser:** See Anheuser-Busch (St Louis, MO)

**Busch:** See Anheuser-Busch (St Louis, MO)

## Cornelius Pass Roadhouse & Brewery
Cornelius Pass Road at Highway 26
Hillsboro, OR 97123

One of the original McMenamin brewpubs, this one was established in 1985 and features an outdoor beer garden.

Annual production: 100 barrels

Other breweries owned by the same company: Edgefield Brewery (Troutdale, OR); Fulton Pub & Brewery (Portland, OR); High Street Brewery & Cafe (Eugene, OR); Highland Pub & Brewery (Gresham, OR); Hillsdale Brewery & Public House (Portland, OR); Lighthouse Brewpub (Lincoln City, OR); McMenamin's (Beaverton, OR); McMenamin's (West Linn, OR); Oak Hills Brewpub (Portland, OR); Thompson Brewery & Public House (Salem, OR)

Major top-fermented brands: Cascade Head, Crystal, Hammerhead, Terminator Stout

Major seasonal brands: Bock, Nut Brown, Purple Haze (Boysenberry-Raspberry Ale), Raspberry Stout, Wheat

## Deschutes Brewery and Public House

1044 NW Bond Street
Bend, OR 97701

This brewpub was founded by Gary Fish in 1988.

Annual production: 14,000 barrels

Flagship brand: Black Butte Porter

Major top-fermented brands: Bachelor Bitter, Black Butte Porter, Bond Street Brown Ale, Cascade Golden Ale, Jubelale, Mirror Pond Pale Ale

GABF Gold Medals: Jubelale, 1990; Strong Ale, 1990

GABF Silver Medals: Jubelale Strong Ale, 1991; Wychick Wheat, 1991; Bond Street Brown Ale, 1993

## Edgefield Brewery

2126 Southwest Halsey Street
Troutdale, OR 97060

This brewery/restaurant was founded by Mike McMenamin in 1993 as the largest of the McMenamin chain of brewery/restaurants and brewpubs. The overall facility, which is a former state poor house, also includes a ballroom, meeting rooms and four to five guest rooms.

Annual production: 1000 barrels

Other breweries owned by the same company: Cornelius Pass Roadhouse & Brewery (Hillsboro, OR); Fulton Pub & Brewery (Portland, OR); High Street Brewery & Cafe (Eugene, OR); Highland Pub & Brewery (Gresham, OR); Hillsdale Brewery & Public House (Portland, OR); Lighthouse Brewpub (Lincoln City, OR); McMenamin's (Beaverton, OR); McMenamin's (West Linn, OR); Oak Hills Brewpub (Portland, OR); Thompson Brewery & Public House (Salem, OR)

Major top-fermented brands: Black Rabbit Porter, Edgefield Extra, Transformer Ale

Major seasonal brands: Edgefield Golden, Edgefield Mild, Raspberry Stout, Troutdale Pale

## Full Sail Brewing
506 Columbia Street
Hood River, OR 97031

This brewery was founded by Irene Firmat, Jerome Chicvar and James Emerson as Hood River Brewing in 1987. It was a companion establishment to the White Cap Pub next door. The name comes from the thousands of windsurfers who come to this section of the Columbia River Gorge to practice their craft under conditions perfectly suited to windsurfing.

Annual production: 55,000 barrels

Other brewery owned by the same company: Full Sail Brewery at the River Place (Portland, OR)

Flagship brands: Full Sail Golden, Full Sail Amber

Major top-fermented brand: Full Sail Pilsner

Major bottom-fermented brands: Full Sail Golden, Full Sail Amber, Full Sail Brown

Major seasonal brands: Wassail Winter Ale, Full Sail Doppelbock, Maibock, Oktoberfest

GABF Gold Medals: Full Sail Amber, 1989; Full Sail Brown, 1989

## Full Sail Brewery at the River Place
The Pilsner Room
307 SW Montgomery
Portland, OR 97201

This brewery/restaurant was founded by Full Sail Brewing in 1992 as an extension of its Hood River operations.

Annual production: 30,000 barrels

Other brewery owned by the same company: Full Sail Brewing (Hood River, OR)

Flagship brands: Full Sail Golden, Full Sail Amber

Major top-fermented brand: Full Sail Pilsner

Major bottom-fermented brands: Full Sail Golden, Full Sail Amber, Full Sail Brown

Major seasonal brands: Wassail Winter Ale, Full Sail Doppelbock, Maibock, Oktoberfest

GABF Gold Medals: Full Sail Amber, 1989; Full Sail Brown, 1989

## Fulton Pub & Brewery
618 SW Nebraska Street
Portland, OR 97201

This brewery/restaurant was founded by Mike McMenamin in 1988 as one of the early brewpubs in his chain.

Annual production: 1000 barrels

Other breweries owned by the same company: Cornelius Pass Roadhouse & Brewery (Hillsboro, OR); Edgefield Brewery (Troutdale, OR); High Street Brewery & Cafe (Eugene, OR); Highland Pub & Brewery (Gresham, OR); Hillsdale Brewery & Public House (Portland, OR); Lighthouse Brewpub (Lincoln City, OR); McMenamin's (Beaverton, OR); McMenamin's (West Linn, OR); Oak Hills Brewpub (Portland, OR); Thompson Brewery & Public House (Salem, OR)

Major top-fermented brands: Cascade Head, Fulton Ale, Nut Brown Ale, Pirhana Pale Ale, Hammerhead Ale, Nebraska Bitter, Ruby (Raspberry) Ale, Terminator Stout

Major seasonal brands: Fruit Ales, Raspberry Stout, Summer Wheat

## High Street Brewery & Cafe
1243 High Street
Eugene, OR 97401

This brewpub was one of the first in the chain of McMenamin family brewpubs. Founded by Mike McMenamin in 1988, it is located in a house built in 1900.

Annual production: 1000 barrels

Other breweries owned by the same company: Cornelius Pass Roadhouse & Brewery (Hillsboro, OR); Edgefield Brewery (Troutdale, OR); Fulton Pub & Brewery (Portland, OR); Highland Pub & Brewery (Gresham, OR); Hillsdale Brewery & Public House (Portland, OR); Lighthouse Brewpub (Lincoln City, OR); McMenamin's (Beaverton, OR); McMenamin's (West Linn, OR); Oak Hills Brewpub (Portland, OR); Thompson Brewery & Public House (Salem, OR)

Major top-fermented brands: Cascade Head, Hammerhead Ale, Ruby (Raspberry) Ale, Terminator Stout

Major seasonal brands: Bock, Kris Kringle, Wheat

## Highland Pub & Brewery
4225 SE 182nd
Gresham, OR 97030

The first brewery in Gresham since Prohibition, Highland Pub & Brewery was founded by Mike McMenamin in 1988 as part of the McMenamin family chain.

Annual production: 1000 barrels

Other breweries owned by same company: Cornelius Pass Roadhouse & Brewery (Hillsboro, OR); Edgefield Brewery (Troutdale, OR); Fulton Pub & Brewery (Portland, OR); High Street Brewery & Cafe (Eugene, OR); Hillsdale

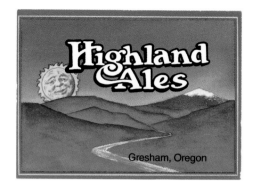

Brewery & Public House (Portland, OR); Lighthouse Brewpub (Lincoln City, OR); McMenamin's (Beaverton, OR); McMenamin's (West Linn, OR); Oak Hills Brewpub (Portland, OR); Thompson Brewery & Public House (Salem, OR)

Major top-fermented brands: Cascade Head, Hammerhead Ale, Ruby (Raspberry) Ale, Terminator Stout

Major seasonal brands: Bock, Kris Kringle, Wheat

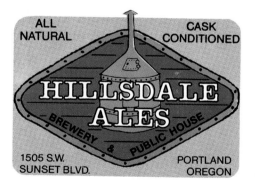

## Hillsdale Brewery & Public House

1505 SW Sunset Boulevard
Portland, OR 97201

This brewpub was founded by Mike McMenamin in February 1984, the first of the 11 breweries in the McMenamin chain of brewpubs and restaurants.

Other breweries owned by the same company: Cornelius Pass Roadhouse & Brewery

(Hillsboro, OR); Edgefield Brewery (Troutdale, OR); Fulton Pub & Brewery (Portland, OR); High Street Brewery & Cafe (Eugene, OR); Highland Pub & Brewery (Gresham, OR); Lighthouse Brewpub (Lincoln City, OR); McMenamin's (Beaverton, OR); McMenamin's (West Linn, OR); Oak Hills Brewpub (Portland, OR); Thompson Brewery & Public House (Salem, OR)

Annual production: 4000 barrels

Flagship brands: Hammerhead, Ruby (Raspberry) Ale, Terminator Stout

Major top-fermented brands: Hammerhead, Ruby (Raspberry) Ale, Terminator Stout

Major seasonal brands: Altman's Alt, Bock, Raspberry Stout

**Hood River Brewing:** See Full Sail Brewing (Hood River, OR and Portland, OR)

## Liberty Brewing

5875 SW Lakeview Drive
Lake Oswego, OR 97035

This brewery was founded by Jim Leuders in 1993.

Annual production: Up to 26,000 barrels

Major top-fermented brand: Three Finger Jack Stout

Major bottom-fermented brands: Amber Lager, Saxer Pilsner

## Lighthouse Brewpub

4157 North Highway 101
Lincoln City, OR 97367-5050

Founded by Mike McMenamin in 1986, this brewpub was the first, and to date only, coastside establishment in the McMenamin family chain of brewpubs.

Annual production: 1000 barrels

Other breweries owned by same company: Cornelius Pass Roadhouse & Brewery (Hillsboro, OR); Edgefield Brewery (Troutdale, OR);

Fulton Pub & Brewery (Portland, OR); High Street Brewery & Cafe (Eugene, OR); Highland Pub & Brewery (Gresham, OR); Hillsdale Brewery & Public House (Portland, OR); McMenamin's (Beaverton, OR); McMenamin's (West Linn, OR); Oak Hills Brewpub (Portland, OR); Thompson Brewery & Public House (Salem, OR)

Major top-fermented brands: Cascade Head, Crystal, Hammerhead Ale, Ruby (Raspberry) Ale, Terminator Stout

Major seasonal brands: Bock, Kris Kringle, Wheat

## McMenamin's

6179 SW Murray Boulevard
Beaverton, OR 97005

This brewpub was founded by Mike McMenamin in 1990 as part of the McMenamin family chain of brewpubs.

Annual production: 100 barrels

Other breweries owned by same company: Cornelius Pass Roadhouse & Brewery (Hillsboro, OR); Edgefield Brewery (Troutdale, OR); Fulton Pub & Brewery (Portland, OR); High Street Brewery & Cafe (Eugene, OR); Highland Pub & Brewery (Gresham, OR); Hillsdale Brewery & Public House (Portland, OR); Lighthouse Brewpub (Lincoln City, OR); McMenamin's (West Linn, OR); Oak Hills Brewpub (Portland, OR); Thompson Brewery & Public House (Salem, OR)

Major top-fermented brands: Cascade Head, Crystal, Hammerhead Ale, Ruby (Raspberry Ale), Terminator Stout

Major seasonal brands: Nut Brown Ale, Stella Blue (Blueberry) Ale

## McMenamin's

2090 SW 8th Avenue
West Linn, OR 97005

This brewpub was founded by Mike McMenamin in 1992 as part of the McMenamin family chain of brewpubs.

Annual production: 1000 barrels

Other breweries owned by same company: Cornelius Pass Roadhouse & Brewery (Hillsboro, OR); Edgefield Brewery (Troutdale, OR); Fulton Pub & Brewery (Portland, OR); High Street Brewery & Cafe (Eugene, OR); Highland Pub & Brewery (Gresham, OR); Hillsdale Brewery & Public House (Portland, OR); Lighthouse Brewpub (Lincoln City, OR); McMenamin's (Beaverton, OR); Oak Hills Brewpub (Portland, OR); Thompson Brewery & Public House (Salem, OR)

Major top-fermented brands: Cascade Head, Crystal, Hammerhead Ale, Ruby (Raspberry Ale), Terminator Stout

Major seasonal brand: Willamette River Bitter

## Mt Hood Brewpub/
## Mt Hood Brewing

87304 Government Camp Loop
Government Camp, OR 97028

The pub originally opened in 1991 and began serving the products of Mt Hood Brewing in 1992. The pub and the brewing company are separately owned and operated.

Annual production: 1000 barrels

Major top-fermented brands: Cloud Cap, Amber Ale, Gypsy Ale, Southside Light, Session Ale, Pinnacle ESB, Ice Axe IPA, Hogsback Oatmeal Stout

Major seasonal brand: Pittock Wee Heavy Scotch Ale

## Oak Hills Brewpub

14740 NW Cornell Road #80
Portland, OR 97229

Founded by Mike McMenamin in 1990, Oak Hills Brewpub is one of 11 brewpubs and restaurants in the chain of McMenamin brewpubs.

Annual production: 1000 barrels

Other breweries owned by same company: Cornelius Pass Roadhouse & Brewery (Hillsboro, OR); Edgefield Brewery (Troutdale, OR); Fulton Pub & Brewery (Portland, OR); High Street Brewery & Cafe (Eugene, OR); Highland Pub & Brewery (Gresham, OR); Hillsdale Brewery & Public House (Portland, OR); Lighthouse Brewpub (Lincoln City, OR); McMenamin's (Beaverton, OR); McMenamin's (West Linn, OR); Thompson Brewery & Public House (Salem, OR)

Major top-fermented brands: Cascade Head, Crystal Ale, Hammerhead Ale, Ruby (Raspberry) Ale, Terminator Stout

Major seasonal brands: Apollo Pale, Golden Oak, Kris Kringle

**Oregon Brewing:** See Rogue (Ashland, OR and Newport, OR) and Bayfront (Newport, OR)

## Oregon Trail Brewery

321 Second Street
Corvallis, Oregon 97333

This brewery was founded in July 1987 in the town of Corvallis, OR, home of Oregon State University.

Annual production: 2400 barrels

Major top-fermented brands: Empirical Brown Ale, Oregon Trail Ale, Oregon Trail Porter, Oregon Trail Stout

## Portland Brewing
2730 NW 31st
Portland, OR 97210

This brewery and brewpub, one of Oregon's largest, was founded on NW Flanders by Fred Bowman and Art Larrance in January 1986. The present brewing facility opened in 1993.

Annual production: 16,000 barrels

Other brewery owned by same company:

Portland Brewing & Brewpub (Portland, OR)

Flagship brands: McTarnahan's Ale, Oregon Honey Beer, Portland Ale

Major top-fermented brands: McTarnahan's Ale, Oregon Honey Beer, Portland Ale, Portland Porter, Portland Stout

Major seasonal brands: Icicle Creek Winter Ale, Malantey's, Octoberfest, Winter Ale

GABF Gold Medal: McTarnahan's Ale, 1992

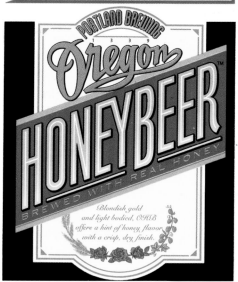

## Rogue Brewery & Tasting Room

Newport Marina
at South Beach
Newport, OR 97365

This brewery was founded by Jack Joyce in 1992 as an expansion facility for his Bayfront Brewery & Public House, located about one mile north across the mouth of the Yaquina River.

Annual production: 6000 barrels

Other breweries owned by same company: Rogue Brewery & Public House (Ashland, OR), Bayfront Brewery & Public House (Newport, OR)

Major top-fermented brands: Golden Ale, Mogul Madness, Mexicali Rogue, Newporter, Rogue Saint Red, Rogue-n-Berry Ale

Major bottom-fermented brand: Waterfront Lager

GABF Gold Medals: Rauchbier, 1990; Old Crustacean, 1993

GABF Silver Medals: Rogue Welkommen, 1991, 1993

## Rogue Brewery & Public House

31-B Water Street
Ashland, OR 97520

The brewery was founded by Jack Joyce in 1988. Located near Oregon's Rogue River, it is owned by Oregon Brewing, which started a second brewpub, the Bayfront Brewery & Public House, in Newport in 1989.

Annual production: Under 6000 barrels

Other breweries owned by same company: Bayfront Brewery & Public House (Newport,

OR), Rogue Brewery & Tasting Room (South Beach/Newport, OR)

Major top-fermented brands: Ashland Amber Ale, Rogue Golden Ale, Shakespeare Oatmeal Stout

GABF Gold Medals: Rauchbier, 1990; Old Crustacean, 1993

GABF Silver Medals: Rogue Welkomemmen, 1991, 1993

**Rolling Rock:** See Latrobe Brewing (Latrobe, PA)

**Schlitz:** See Stroh Brewing (Detroit, MI)

## Steelhead Brewery & Cafe

199 East 5th Avenue
Eugene, OR 97401

Steelhead is a brewpub near the University of Oregon campus that was founded in 1991.

Annual production: 1200 barrels

Major top-fermented brands: Amber Ale, Bombay Bomber, IPA, Station Square Stout

Major seasonal brands: French Pete's Porter, Ginger Bell's, Oatmeal Stout, Steelhead Cream Ale, Time Warp Weizenbock

GABF Gold Medals: Steelhead Amber, 1991; Steelhead Stout, 1991

## Thompson Brewery & Public House

3575 Liberty Road South
Salem, OR 97302

This brewpub was founded by Mike McMenamin in 1992 as part of his McMenamin chain of brewpubs. It was the first brewery to be started in Oregon's capital city in over three decades.

Annual production: Under 500 barrels

Other breweries owned by same company: Cornelius Pass Roadhouse & Brewery (Hillsboro, OR); Fulton Pub & Brewery (Portland, OR); High Street Brewery & Cafe (Eugene, OR); Highland Pub & Brewery (Gresham, OR); Hillsdale Brewery & Public House (Portland, OR); Lighthouse Brewpub (Lincoln City, OR); McMenamin's (Beaverton, OR); McMenamin's (West Linn, OR); Oak Hills Brewpub (Portland, OR)

Major top-fermented brands: Cascade Head, Crystal Ale, Hammerhead Ale, Ruby (Raspberry) Ale, Terminator Stout

Major seasonal brands: Thompson Kriek, Oktoberfest, Wheat

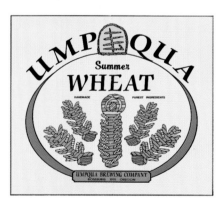

## Umpqua Brewing

328 SE Jackson
Roseburg, OR 97470

This brewpub was founded by Michael Murphy, Marco Yohai and Charlie Hanks in 1991. Umpqua Brewing was named for the Umpqua River and the local region. The logo, a petroglyph of the region, is from the Yoncalla boulder, 30 miles north of the brewery. Its exact meaning is unknown, but the word 'umpqua' means 'overflowing, satisfying and abundant.'

Annual production: 500-700 barrels

Flagship brands: Roseburg Red, Summer Wheat

Major seasonal brands: Double Red Barley Wine, Festive Ale, Kölsch, Nebo Bock, Perry's Old Ale, Rose Garden White

**Henry Weinhard's:** See Blitz-Weinhard (Portland, OR)

## Widmer Brewing

The Heathmen Bakery & Pub
901 SW Salmon
Portland, OR 97205

This brewpub was founded by Kurt and Rob Widmer and named 1988 Portland Restaurant of the Year.

Annual production: Under 500 barrels

Other breweries owned by same company: The Widmers operate three brewpubs in the Portland, OR area.

Flagship brand: Widmer

Major top-fermented brands: Altbier, Hefeweizen, Weizenbier

Major bottom-fermented brand: Bockbier

Major seasonal brands: Festbier, Märzenbier, Oktoberfestbier, Rauchbier

GABF Silver Medal: Widmer Alt, 1987

## Widmer Brewing

929 North Russell Street
Portland, OR 97227

Widmer Brewing was founded by by Kurt Widmer in 1984 and was originally located on NW Lovejoy in Portland. It was the second microbrewery to be established in Portland and is the largest microbrewery in Oregon, a

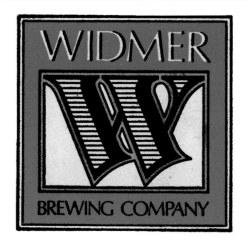

state noted for its vast proliferation of small breweries.

Annual production: 30,000 barrels

Other breweries owned by same company: The Widmers operate three brewpubs in the Portland, OR area.

Flagship brand: Widmer

Major top-fermented brands: Altbier, Hefeweizen, Weizenbier

Major bottom-fermented brand: Bockbier

Major seasonal brands: Festbier, Märzenbier, Oktoberfestbier, Rauchbier

GABF Silver Medal: Widmer Alt, 1987

## Widmer Brewing #2

923 SW 9th
Portland, OR 97205

This brewery was founded by Kurt Widmer in 1990 as an expansion site for the North Russell facility.

Annual production: 2600 barrels

Other breweries owned by same company: The Widmers operate three brewpubs in the Portland, OR area.

Flagship brand: Widmer

Major top-fermented brands: Altbier, Hefeweizen, Weizenbier

Major bottom-fermented brand: Bockbier

Major seasonal brands: Festbier, Märzenbier, Oktoberfestbier, Rauchbier

GABF Silver Medal: Widmer Alt, 1987

## Wild River Brewing & Pizza Company

249 North Redwood Highway
Cave Junction, OR 97523

This brewpub, formerly known as Pizza Deli & Brewery, was founded by Jerry and Bertha Miller in 1990. The Pizza Deli opened as a restaurant in 1975 and began brewing beer in 1990.

Annual production: 1000 barrels

Flagship brand: Wild River

Major top-fermented brand: Wild River ESB, Wild River Hefe-Weizen, Wild River Nut Brown Ale

Major bottom-fermented brand: Wild River Harbor Lights Kölsch

Major seasonal brands: Wild River Blackberry Porter, Wild River Cave Bear Barley Wine, Wild River Double Eagle Russian Imperial Stout, Wild River Oktoberfest, Wild River Snug Harbor Old Ale, Wild River Weizen-Bock

GABF Silver Medal: Wild River Nut Brown Ale, 1992

## Willamette Brewing

120 Commercial Street NE
Salem, OR 97301

The brewery was founded by Jeff Cruise in 1991 in a former livery stable that also had served as a bowling alley.

Annual production: 1200 barrels

Major top-fermented brands: Durbin Golden Ale, Millrace Amber Ale, Santiam Porter

Major bottom-fermented brands: Capitol Rush Light, Cruise Bock, Willamette Wheat

Major seasonal brand: Helles Bock

# WASHINGTON AND ALASKA

**Samuel Adams:** See Boston Beer Company (Boston, MA) and Philadelphia Brewing (Philadelphia, PA)

## Alaskan Brewing
Douglas, AK 99824

This brewery was founded by Geoff and Marcy Larson as Chinook Alaskan Brewing & Bottling Company in 1986. The name was shortened to Alaskan Brewing Company in 1989. It is the first brewing company built in Alaska since Prinzbräu Brewing closed in 1979.

Annual production: 14,000 barrels

Flagship brands: Alaskan Amber Beer, Alaskan Pale Ale

Major top-fermented brand: Alaskan Smoked Porter

Major seasonal brands: Alaskan Arctic Ale, Alaskan Autumn Ale, Alaskan Wheat Beer, Alaskan Winter Stock Ale, Break Up Bock

GABF Gold Medals: Alaskan Amber Beer, 1987, 1988, 1990; Alaskan Smoked Porter, 1991, 1992, 1993; Alaskan Autumn Ale, 1991

GABF Silver Medals: Alaskan Smoked Porter, 1990; Alaskan Autumn Ale, 1989, 1990

The Chicago Beer Society, Best of Show & Gold Medal Ale: Alaskan Amber Beer, 1990, 1991

Chefs in America Gold Medal for Excellence: Alaskan Amber Beer, 1990, 1991, 1992; Alaskan Pale Ale, 1993, 1994

## Big Time Brewing
Brewery & Alehouse
4133 University Way NE
Seattle, WA 98105

This brewery and ale house were founded by Reid Martin in December 1988.

Annual production: 1000 barrels

Other breweries owned by the same company: Reid and his brother John also founded Triple Rock Brewing in Berkeley, CA and John founded the Twenty Tank Brewery in San Francisco (1990).

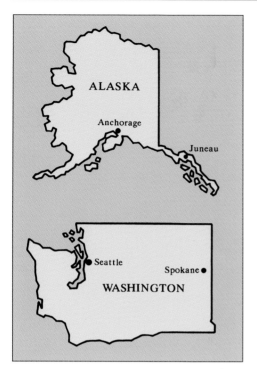

## California & Alaska Street Brewery
4720 California Avenue SW
Seattle, WA 98116

This brewery was founded in 1991.

Annual production: 500 barrels

Major top-fermented brands: Admiral ESB, Alki Ale, Fauntleroy Stout, Hi-Yu Brown Ale, Junction Gold, Vashon Old Stock

Major seasonal brands: Irish Porter, West Seattle Weisse

Major top-fermented brands: Prime Time Pale Ale, Atlas Amber, Coal Creek Porter

GABF Gold Medals: Old Wooly Barley Wine, 1990; Prime Time Pale Ale, 1990; Coal Creek Porter, 1990

GABF Silver Medal: Prime Time (Blonde Ale), 1993

## Bird Creek Brewery
310 East 76th, Unit B
Anchorage, AK 99518

This brewery was founded by Ike Kelly in 1991.

Annual production: 600 barrels

Flagship brand: Old 55 Pale Ale

Major top-fermented brands: Anchorage Ale, Denali Style Ale

**Budweiser:** See Anheuser-Busch (St Louis, MO)

**Busch:** See Anheuser-Busch (St Louis, MO)

## Fish Brewing Company & Fishbowl Pub
515 Jefferson
Olympia, WA 98501

This brewery was founded by Crayne and Mary Horton in 1993. It is the only brewery in Washington's state capital. The famous 'Olympia' brand is brewed by Pabst in the old Olympia Brewing facility in neighboring Tumwater.

Annual production: 1000 barrels

Flagship brand: Fish Tale Pale Ale

Major top-fermented brands: Fish Eye IPA, Trout Stout, Mudshark Porter

Major bottom-fermented brand: Fishbone Bock

Major seasonal brand: Leviathan Barleywine

## Fort Spokane Brewery
401 West Spokane Falls Boulevard
Spokane, WA 99201

This brewpub was founded in 1989 by James Bochemuehl, the great-great-grand nephew of the original founders, Bernard and Max Bochemuehl, who opened their Fort Spokane Brewery in 1889 and closed it in 1900.

Annual production: 1456 barrels

Major top-fermented brands: Blond Alt, Border Run, Bulldog Stout, FSB Pale, Red Alt

Major seasonal brands: Holiday Ale, Octoberfest

## Hale's Ales
5634 East Commerce Street
Spokane, WA 99212-1307

Hale's Ales is a brewery founded by Michael Hale in 1983 in Colville, the third microbrewery to open in Washington. A second facility was opened in Kirkland, WA in 1986, and the Colville operation moved to Spokane in 1991.

Annual production: 8500 barrels

Other brewery owned by the same company: Hale's Ales Moss Bay Brewery (Kirkland, WA)

Flagship brand: Pale American Ale

Major top-fermented brands: Hale's Special Bitter, Celebration Porter, Washington Wheat, Irish Ale, Cascade Mist, O'Brien's Harvest Ale, Wee Heavy

Major seasonal brands: Irish Ale, Wee Heavy, Harvest Ale

## Hale's Ales
## Moss Bay Brewery
109 Central Way
Kirkland, WA 98033

This brewery was founded by Michael Hale in 1983.

Hale's Ales was originally founded by Michael Hale in Colville in 1983. A second facility was opened here in Kirkland, WA in 1986.

Annual production: 8500 barrels

Other brewery owned by the same company: Hale's Ales (Spokane, WA)

Flagship brand: Pale American Ale

Major top-fermented brands: Hale's Special

Bitter, Celebration Porter, Washington Wheat, Irish Ale, Cascade Mist, O'Brien's Harvest Ale, Wee Heavy, Moss Bay Amber, Moss Bay Extra, Moss Bay Stout

Major seasonal brands: Irish Ale, Wee Heavy, Harvest Ale

**Hamm's:** See Pabst (Tumwater, WA)

## Hart Brewing
110 West Marine Drive
Kalama, WA 98625

This brewery overlooking the Columbia River north of Portland was founded by Beth Harwell and Tom Baune in 1984.

Annual production: 33,000 barrels

Other brewery owned by the same company: Hart Brewing, Inc, owns Kemper Brewing (Poulsbo, WA), as well as Hart Brewing

Flagship brands: Wheaten, Pyramid

Major top-fermented brands: Pyramid Pale, Hefeweizen, Best Brown, Amber Wheat, Espresso Stout

Major seasonal brands: Snow Cap Ale (winter), Wheaten Bock (spring)

GABF Gold Medal: Pacific Crest Ale, 1990

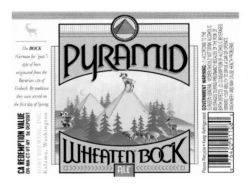

## Hazel Dell Brewpub
8513 NE Highway 99
Vancouver, WA 98665

This brewpub was founded in August 1993.

Annual production: 500 barrels

Flagship brand: Red Zone Pale Ale

Major top-fermented brands: Captain Moran's Irish Stout, Red Zone Pale Ale, Steinweizen (wheat ale)

Major seasonal brand: Oktoberfest

## Kemper Brewing
22381 Foss Road
Poulsbo, WA 98370

This brewery was founded by Andrew Thomas and Will Kemper in 1984 and originally located in the Foss Meat Packing Plant building on Bainbridge Island. The brewery was moved to Poulsbo in 1986.

Annual production: 6900 barrels

Other brewery owned by the same company: Kemper Brewing is owned by Hart Brewing, Inc (Kalama, WA)

Flagship brand: Thomas Kemper

Major bottom-fermented brands: Thomas Kemper Hefe-Weizen, Thomas Kemper Integralé, Thomas Kemper Pale Lager, Thomas Kemper Pilsner, Thomas Kemper Weizen-Berry

Major seasonal brands: Thomas Kemper Oktoberfest, Thomas Kemper Rolling Bay Bock, Thomas Kemper Winterbräu

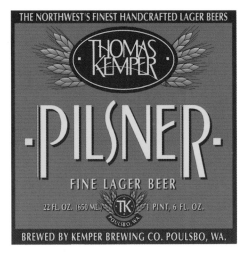

## Leavenworth Brewing
636 Front Street
Leavenworth, WA 98826

This brewpub was founded in 1992.

Annual production: Under 500 barrels

Major top-fermented brands: Bull's Tooth Porter, Escape Altbier

Major bottom-fermented brands: Friesian Pilsner, Whistling Pig Wheat

Major seasonal brands: Christmas Bock, Mai Bock, Oktoberfest

## Maritime Pacific Brewing
1514 NW Leary Way
Seattle, WA 98107

This brewery was founded in 1990.

Annual production: 1800 barrels

Flagship brand: Flagship Red Ale

Major top-fermented brands: Clipper Gold Wheat Ale, Islander Pale, Nighwatch

Major seasonal brands: Bosun's Black, Maibock, Jolly Roger Christmas Ale, Navigator Dark, O'Leary's Irish, Windfest, Windjammer, Dark Wheat Ale

**Michelob:** See Anheuser-Busch (St Louis, MO)

**Moss Bay:** See Hale's Ales (Kirkland, WA)

**O'Doul's:** See Anheuser-Busch (St Louis, MO)

**Olympia:** See Pabst (Tumwater, WA)

## Onalaska Brewing
248 Burchett Road
Onalaska, WA 98570

This brewery was founded by Dave Moorehead in 1991.

Annual production: 160 barrels

Major top-fermented brands: Onalaska Ale, Red Dog Ale

## Pabst Brewing
Olympia Brewery
Tumwater, WA 98507

The original Olympia Brewing Company evolved from the Capital Brewing Company, established in Tumwater on the outskirts of Olympia (the capital of Washington) by Leopold Schmitt in 1896. Renamed Olympia Brewing in 1902, it was acquired by the Pabst Brewing Company in 1985, two years after Olympia had acquired the Theodore Hamm Brewing Company of St Paul, MN.

Annual production: 4,500,000 barrels

Other breweries owned by same company: The Pabst Brewing Company also operates the Pabst Brewery (Milwaukee, WI) and the Pearl Brewery (San Antonio, TX).

Flagship brand: Olympia

Major bottom-fermented brands: Buckhorn,

Buckhorn Light, Hamm's, Hamm's Draft, Hamm's Special Light, Lucky Lager, MAXX Special Lager, Olde English 800, Olympia, Olympia Gold, Pabst Blue Ribbon, Pabst Light

GABF Gold Medals: Pearl Lager Beer, 1991; Olde English 800, 1991; Olympia Dry, 1993

GABF Silver Medals: Pabst Blue Ribbon, 1990; Olde English 800, 1990

## Pacific Northwest Brewing
322 Occidental Avenue South
Seattle, WA 98104

This brewpub was founded by Richard Wrigley in 1989 near Seattle's sports complex, the King Dome.

Annual production: Under 500 barrels

Major top-fermented brands: Amber, Blonde Ale, Bitter, Cream Porter, Gold Ale, Stout

Major seasonal brands: Christmas Gold, Christmas Mild

## Pike Place Brewery
1432 Western Avenue
Seattle, WA 98101

This small but excellent brewery was founded in October 1989 by internationally known beer importer Charles Finkel in the Pike Place Market. It is owned jointly by Finkel and brewmaster John Farias, who oversees the brewing of Pike Place Pale Ale and other specialty beers.

Annual production: 1700 barrels

Flagship brand: Pike Place Pale Ale

Major top-fermented brands: Birra Perfetto, East India Pale Ale, Old Bawdy Barley Wine, Pike Place Pale Ale, Rosanna Red Chili Ale

GABF Silver Medal: Old Bawdy Barley Wine, 1993

**Pyramid:** See Hart Brewing (Kalama, WA)

## Rainier Brewing
3100 South Airport Way
Seattle, WA 98124

Rainier, named for Washington's highest mountain and Seattle's premier hometown brand for most of the twentieth century, was first brewed by Seattle Brewing & Malting between 1906 and 1915. After Prohibition, German-Canadian brewer Emil Sick arrived in Seattle determined to start a chain of breweries in the Northwest. He revived Seattle Brewing and renamed it Rainier Brewing. It was his flagship as he acquired breweries in Spokane, WA; Lethbridge, AL; Salem, OR; Missoula, MT; and Great Falls, MT.

Rainier remained prominent during the 1935-1955 period, both as a lager brand and the name of the brewery and also as the name of Seattle's Pacific Coast League baseball

team, which Sick also owned. In 1958, Sick sold his brewing operations to Molson of Canada, who in turn sold Rainier Brewing to Heileman in 1977. The Rainier brand name was retained by both companies.

Annual production: 50,000 barrels

Other brewery owned by same company: Rainier is a subsidiary of G Heileman Brewing (La Crosse, WI).

Flagship brand: Rainier

Major top-fermented brand: Rainier Ale

Major bottom-fermented brands: Rainier, Rainier Dry, Rainier Light

GABF Gold Medal: Rainier (American Lager), 1990

## Red Hook Ale Brewery
3400 Phinney Avenue North
Seattle, WA 98103

This brewery, Seattle's first in several decades, was founded by Paul Shipman as the Independent Ale Brewery in 1982. The Trolleyman Pub was opened in 1998, and both are located in the old home of the Seattle Electric Railway, the Fremont trolley car barn in the city's Ballard district.

Annual production: 73,000 barrels

Other brewery owned by the same company: Redhook Ale Brewery (Woodinville, WA)

Major top-fermented brands: Ballard Bitter, Blackhook Porter, Wheathook, Blueline specialty beers, Redhook ESB, Winterhook Christmas Ale

Major seasonal brands: Blueline specialty beers, Winterhook Christmas Ale

## Redhook Ale Brewery
14300 NE 145th Street
Woodinville, WA

The original Redhook Ale Brewery was brewery was founded by Paul Shipman as the Independent Ale Brewery in 1982 in Seattle, WA. This second location opened in August 1994.

Annual production: Over 1000 barrels

Other brewery owned by the same company: Redhook Ale Brewery & Trolleyman Pub (Seattle, WA)

Major top-fermented brands: Ballard Bitter, Blackhook Porter, Blueline specialty beers, Redhook ESB, Wheathook

Major seasonal brands: Blueline specialty beers, Winterhook Christmas Ale

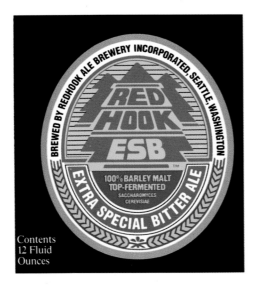

**Rolling Rock:** See Latrobe Brewing (Latrobe, PA)

## Roslyn Brewing
33 Pennsylvania Avenue
Roslyn, WA 98941

The brewery was founded by Roger Beardsley and Dino Enrico in 1990, although an original brewery was founded as the Roslyn Brewing and Malting Company in 1889 (some sources say 1891) by William Dewitt and Frank Groger. It closed in 1913 with the enactment of Prohibition.

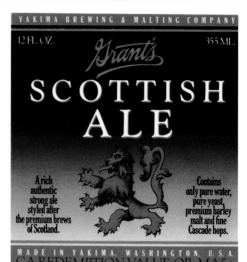

Annual production: 350 barrels

Flagship brand: Roslyn Beer

Major brands: Brookside Beer, Roslyn Beer

**Schlitz:** See Stroh Brewing (Detroit, MI)

## Yakima Brewing & Malting
Grant's Brewery Pub
32 North Front Street
Yakima, WA 98901

This brewery and pub were founded by Herbert 'Bert' Grant in 1982.

Located in a late 1800s railroad station, Grant's Brewery Pub was the first to open in the United States since Prohibition and is located in the heart of North America's greatest hop-growing region.

The brewery operation of Yakima Brewing & Malting is located three miles away. Under the direction of founder Herbert Grant, the brewery produces beer for both the retail market and Grant's brewpub.

Annual production: 20,000 barrels

Flagship brand: Grant's

Major top-fermented brands: Grant's Celtic Ale, Grant's Imperial Stout, Grant's Pale Ale, Grant's Scottish Ale, Grant's Spice Ale, Grant's Weis Beer

GABF Silver Medal: Grant's Imperial Stout, 1987

# WESTERN AND PRAIRIE CANADA

## Barley Mill Brewpub
6807 Rochdale Boulevard NW
Regina, Saskatchewan S4X 2Z2

This brewpub was founded in 1989 and is one of the brewpubs in the Dunn Group.

Annual production: Over 500 hectolitres

Other brewery owned by the same company: Bonzini's Brew Pub (Regina, Saskatchewan)

Major top-fermented brand: George Edgar Ale

**Produced by**
**Big Rock Brewery • Calgary, Alberta, Canada**
341 ml                                    11.5 fl.oz

Major bottom-fermented brands: Barley Mill Classic Lager, Castaway Electric Pilsner, Golden Grain Lager, Prairie Lager

## Big Rock Brewery
6403 35th Street SE
Calgary, Alberta T2C 1N2

This brewery was founded by Ed McNally in 1986.

Annual production: Under 150,000 hectolitres

Other brewery owned by same company: Big Rock Brewery (Edmonton, Alberta)

Flagship brands: Traditional Ale, Warthog Ale

Major top-fermented brands: Bitter, Cock o' the Rock Porter, McNally's Extra, Pale Ale, Royal Coachman, Traditional Ale, Warthog Ale

Major bottom-fermented brand: XO Lager

## Big Rock Brewery
10012 29th Avenue
Edmonton, Alberta T2C 1N2

This brewery was founded by Ed McNally in 1985.

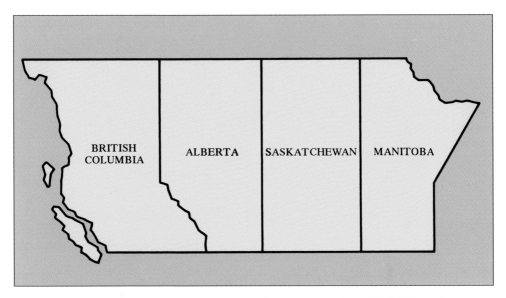

Annual production: 150,000 hectolitres

Other brewery owned by the same company: Big Rock Brewery (Calgary, Alberta)

Flagship brands: Traditional Ale, Warthog Ale

Major top-fermented brands: Buzzard Breath Ale, Traditional Ale, Warthog Ale

Major seasonal brand: Cold Cock Winter Porter

## Bonzini's Brew Pub
4634 Albert Street South
Regina, Saskatchewan S4S 6B4

This brewpub was founded by Dave Dunn in 1991.

Annual production: Under 500 hectolitres

Other brewery owned by same company: Barley Mill Brewpub (Regina, Saskatchewan)

Major top-fermented brands: Black & Tan, Nut Brown Ale, Red Tail Ale

Major bottom-fermented brands: Bear Lager, Great Plains Pilsener

## Brewsters Brew Pub & Brasserie
834 11th Avenue SW
Calgary, Alberta T2R 0E5

This brewery/restaurant was founded by the Lanigan brothers and their wives in 1991.

Annual production: 900 hectolitres

Other breweries owned by the same company: Brewsters Brew Pub & Brasserie (Calgary, Alberta), Brewsters Brew Pub & Brasserie (Moose Jaw, Saskatchewan), Brewsters Brew Pub & Brasserie (Regina, Saskatchewan)

Flagship brand: Hammerhead Red Ale

Major top-fermented brands: Big Horn Bitter, Blue Monk Barley Wine, Hammerhead Red Ale, Palliser Pale Ale, Shaughnessy Stout, Bow Valley Brown Ale

Major bottom-fermented brands: Continental Light Lager, Flying Frog Lager, Original Lager, Wild West Wheat Beer, Ernest Bay Premium Pilsner

Major seasonal brands: Cranberry Ale, Honey Wheat, Spring Bock

### Brewsters Brew Pub & Brasserie
755 Lake Bonavista Drive
Calgary, Alberta T2J 0N3

This brewery/restaurant, overlooking Lake Bonavista, was founded by the Lanigan brothers and their wives in 1992.

Annual production: 900 hectolitres

Other breweries owned by the same company: Brewsters Brew Pub & Brasserie (Calgary, Alberta), Brewsters Brew Pub & Brasserie (Moose Jaw, Saskatchewan)

## Brewsters Brew Pub & Brasserie

8 Main Street North
Moose Jaw, Saskatchewan S6H 3J6

This brewery/restaurant was founded in the Cornerstone Inn by the Lanigan brothers and their wives in 1991.

Annual production: 900 hectolitres

Other breweries owned by the same company: Brewsters Brew Pub & Brasserie (2 in Calgary, Alberta), Brewsters Brew Pub & Brasserie (Regina, Saskatchewan)

Flagship brand: Hammerhead Red Ale

Major top-fermented brands: Big Horn Bitter, Blue Monk Barley Wine, Hammerhead Red Ale, Palliser Pale Ale, Shaughnessy Stout, Bow Valley Brown Ale

Major bottom-fermented brands: Continental Light Lager, Flying Frog Lager, Original Lager, Wild West Wheat Beer, Ernest BAy Premium Pilsner

Major seasonal brands: Cranberry Ale, Honey Wheat, Spring Bock

## Brewsters Brew Pub & Brasserie

1832 Victoria Avenue East
Regina, Saskatchewan S4N 7K3

This brewery/restaurant was founded by the Lanigan brothers and their wives in 1989.

Annual production: 900 hectolitres

Other breweries owned by the same company: Brewsters Brew Pub & Brasserie (2 in Calgary, Alberta), Brewsters Brew Pub & Brasserie (Moose Jaw, Saskatchewan)

Flagship brand: Hammerhead Red Ale

Major top-fermented brands: Big Horn Bitter, Blue Monk Barley Wine, Hammerhead Red Ale, Palliser Pale Ale, Shaughnessy Stout, Bow Valley Brown Ale

Major bottom-fermented brands: Continental Light Lager, Flying Frog Lager, Original Lager, Wild West Wheat Beer, Ernest Bay Premium Pilsner

Major seasonal brands: Cranberry Ale, Honey Wheat, Spring Bock

## Buckerfield Brewery

Swan's Brewpub
506 Pandora Avenue
Victoria, British Columbia V8W 1N6

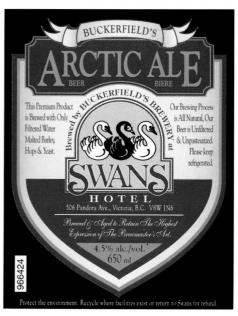

This brewpub was founded by Michael Williams in 1989 in Buckerfields' Seed Warehouse. The 1913 building has been remodeled into an English neighborhood pub with a 29-room hotel, the Foul Fish Cafe and a Wine and Beer Shoppe.

Annual production: 1700 hectolitres

Flagship brand: Arctic Ale

Major top-fermented brands: Appleton Brown, Buckerfield's Bitter, Pandora Pale, Riley's Scotch Ale, Swan's Arctic, Swan's Oatmeal Stout

Major bottom-fermented brand: Old Towne Bavarian Lager

Major seasonal brands: Beacon Hill Lager, Dragon Lady Porter, Judge Begbie's Dark Lager, Swan's Wheat Beer

## Bushwakker Brewing

2206 Dewdney Avenue
Regina, Saskatchewan S4R 1H3

This brewpub was founded in 1992 in the Strathdee Centre Mall.

Annual production: Over 500 hectolitres

Major top-fermented brands: Granny's Bitter, Palliser Porter, Regina Pale

Major bottom-fermented brands: Last Mountain Lager, Northern Lights Lager, Stubble Jumper Pils

Major seasonal brands: Baron Bock, Chinook ESB, Cyclone Barleywine, Harvest Märzen, Wakky Wheat Bock

## Canadian Heritage Brewing

3131 Chatham Street
Richmond, British Columbia V7E 2Y4

Annual production: Under 500 hectolitres

**Caribou:** See Western (Prince George, British Columbia)

**Carling O'Keefe:** See Molson (Toronto, Ontario)

## Clark's Crossing Brewpub

3030 Diefenbaker
Saskatoon, Saskatchewan S7L 7K2

This brewpub was founded in 1990.

Annual production: Under 500 hectolitres

Major top-fermented brand: Wheat Ale

Major bottom-fermented brands: Lager, Pilsner

## Columbia Brewing
## Labatt Breweries of
## British Columbia

1220 Erickson
Creston, British Columbia V0B 1G0

Annual production: 300,000 hectolitres

Other breweries owned by the same company: Columbia is a division of Labatt Brew-

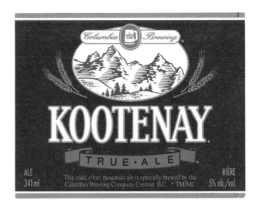

ing. See Labatt Breweries, Ltd (London, Ontario) for a list of Labatt breweries.

Major top-fermented brand: Kootenay

Major bottom-fermented brands: Glacier Light, Kokanee

## Drummond Brewing

2210 Baetz Avenue
Red Deer, Alberta T4R 1W5

This major regional brewery was founded in 1985.

Annual production: 250,000 hectolitres

Flagship brand: Drummond Premium Lager

Major bottom-fermented brands: Black Wolf, Celtic Gold, Drummond Draft-in-a-Can, Drummond Dry, Drummond Dry Light, Drummond Light, Drummond Premium Lager, No Name, No Name Light, Wolfsbräu Amber

## Fox & Hounds Brewpub
7 Assiniboine Drive
Saskatoon, Saskatchewan S7K 4C1

This English-style brewpub was founded as Miners Brewpub in 1989, and later reopened as the Fox & Hounds.

Annual production: Under 500 hectolitres

Major top-fermented brand: Dark Ale

Major bottom-fermented brands: Light Lager, Original Lager, Pilsner

Major seasonal brand: Cranberry Christmas Wheat

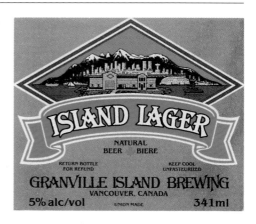

## Granville Island Brewing
1441 Cartwright Street
Vancouver, British Columbia V6H 3R7

One of Canada's original microbreweries, Granville Island was founded on the island of the same name in 1984. It was acquired by Pacific Western Brewing in 1989.

Annual production: 50,000 hectolitres

Major top-fermented brand: Lord Granville Pale Ale

Major bottom-fermented brands: Island Bock, Island Lager, Island Lager Light

## Great Western Brewing
519 2nd Avenue North
Saskatoon, Saskatchewan S7J 2C6

Annual production: 200,000 hectolitres

Major top-fermented brand: Gibbs Ale

Major bottom-fermented brands: Christmas Goose Malt Liquor, Great Western Gold, Great Western Lager, Great Western Light, Prairie 3.2, Saskatchewan

## Horseshoe Bay Brewing
6695 Nelson Avenue
West Vancouver, British Columbia V7W 2B2

Although several microbreweries existed in California at the time, when John Mitchell began brewing and purveying beer at his Troller Pub/Horseshoe Bay Brewing Company in 1982, it became the first brewpub to open in North America. The brewery closed in 1987. In the meantime, Mitchell founded Spinnakers (Victoria, British Columbia) in 1984. Horseshoe Bay reopened in 1989 as a brewery but not a brewpub.

Annual production: Under 1000 hectolitres

Major top-fermented brands: Bay Ale, IPA, Nut Brown Raspberry Triple

Major seasonal brand: Christmas Ale

**Kokanee:** See Columbia Brewing (Creston, British Columbia)

### Labatt's Alberta Brewery
4415 Calgary Trail
Edmonton, Alberta T5J 2P2

This brewery was built by Labatt and opened in June 1964.

Annual production: 750,000 hectolitres

Other breweries owned by the same company: Labatt Breweries of Canada's flagship brewery is in London, Ontario. The company also operates breweries in New Westminster, British Columbia; Winnipeg, Manitoba; St John, New Brunswick; St John's, Newfoundland; Etobicoke, Ontario; and La Salle, Quebec.

Flagship brand: Labatt's Blue

Major bottom-fermented brands: Bud Light, Budweiser, Club Lager, Labatt's Blue, Labatt Lite, Lucky Lager

### Labatt Breweries, British Columbia
210 Brunette Street
New Westminster, British Columbia V3L 4Z2

In 1958, Labatt acquired Lucky Lager Breweries, Ltd of British Columbia, of which this was the flagship facility. Labatt also owned a major stake in Lucky Lager Breweries in the United States until 1971.

Annual production: 770,000 hectolitres

Other breweries owned by the same company: Labatt Breweries of Canada's flagship

brewery is in London, Ontario. The company also operates breweries in Edmonton, Alberta; Winnipeg, Manitoba; St John, New Brunswick; St John's, Newfoundland; Etobicoke, Ontario; and La Salle, Quebec.

Flagship brand: Labatt's Blue

Major bottom-fermented brands: Budweiser, Guinness, Labatt's Blue, Labatt's Extra Stock, Labatt Lite

### Labatt's Manitoba Brewery
1600 Notre Dame Avenue
Winnipeg, Manitoba K2W 3S5

This brewery evolved from the Winnipeg Brewery, built in 1873 on the banks of Colony Creek near downtown Winnipeg. It was acquired in 1885 by Patrick Shea and John McDonagh. After McDonagh's death, Shea expanded and modernized what was then known as Shea's Winnipeg Brewery. It was acquired by Labatt's in November 1953 and managed by John Labatt, a descendent of the founder, who moved the facility to its present location. In 1972, a new brewhouse was built.

Annual production: 538,000 hectolitres

Other breweries owned by the same company: Labatt Breweries of Canada's flagship brewery is in London, Ontario. The company also operates breweries in Edmonton, Alberta;

New Westminster, British Columbia; St John, New Brunswick; St John's, Newfoundland; Etobicoke, Ontario; and La Salle, Quebec.

Flagship brand: Labatt's Blue

Major top-fermented brands: Country Club Stout, Labatt's 50 Ale, Velvet Cream Stout

Major bottom-fermented brands: Club Lager, Labatt's Blue, Labatt's Extra Dry, Labatt Lite, Lucky Lager

### Lethbridge Brewery
Lethbridge, Alberta T1J 4A2

This facility was founded in 1901 by Fritz Sick, whose son, Emil Sick, used it as the springboard to build an American brewing empire based at the Rainier Brewery in Seattle and which included breweries in Oregon and Montana. In 1958, Sick sold his operations to Molson, who sold Rainier to G Heileman and Lethbridge to Molson, although the latter was operated for over 30 years by Molson under the Lethbridge name.

Annual production: 520,000 hectolitres

Other breweries owned by the same company: The Lethbridge Brewery has been a Molson subsidiary since 1958. Molson also operates breweries in Barrie, Ontario; Edmonton, Alberta; Etobicoke, Ontario (a former Carling O'Keefe plant); Montreal, Quebec; Regina, Saskatchewan; St John's, Newfoundland; Vancouver, British Columbia; and Winnipeg, Manitoba.

Flagship brand: Lethbridge Pilsner

### Molson Breweries
10439-121st Street
Edmonton, Alberta T5N 1L3

This brewery was founded in 1892.

Annual production: 450,000 barrels

Other breweries owned by the same company: Barrie, Ontario; Edmonton, Alberta; Etobicoke, Ontario (a former Carling O'Keefe plant); Montreal, Quebec; Regina, Saskatchewan; St John's, Newfoundland; Vancouver, British Columbia; and Winnipeg, Manitoba. Sick's Lethbridge Brewery (Lethbridge, Alberta) has been a Molson subsidiary since 1958.

Flagship brand: Molson Golden

Major bottom-fermented brands: Blackhorse Beer, Carling Black Label, Coors, Coors Light, Dominion Ale, India Beer, Molson Canadian, Molson Canadian Light, Molson Golden, Molson Special Dry, Old Vienna, O'Keefe Extra Old Stock, Pilsner Old Style, Rickard's Red

Major awards received: Monde Selection Gold Medals: India Beer, 1971, 1982, 1984; Molson Canadian, 1984

## Molson Breweries
1300 Dewdney Avenue
Regina, Saskatchewan S4R 1G4

This brewery was Molson's original Saskatchewan facility.

Annual production: 330,000 hectolitres

Other breweries owned by the same company: Barrie, Ontario; Edmonton, Alberta; Etobicoke, Ontario (a former Carling O'Keefe plant); Montreal, Quebec; St John's, Newfoundland; Vancouver, British Columbia; and Winnipeg, Manitoba. Sick's Lethbridge Brew-

ery (Lethbridge, Alberta) has been a Molson subsidiary since 1958.

Flagship brand: Molson Golden

Major bottom-fermented brands: Bohemian, Calgary Export, Coors, Coors Light, Molson Canadian, Molson Canadian Light, Molson Special, Molson Special Dry, O'Keefe Extra Old Stock, Old Vienna, OV Light, Pilsner Old Style

Major awards received: Monde Selection Gold Medals: India Beer, 1971, 1982, 1984; Molson Canadian, 1984

## Molson Breweries
1550 Burrard Street
Vancouver, British Columbia V6J 3G5

This brewery was built by Molson in the 1940s.

Annual production: 1,200,000 hectolitres

Other breweries owned by the same company: Barrie, Ontario; Edmonton, Alberta; Etobicoke, Ontario (a former Carling O'Keefe plant); Montreal, Quebec; Regina, Saskatchewan; St John's, Newfoundland; and Winnipeg, Manitoba. Sick's Lethbridge Brewery (Lethbridge, Alberta) has been a Molson subsidiary since 1958.

Flagship brand: Molson Golden

Major bottom-fermented brands: Blackhorse Beer, Carling Black Label, Carling Pilsner, Coors Banquet, Coors Light, Foster's, Kirin, Kirin Draft, Kirin Dry, Kirin Light, Kronenbräu, Miller Genuine Draft, Miller High Life, Miller Lite, Molson Canadian, Molson Light, Pilsner Old Style, Rickard's Red, Toby

Major awards received: Monde Selection Gold Medals: India Beer, 1971, 1982, 1984; Molson Canadian, 1984

## Molson Breweries
77 Redwood Avenue
Winnipeg, Manitoba R2W 5J5

This brewery was founded by the Drewry Family in 1887. It later became a Carling O'Keefe brewery, and in 1989 it was acquired by Molson.

Annual production: 400,000 hectolitres

Flagship brand: Old Vienna (OV)

Major bottom-fermented brands: Arctic Bay, Carling Black Label, O'Keefe Extra Old Stock, Old Vienna, Old Vienna Light, Miller High Life, Miller Lite, Molson Special, Molson Special Dry, Molson Canadian, Standard Lager

Annual production: 75,000 hectolitres

Flagship brand: Extra Special Pale Ale

Major top-fermented brand: Extra Special Pale Ale

Major bottom-fermented brand: Premium Lager

Major Seasonal brand: Spring Pilsner

Major award received: 1991 Canadian Award for Business Excellence, Certificate of Merit

## Nelson Brewing
512 Latimer Street
Nelson, British Columbia V1L 4T9

This brewery was founded by Paddy Glenny and Dieter Feist in 1991, who purchased the Nelson brand name from the heirs of the first Nelson Brewery, which opened at this location in 1893.

Annual production: 4500 hectolitres

Major top-fermented brand: Old Brewery Ale

Major bottom-fermented brand: Silver King Lager

## Okanagan Spring Brewery
2801-27A Avenue
Vernon, British Columbia V1T 1T5

This brewery was founded by German immigrants Jakob Tobler and Buko von Krosigk in 1985.

## Pacific Western Brewing
641 N Nechako Road
Prince George, British Columbia V2K 4M4

This brewery was founded in 1957 on a freshwater spring under the name Caribou Brewing Company, Ltd. Five years later it was bought by Carling O'Keefe and promptly auctioned off. It was purchased by Ben Ginter and rechristened Tartan Breweries. Ginter's popular products, Uncle Ben's Beer and Uncle Ben's Malt Liquor, carried the company successfully until he attempted to expand. He ran out of cash building a second brewery at Richmond, British Columbia. In 1978, the brewery was purchased by Nelson Skalbania, who renamed it Canadian Gold Brewing. It was sold again in 1981 to WR Sharpe (formerly of Canada Dry) and his associates, who operated it as the Old Fort Brewing Company until 1984, when the

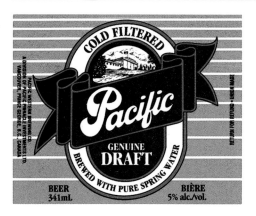

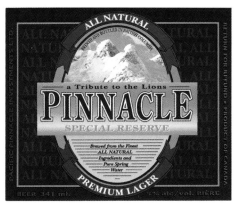

Major bottom-fermented brands: Canterbury, Pacific Dry, Pacific Genuine Draft, Pacific Pilsner, Pinnacle Special Reserve, Traditional Lager Dry Ice

## Prairie Inn Neighborhood Pub & Cottage Brewery

7806 East Saanich Road
Saanichton, British Columbia V0S 1M0

This brewpub was founded in 1983.

Annual production: Under 500 hectolitres

## Saskatoon Brewing

2105 8th Street East #32
Saskatoon, Saskatchewan S7H 0T8

The brewery, as well as Cheers Brewpub & Restaurant, was founded by Russ Turner in 1990.

Annual production: 2200 hectolitres

Flagship brands: Big Sky Pale Ale, Prairie Dark Ale

Major bottom-fermented brands: Arctic Pilsner, Blackstrap Bock, Classic Lager, Wheat Beer (Weizen)

Major seasonal brands: Christmas Ale, Oktoberfest

## Shaftebury Brewing

1973 Pandora Street
Vancouver, British Columbia V5L 5B2

This brewery was founded by Tim Witting and Paul Beaton in 1987.

Annual production: 15,000 hectolitres

Flagship brand: Shaftebury Cream Ale

name was changed to Pacific Western Brewing.

By 1984, Pacific Western had a seven percent share of the British Columbia market and had embarked on an aggressive marketing campaign aimed at the North American West Coast. In 1989, Pacific Western purchased Simcoe Brewing in Ontario and Granville Island Brewing in Vancouver. Granville Island Brewing was among the largest of the smaller breweries that opened in British Columbia in the early 1980s. Its brands included Island Lager Beer and Island Bock Beer. Also in 1989, Pacific Western purchased the Calona Winery from Hublein.

Annual production: 200,000 barrels

Other brewery owned by the same company: Granville Island Brewing (Victoria, British Columbia).

Flagship brand: Pacific Genuine Draft

Major top-fermented brands: Extra Special Bitter, Rainforest Amber Ale, Wheat Ale

Major seasonal brand: Wheat Ale (summer)

## Spinnakers Brewpub
308 Catherine Street
Victoria, British Columbia V9A 3S8

This brewpub was founded by John Mitchell in 1984 after he left Horseshoe Bay Brewing. Horseshoe Bay, which Mitchell founded in 1982, was the first microbrewery in Canada and the first brewpub in North America.

Annual production: 1800 hectolitres

Flagship brand: Mitchell's ESB

## Sunshine Coast Breweries
1298 Wharf Avenue
Sechelt, British Columbia V0N 3A0

Annual production: Under 500 hectolitres

## Vancouver Island Brewing
6809 Kirkpatrick Crescent, RR #3
Victoria, British Columbia V8X 3X1

This brewery was founded in British Columbia's provincial capital in 1984.

Annual production: 13,000 hectolitres

Flagship brand: Hermann's Dark Lager

Major top-fermented brand: Piper's Pale Ale

Major bottom-fermented brand: Victoria Lager

## Whistler Brewing Company
1209 Alpha Lake Road
Whistler, British Columbia V0N 1B1

This brewery was founded near the Whistler ski area by Jenny Hieter and Rob Mingay in 1989.

Annual production: 12,000 hectolitres

Flagship brand: Whistler Premium Lager

Major bottom-fermented brands: Black Tusk, Whistler's Mother, Whistler Premium Lager

Major awards received: Best Microbrewed Beer in British Columbia (Premium Lager): *Vancouver* Magazine, 1990

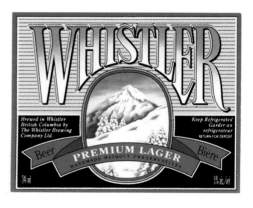

# EASTERN CANADA

## Algonquin Brewing
One Old Brewery Lane
Formosa, Ontario N0G 1W0

This brewery was opened by Evan W Hayter II as Northern Algonquin, Ltd in 1988 in the former Formosa Spring Brewery, which dated from 1870 and had closed in its centennial year of 1970.

Annual production: 90,000 hectolitres

Flagship brand: Formosa Springs Cold Filtered Draft Beer

Major top-fermented brand: Algonquin Special Reserve Ale

Major bottom-fermented brands: Algonquin Country Lager, Algonquin Light, Algonquin Royal Amber Lager, Formosa Springs Light

Major seasonal brand: Formosa Springs Bavarian Bock

Major awards received: Monde Selection (Brussels) 1992-1993: Algonquin Special Reserve Ale (Grand Gold Medal), Formosa Springs Cold Filtered Draft (Gold Medal), Algonquin Royal Amber Lager (Gold Medal), Formosa Springs Light (Silver Medal)

## Amstel Brewery Canada
201 Burlington Street East
Hamilton, Ontario L8L 4H2

Formerly Hamilton Breweries, this brewery began operations in 1981 and is now owned entirely by Heineken NV of the Netherlands. The products brewed here include Steeler

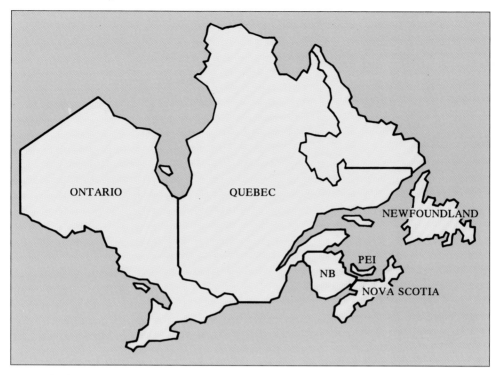

Lager, which is considered Hamilton's 'hometown' beer, and Grizzly, a lager originally brewed only for the United States export market but now available in Ontario as well.

A major part of Amstel's operation is, of course, devoted to brewing the parent company's Amstel and Amstel Light brands, but it also brews Henninger and Peroni beers under license from the respective German and Italian breweries who originated these brands.

Annual production: 300,000 hectolitres

Flagship brands: Amstel, Grizzly

Major bottom-fermented brands: Amstel, Amstel Light, Grizzly, Henninger Export, Henninger Meister Pils, Peroni

### Amsterdam Brasserie & Brewpub
133 John Street
Toronto, Ontario M5V 2E4

Dating from 1986, Amsterdam is the first brewpub in Toronto, and is particularly popular with Blue Jays fans during baseball season.

Annual production: Over 1000 hectolitres

Major top-fermented brands: Bitter, Nut Brown Ale

Major bottom-fermented brand: Lager

Major seasonal brands: Amber Weiss, Blonde Ale, Christmas Bock, Oktoberfest, Rauchbier, Spring Bock

## Barb's Union Station Pub & Eatery

4396 Steeles Avenue East
Markham, Ontario L3R 9W1

This brewpub was founded in 1992.

Annual production: Under 500 hectolitres

Major top-fermented brand: Barb's Union Station Ale

Major bottom-fermented brand: Lager

**Barney's Pub:** See CEEP's (London, Ontario)

## Blue Anchor Restaurant & Brewpub

47 West Street SE
Orillia, Ontario L3V 5G5

A twentieth century replica of a fifteenth century English pub in a nineteenth century Canadian building, this brewpub was founded in 1988. Blue Anchor was a brand name used by the Newfoundland Brewery, which was built in St John's in 1892 and acquired by Molson in 1962.

Annual production: Under 500 hectolitres

Major top-fermented brand: Bitter Amber Ale

Major bottom-fermented brand: Lager

## Brasal Allemande Brewery

8477 Rue Cordner
La Salle, Quebec H8N 2X2

This German-style lager brewery was founded by the Jagermann family in 1989.

Annual production: 20,000 hectolitres

Flagship brand: Hopps Bräu Beer

Major bottom-fermented brands: Brasal Light Beer, Brasal Spécial Beer

Major seasonal brand: Brasal Bock Beer

Major award received: Super Salon Alimentation International, 1991

## Brasseurs du Nord, Inc

875 Boulevard Michèle-Bohec
Blainville, Quebec J7C 5E7

This major new Canadian brewery was founded in 1987.

Annual production: 22,000 hectolitres

Flagship brand: Borèale

Major top-fermented brands: Borèale Rousse, Borèale Blonde, Borèale Noire, Borèale Forte

## Brax 'n' Brew

4230 Sherwoodtowne Boulevard
Mississauga, Ontario L4Z 2G6

This brewpub was founded in about 1989 as the Luxembourg Brewpub but was renamed for its new owner, Brax Diab.

Annual production: Under 500 hectolitres

Major top-fermented brand: Knight's Ale

Major bottom-fermented brand: Harvester

Major seasonal brands: IPA, Märzen, Winter Warmer

## Brick Brewing

181 King Street South
Waterloo, Ontario N2J 1P7

This brewery was founded by Jim Brickman in 1984.

Annual production: 100,000 hectolitres

Flagship brand: Brick Premium Lager

Major bottom-fermented brands: Brick Amber Dry, Henniger, Kaiser Pils, Pacific Real Draft, Red Baron

Major seasonal brand: Brick Anniversary Bock

Major awards received: Monde Selection (Brussels, Luxemburg, Barcelona, Amsterdam): 11 gold medals for quality, 1990, 1991, 1992, 1993

**Carling O'Keefe:** See Molson (Toronto, Ontario)

## CC's Brewpub
6981 Mill Creek Drive, Unit 1
Mississauga, Ontario L5N 6B8

This brewpub evolved from an existing restaurant and began brewing in 1991.

Annual production: Under 500 hectolitres

Flagship brand: CC's Own Lager

## La Cervoise
4457 St Laurent Boulevard
Montreal, Quebec H2W 1Z8

This brewery was founded by Jean-Pierre Trepanier in 1988.

Annual production: 700-800 hectolitres

Flagship brand: La Futée

Major bottom-fermented brands: La Futèe, La Main

Major seasonal brands: Hydromel, Oktoberfest (a different style—wheat, bitter, etc—is offered every week on a rotating basis)

## CEEP's Brewpub
Barney's Pub
671 Richmond Street
London, Ontario N6A 3G7

This single small brewery began brewing in

1991, servicing two adjacent pubs. Barney's is a more traditional pub, while CEEP's is a student-oriented sports bar. Both are near the University of Western Ontario campus.

Annual production: 300 hectolitres

Flagship brand: CEEP's Lager

Major seasonal brand: Wheat

## Charley's Tavern
4715 Tecumseh Road East
Windsor, Ontario N8T 1B6

This brewpub evolved from an existing sports bar and began brewing in about in 1992.

Annual production: Under 500 hectolitres

Major top-fermented brands: Timeout Ale, Timeout Lager

## Cheval Blanc
809 Ontario Street
Montreal, Quebec H2L 1P1

Quebec's first brewpub was founded by Jerome Denys in 1987 in an old tavern, operated by the Denys family since 1937. In true Canadian fashion, Cheval Blanc produces their unique Maple Syrup Beer.

Annual production: Under 500 hectolitres

Major top-fermented brands: Amber Ale, Brown Ale, Golden Ale, Pale Ale

Major seasonal brands: Cap Tourmente, Loch Ness Scottish Ale, Maple Syrup, Titanic

## Conners Brewing
227 Bunting Road
St Catharines, Ontario L2M 3Y2

This brewery was founded in Don Mills, Ontario in 1986, closed in 1990 and was reopened later in the same year by new owners, Marc Bedard and Glen Dalzell. Annual production: 17,500 barrels

Flagship brand: Best Bitter

Major top-fermented brands: Ale, Best Bitter,

Imperial Stout, Special Draft

Major bottom-fermented brand: Premium Lager

Major award received: International Wine & Food Show 1992: Best Bitter (silver)

## Creemore Springs Brewery
139 Mill Street
Creemore, Ontario L0M 1G0

This brewery was founded by John Wiggins in 1987 in the restored 1890s May Hardware Store building. Creemore uses the slogan 'A hundred years behind the times—brewing good old-fashioned lager the pure and natural way.'

Annual production: 15,000 hectolitres

Flagship brand: Creemore Springs Premium Lager

Major bottom-fermented brand: Creemore Springs Premium Lager

Major awards received: Ontario Food & Beer Show: Creemore Springs Premium Lager (Gold Medal), 1990, 1991

## Crocodile Club
5414 Gatineau
Montreal, Quebec H3G 1Z5

This brewpub was founded by Bernard Ragueneau in 1988, with the decor being a French Canadian interpretation of a blend of California and possibly South Florida motifs.

Annual production: 450 hectolitres

Other brewery owned by the same company: Crocodile Club St Laurent (Montreal, Quebec)

Major top-fermented brand: La Crocodile Pale Ale

## Crocodile Club St Laurent
4238 St Laurent
Montreal, Quebec H2W 1Z3

This brewery/restaurant was founded in 1989 and features French *haute cuisine* and a disco.

Annual production: 1000 hectolitres

Other brewery owned by the same company: Crocodile Club (Montreal, Quebec)

Major top-fermented brand: La Crocodile Pale Ale

## Denison's
75 Victoria Street
Toronto, Ontario M5C 2B1

This brewery/restaurant was founded by Luitpold Prinz Von Bayern (Leopold, Prince Of Bavaria) and a limited partnership in 1989.

Growler's Bar and Conchy Joe's Oyster bar are adjacent.

Annual production: 1100 hectolitres

Flagship brand: Royal Dunkel (dark Munich-style lager)

Major top-fermented brand: Weizen-Hefeweizen Beer

Major bottom-fermented brand: Growler's Lager (filtered and unfiltered)

Major seasonal brands: Bock, Spezial, Märzen, Weizen

**Formosa Spring Brewery:** See Algonquin Brewing (Formosa, Ontario) and Molson Breweries (Barrie, Ontario)

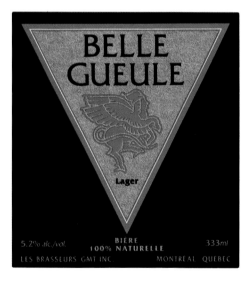

## GMT Brasseurs
5710 Garnier Street
Montreal, Quebec H2G 2Z7

This brewery was founded by Gilbert Gravel, André Martineau and Yves Thibault in 1988.

Annual production: 12,000 hectolitres

Flagship brand: Belle Gueule

Major bottom-fermented brands: Belle Gueule, Tremblay

## Golden Lion Brewing

6 College Street
Lennoxville, Quebec J1M 1Z6

This brewpub was founded by Stan Groves in 1986 in an English-style pub that had existed since 1973. The food now includes Louisiana and Mexican cuisine.

Annual production: 500 hectolitres

Flagship brand: Lion's Pride

Major top-fermented brands: Bishop's Best Bitter, Lion's Pride, Township's Pale Ale

Major seasonal brands: Biere D'Amour, Blackfly Stout, Santa's Suds

Major awards received: Best Beer in Lenoxville/Ascot, 1993; Kenny Morrison's 'Hey Good Buddy—Buy Me a Beer' Award, 1994

## Granite Brewery

1222 Barrington Street
Halifax, Nova Scotia B3J 1Y4

This establishment was founded by Kevin Keefe in 1985 as the first Canadian microbrewery and brewpub outside British Columbia. It is located in the Henry House, the landmark home of William Alexander Henry, father of the Canadian Constitution.

Annual production: 600 hectolitres

Other brewery owned by the same company: Granite Brewery Ontario (Toronto, Ontario)

Flagship brand: Best Bitter

Major top-fermented brand: Peculiar

## Granite Brewery Ontario

245 Eglington Avenue East
Toronto, Ontario M4P 3B7

This brewpub was founded in 1991 by Kevin Keefe, the founder of Granite Brewing (Halifax, Nova Scotia), the first brewpub outside British Columbia.

Annual production: 600 hectolitres

Other brewery owned by the same company: Granite Brewery (Halifax, Nova Scotia)

Flagship brands: Best Bitter, Best Bitter Special, Peculiar (dry hopped)

Major top-fermented brand: Best Bitter, Best Bitter Special, Keefe's Irish Stout, Peculiar, Summer Ale

Major seasonal brand: Summer Ale

## Great Lakes Brewing

30 Queen Elizabeth Boulevard
Etobicoke, Ontario M8Z 1L8

This brewery was founded by Bruce Cornish, who sold it in 1991. Bottling and canning for export began in 1995.

Annual production: 27,600 hectolitres

Flagship brand: Great Lakes Lager

**Grizzly:** See Amstel (Hamilton, Ontario)

**Growler's:** See Denison's (Toronto, Ontario)

**Hamilton:** See Amstel (Hamilton, Ontario)

## Hart Breweries
175 Industrial Avenue
Carleton Place, Ontario K7C 3V7

This brewery was founded by a limited partnership of Jonathan Hatchell and Lorne Hart in 1991. The brewer is Keith Hart.

Annual production: 5800 hectolitres

Flagship brand: Hart Amber Ale

Major top-fermented brands: Amber Ale, Cream Ale, Dragon's Breath Hardy Stout, Pale Ale

Major seasonal brand: Porter (fall)

Major award received: International Wine & Food Show 1992: Gold Medal (Ale Category)

## Heidelberg Restaurant & Brewery
2 King Street
Heidelberg, Ontario N0B 1Y0

A hub of local activity since 1838, the Old Heidelberg Restaurant became a brewpub in 1986.

Annual production: Under 500 hectolitres

Flagship brand: Our Beer

**Keith's:** See Oland (Halifax, Nova Scotia)

**Kooteney:** See Columbia Brewing (Creston, British Columbia)

## L'Inox
37 Rue Street André
Quebec City, Quebec G1K 8T3

Now a brewpub, L'Inox evolved from a tavern and began brewing in 1987.

Annual production: Under 500 hectolitres

Major top-fermented brands: Bitter, Transit, Trouble Fete

Major seasonal brands: Stout, Viking (mead)

## Kingston Brewing
34 Clarence Street
Kingston, Ontario K7L 4V1

The brewery, and the adjacent The Pilot House of Kingston Pub, were founded in 1986. The Pilot House features a large collection of breweriana.

Annual production: Under 500 hectolitres

## Labatt's Breweries

150 Simcoe Street
London, Ontario N6A 4M3

Labatt's Breweries, Ltd, (formerly John Labatt, Ltd) dates to a brewery built in 1828 in London, Ontario by innkeeper George Balkwill. This brewing company was sold to William and George Snell in 1832 (brewers in Ontario since 1828) and to Samuel Eccles and John Labatt in 1847. In 1853, Labatt became the sole owner of the present company and renamed the company for himself. The Simcoe Street brewery has continued to evolve and expand ever since.

Labatt Breweries, Ltd was, until the 1989 merger of Molson and Carling O'Keefe, the largest brewing company in Canada. The company also owns a controlling interest in Latrobe Brewing (Latrobe, PA, USA) and Birra Moretti (Udine, Italy).

In 1993, Molson and Labatt in Canada, and Anheuser-Busch and Miller in the United States, began to market 'ice' beer. Developed and patented by Labatt, ice beer is a pale lager which is quickly chilled to sub-freezing temperatures after brewing but before final fermentation. The result is the formation of ice crystals in the beer, which are removed to produce a beer with roughly twice the alcohol content of typical mass market lagers.

Annual production: 1,700,000 hectolitres

Other breweries owned by the same company: Labatt Breweries also operates breweries in Edmonton, Alberta; New Westminster, British Columbia; Winnipeg, Manitoba; St John, New Brunswick; St John's, Newfoundland; Etobicoke, Ontario; and La Salle, Quebec.

Flagship brand: Labatt's Blue

Major top-fermented brand: Labatt's 50 Ale

Major bottom-fermented brands: Budweiser, Carlsberg, Carlsberg Light, John Labatt Classic, Labatt's Blue, Labatt's Blue Light, Labatt's Extra Dry, Labatt Lite

## Labatt's New Brunswick Brewery

Simms Street
Saint John W, New Brunswick E2M 4X7

This brewery was acquired by Labatt in the 1971 acquisition of Oland & Son, Ltd (See Oland).

Annual production: 382,000 hectolitres

Other breweries owned by the same com-

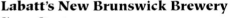

pany: Labatt Breweries of Canada's flagship brewery is in London, Ontario. The company also operates breweries in Edmonton, Alberta; New Westminster, British Columbia; Winnipeg, Manitoba; St John's, Newfoundland; Etobicoke, Ontario; and La Salle, Quebec.

Flagship brand: Labatt's Blue

Major top-fermented brands: Keith's IPA, Labatt's Blue, Labatt's 50 Ale

Major bottom-fermented brands: Labatt Lite, Oland Export, Oland Schooner

## Labatt's Newfoundland Brewery
Leslie Street
St John's, Newfoundland A1E 3Y4

This brewery was founded by the Brownrigg family in 1933 and known as Bavarian Brewing, Ltd. It was purchased by the Labatt Brewing Company in 1962.

Annual production: 250,000 hectolitres

Other breweries owned by the same company: Labatt Breweries of Canada's flagship brewery is in London, Ontario. The company also operates breweries in Edmonton, Alberta; New Westminster, British Columbia; Winnipeg, Manitoba; St John, New Brunswick; Etobicoke, Ontario; and La Salle, Quebec.

Flagship brand: Labatt's Blue

Major top-fermented brands: Labatt's 50 Ale

Major bottom-fermented brands: Blue Star, Carling Black Label, Jockey Club, Labatt's Blue, Labatt's Extra Dry, Labatt Lite

## Labatt Breweries of Ontario
50 Resources Road
Etobicoke, Ontario M9P 3V7

Annual production: 1,720,000 hectolitres

Other breweries owned by the same company: Labatt Breweries of Canada's flagship brewery is in London, Ontario. The company also operates breweries in Edmonton, Alberta; New Westminster, British Columbia; Winnipeg, Manitoba; St John, New Brunswick; St John's, Newfoundland; and La Salle, Quebec.

Flagship brand: Labatt's Blue

Major top-fermented brand: Labatt's 50 Ale

Major bottom-fermented brands: Carlsberg, Carlsberg Light, Labatt Blue, Labatt's Blue Light, Schooner

## La Brasserie Labatt
50 Labatt Avenue
La Salle, Quebec H8R 3E7

This brewery was built by Labatt and opened in 1955.

Annual production: 2,300,000 hectolitres

Other breweries owned by the same com-

pany: Labatt Breweries of Canada's flagship brewery is in London, Ontario. The company also operates breweries in Edmonton, Alberta; New Westminster, British Columbia; Winnipeg, Manitoba; St John, New Brunswick; St John's, Newfoundland; and Etobicoke, Ontario.

Flagship brand: Labatt's Blue

## Lighthouse Brewpub
143 Duke Street
Bowmanville, Ontario L1C 2W4

This small brewpub was founded at the Flying Dutchman Hotel in 1990.

Annual production: Under 500 hectolitres and brewed on an irregular basis

Flagship brand: Lighthouse

## Lion Brewery, Museum & Malt House
59 King Street North
Waterloo, Ontario N2J 2X2

This brewery/restaurant was founded in 1987 in the 1842 Huether Hotel, which originally housed a brewery and inn. Two unique features of this establishment are the breweriana collection and the adjacent do-it-yourself brewing facility known as The Beer Factory.

Annual production: Under 500 hectolitres

Major top-fermented brands: Huether Premium, Lion Lager, Lion Light

Major bottom-fermented brands: Adlys Ale, English Ale

## McAuslan Brewing
4850 Rue Street, Ambroise, Bureau 100
Montreal, Quebec H4C 3N8

Quebec's first microbrewery was founded by Peter McAuslan in 1989 near the historic Lanchine Canal and Atwater Outdoor Market.

Annual production: Under 500 hectolitres

Major top-fermented brands: Griffon Brown, Griffon Extra Pale, St Ambroise Pale, St Ambroise Oatmeal Stout

## Marconi's Restaurant & Brewery
262 Carlingview
Etobicoke, Ontario M9W 5G1

This brewery/restaurant was founded near the Toronto airport in 1990 at the Journey's End Suites. Their Superiore brand is brewed under contract by Algonquin Brewing.

Annual production: Under 1500 hectolitres

Major bottom-fermented brands: Marconi's Dry Light, Marconi's European Lager

Major seasonal brands: Christmas, Octoberfest

## Massawippi Brewing
33 Winder
Lennoxville, Quebec J1M 1Z6

This brewery was founded as the Pilsen Brewpub in North Hatley in 1986, but the brewery was moved to Lennoxville when the Pilsen was sold.

Annual production: Under 1500 hectolitres

Major top-fermented brands: Massawippi Bitter, Massawippi Dutch

Major bottom-fermented brand: Massawippi Quai

Major seasonal brand: Massawippi Stout

## Master's Brasserie & Brewpub
330 Queen Street
Ottawa, Ontario K1A 5A5

This brewery/restaurant was founded at the Skyline Hotel.

Annual production: Under 500 hectolitres

Major top-fermented brand: Master's Ale

Major bottom-fermented brand: Master's Lager

## Molson Breweries of Canada

2 International Boulevard
Toronto, Ontario M9W 1A2

Molson is the largest brewing company in Canada and the oldest brewing company in the entire Western Hemisphere. The history of brewing in Canada is similar to that of the United States—involving a well-developed home brewing activity and an active brewpub scene by the eighteenth century. The first big name in commercial Canadian brewing was John Molson. From the English county of Lincolnshire, Molson arrived in Montreal in 1782 armed with a copy of John Richardson's *Theoretical Hints on the Improved Practice of Brewing.* The people of Quebec, predominantly French, preferred wine, so there was little of a brewing tradition in this province. Since imported English beer sold for more than rum in Montreal, the city's beer drinkers welcomed John Molson's first brewery, which began brewing in 1786. Today, Molson Breweries (Brasseries Molson in Quebec) is headquartered in Toronto.

Molson's flagship brand, Molson Golden, is a national brand in Canada and the biggest selling Canadian export brew in the United States. Other Molson beers include Molson Canadian Lager, Molson Light (Legère), Molson Export Ale and Export Light Ale. Special regional beers brewed by Molson's western breweries (British Columbia, Alberta, Manitoba and Saskatchewan) are Bohemian, Brador, Edmonton Export Lager, Frontier Beer, Imperial Stout, Old Style and Royal Stout. Regional beers brewed by Molson in eastern Canada include Molson Bock, Molson Cream

Porter, Molson Diamond, Molson Oktoberfest India Beer and Laurentide Ale. Molson also brews Löwenbräu under license from Löwenbräu in Munich. Since 1987, Molson has brewed Coors in Canada, under license from the Colorado brewery, and in 1988 Molson started contract production of Kirin Beer from Japan.

Annual production: See the individual breweries listed below.

Other breweries owned by the same company: Edmonton, Alberta; Etobicoke, Ontario (a former Carling O'Keefe plant); Montreal, Quebec; Regina, Saskatchewan; St John's, Newfoundland; Vancouver, British Columbia; and Winnipeg, Manitoba. Sick's Lethbridge Brewery (Lethbridge, Alberta) has been a Molson subsidiary since 1958.

Flagship brand: Molson Golden

Major awards received: Monde Selection Gold Medals: India Beer, 1971, 1982, 1984; Molson Canadian, 1984

## Molson Breweries
1 Big Bay Point Road
Barrie, Ontario L4M 4T2

This brewery was founded in 1971 as the Formosa Spring Brewery and was acquired by Molson in 1974.

Annual production: 2,500,000 hectolitres

Other breweries owned by the same company: Edmonton, Alberta; Etobicoke, Ontario (a former Carling O'Keefe plant); Montreal, Quebec; Regina, Saskatchewan; St John's, Newfoundland; Vancouver, British Columbia; and Winnipeg, Manitoba. Sick's Lethbridge Brewery (Lethbridge, Alberta) has been a Molson subsidiary since 1958.

Flagship brand: Molson Golden

Major top-fermented brands: Club Ale, Molson Stock Ale

Major bottom-fermented brands: Brador, Coors, Coors Light, Löwenbräu, Molson Canadian, Molson Canadian Light, Molson Dry, Molson Export, Molson Golden, Molson Light, Molson Special Dry

Major awards received: Monde Selection Gold Medals: India Beer, 1971, 1982, 1984; Molson Canadian, 1984

## Molson Breweries
1 Carlingview Drive
Etobicoke, Ontario M9W 5E5

This brewery was built by Carling O'Keefe and was acquired by Molson in 1989.

Annual production: 3,500,000

Other breweries owned by the same company: Barrie, Ontario; Edmonton, Alberta; Etobicoke, Ontario (a former Carling O'Keefe plant); Montreal, Quebec; Regina, Saskatchewan; St John's, Newfoundland; Vancouver, British Columbia; and Winnipeg, Manitoba.

Sick's Lethbridge Brewery (Lethbridge, Alberta) has been a Molson subsidiary since 1958.

Flagship brand: Molson Golden

Major top-fermented brand: O'Keefe Ale

Major bottom-fermented brands: Amstel, Amstel Light, Arctic Bay, Carling Black Label, Calgary, Cinci Cream, Coors, Coors Light, Foster's, Molson Canadian, Molson Export, Molson Canadian Light, Molson Golden, Molson Light, Molson Special Dry, O'Keefe Extra Old Stock, Old Vienna, Richard's Red, Toby

Major awards received: Monde Selection Gold Medals: India Beer, 1971, 1982, 1984; Molson Canadian, 1984

## La Brasserie Molson
1555 Notre Dame Street East
Montreal, Quebec H2L 2R5

This brewery was founded by John Molson in 1786. Although it has been completely rebuilt and greatly expanded over the past two centuries, this is the original and still flagship brewery of the Western Hemisphere's oldest brewing company.

Annual production: 4,000,000 hectolitres

Other breweries owned by the same company: Barrie, Ontario; Edmonton, Alberta; Etobicoke, Ontario (a former Carling O'Keefe plant); Regina, Saskatchewan; St John's, Newfoundland; Vancouver, British Columbia; and Winnipeg, Manitoba. Sick's Lethbridge Brewery (Lethbridge, Alberta) has been a Molson subsidiary since 1958.

Flagship brand: Molson Golden

Major top-fermented brands: Dow Ale, O'Keefe Ale, Champlain Porter

Major bottom-fermented brands: Arctic Bay, Brador, Carling Black Label, Coors Banquet, Coors Legère, Kirin, Miller High Life, Miller Lite, Molson Canadian, Molson Export, Molson Golden, Molson Light, Molson Special Dry, O'Keefe Extra Old Stock, Old Vienna, Richard's Red, Stella Artois

Major awards received: Monde Selection Gold Medals: India Beer, 1971, 1982, 1984; Molson Canadian, 1984

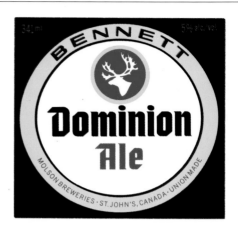

## Molson Breweries
Circular Road
St John's, Newfoundland A1C 5W1

This brewery was originally opened in 1893 as the Newfoundland Brewery. It adopted the Newfoundland dog as its logo in 1925, and the principal brands included Blue Anchor Pale and Blue Anchor Stout. The facility was acquired by Molson in 1962 and expanded over the years, with a new brewhouse being added in 1976.

Annual production: 250,000 hectolitres

Other breweries owned by the same company: Barrie, Ontario; Edmonton, Alberta; Etobicoke, Ontario (a former Carling O'Keefe plant); Montreal, Quebec; Regina, Saskatchewan; Vancouver, British Columbia; and Winnipeg, Manitoba. Sick's Lethbridge Brewery

(Lethbridge, Alberta) has been a Molson subsidiary since 1958.

Flagship brand: Molson Golden

Major top-fermented brands: Coors Light, Dominion Ale, Extra Old Stock, Miller High Life, Miller Lite

Major bottom-fermented brands: Blackhorse Beer, India Beer, Molson Canadian, Molson Canadian Light

Major awards received: Monde Selection Gold Medals: India Beer, 1971, 1982, 1984; Molson Canadian, 1984

## Moosehead Breweries
656 Windmill Road
Dartmouth, Nova Scotia B2Y 3Y3

In 1867, using family recipes brought from England, John and Susannah Oland began brewing ale in their back yard in Dartmouth, Nova Scotia. It proved so popular, the Olands produced larger quantities of their 'good salable ale' to supply the army and navy. With an investment of $7000, the 'Army & Navy Brewery' was formed on the Dartmouth, Nova Scotia waterfront, facing Halifax. Three years later, when John Oland was killed after falling from his horse, Susannah was forced to sell a controlling interest in the brewery. In 1877, an inheritance enabled Susannah to buy back control of the brewery, which she renamed 'S Oland Sons & Co.'

After her death in 1886, her youngest son, George WC Oland, took over the brewery. Because of economic hardships resulting from Prohibition, the majority of Canada's Maritime breweries were forced to sell to an English syndicate in 1895, but unlike the others, the Olands later regained control of their brewery.

In 1917, an explosion caused by the collision of two ships in Halifax Harbor destroyed the brewery, and Susannah's son and brewmaster Conrad Oland was killed and his brother John injured. The following year, George Oland and his eldest son, George Bauld Oland, with insurance money from the

explosion, purchased the Simeon Jones Brewery and renamed it the Red Ball Brewery.

Although Prohibition was still in effect and the Olands were permitted to brew only two percent alcohol beer, they made enough through the New Brunswick operation to return to Halifax and build a new brewery. In 1928, George Oland took over Ready's Breweries in Saint John and called his new company New Brunswick Breweries, Ltd. In 1931, he rechristened his ale 'Moosehead.' In 1947, the company name was changed from New Brunswick Breweries, Ltd to Moosehead Breweries, Ltd, and Ready's Pale Ale was renamed 'Moosehead Pale Ale' to mark the

company's entry into the Nova Scotia market. In 1971, the Halifax branch of the Oland family, which ran a competitive operation called Keith's Brewery, sold Keith's to Labatt. This left Moosehead Breweries with plants in Saint John, New Brunswick, and Dartmouth, Nova Scotia, making it the last major independent Canadian brewery.

In 1978, Moosehead entered the United States market with bottled Moosehead Canadian Lager beer, and in 1984 Moosehead draft beer was introduced. By the 1990s, Moosehead was available in all 50 states and was ranked as the seventh largest import beer out of 450 brands. In 1985, Moosehead arrived in England, distributed by Whitbread. Ironically, it was not until May 1992 that Moosehead Breweries introduced its beer in the Canadian provinces of Ontario, British Columbia, Alberta and Newfoundland, and in 1993, Moosehead was launched in Manitoba.

Annual production: 350,000 hectolitres

Other brewery owned by the same company: Moosehead Breweries (St John, New Brunswick)

Flagship brand: Moosehead Beer

Major top-fermented brand: Ten Penny Old Stock Ale

Major bottom-fermented brands: Alpine Genuine Cold Filtered, Alpine Lager, Alpine Light, Molson Canadian, Moosehead Beer, Moosehead Light, Moosehead Premium Dry, Moosehead Canadian Lager

## Moosehead Breweries
89 Main Street
Saint John, New Brunswick E2M 3H2

This brewery began as Ready's Breweries, Ltd, and was acquired in 1928 by George WC Oland and his son, George Bauld Oland. They renamed it New Brunswick Breweries, Ltd, but because of the prominence of the flagship brand the company became Moosehead Breweries, Ltd in 1947. A second Moosehead Brewery was erected in Dartmouth, Nova

Scotia, the original home of George WC Oland's parents, John and Susannah Oland, who had founded the brewing company in 1867.

Other brewery owned by the same company: Moosehead Breweries (Dartmouth, Nova Scotia)

Flagship brand: Moosehead Beer

Major top-fermented brands: Moosehead Pale Ale, Ten Penny Old Stock Ale

Major bottom-fermented brands: Alpine Genuine Cold Filtered, Alpine Lager, Alpine Light, Molson Canadian, Moosehead Beer, Moosehead Canadian Lager, Moosehead Light, Moosehead Light Canadian Beer, Moosehead Premium Dry

## Niagara Falls Brewing

6863 Lundy's Lane
Niagara Falls, Ontario L2G 1V7

This brewery was founded by Mario and Bruno Criveller in 1989.

Annual production: 10,000 hectolitres

Flagship brand: Eisbock Strong Beer (8% alcohol/volume)

Major top-fermented brand: Gritstone Premium Ale

Major bottom-fermented brand: Trapper Cold Filtered Draft

Major seasonal brand: Eisbock Strong Beer

**Northern Algonquin:** See Algonquin (Formosa, Ontario)

## Northern Breweries

503 Bay Street
Sault Ste Marie, Ontario P6A 5L9

This brewery was founded in 1989 by Casimir Kocot and Andrew Short as Soo Falls Brewing. In 1960, it became part of Doran's Northern Ontario Breweries, which was purchased by Carling O'Keefe in 1971, and which has been employee-owned as Northern Breweries since 1977.

Annual production: 100,000 hectolitres

Other breweries owned by the same company: also operates plants in Thunder Bay and Sudbury, Ontario.

Flagship brand: Northern

Major top-fermented brand: Northern Ale

Major bottom-fermented brands: Superior Lager, 55 Lager, Thunder Bay Lager, Encore Light, Edelbräu, Northern Extra Light, Northern Draught

### Northern Breweries

185 Lorne Street
Sudbury, Ontario

This brewery was founded in in 1907 by JJ Doran as Sudbury Brewing & Malting. In 1960, it became part of Doran's Northern Ontario Breweries, which was purchased by Carling O'Keefe in 1971, and which has been employee-owned as Northern Breweries since 1977.

Annual production: 170,000 hectolitres

Other breweries owned by the same com-

pany: also operates plants in Sault Ste Marie and Thunder Bay, Ontario.

Flagship brand: Northern

### Northern Breweires

154 North Algoma Street
Thunder Bay, Ontario P7B 5E7

This brewery was founded in 1876 by Conrad Gehl as Kakabeka Falls Brewing. In 1960, it became part of Doran's Northern Ontario Breweries, which was purchased by Carling O'Keefe in 1971, and which has been employee-owned as Northern Breweries since 1977.

Annual production: 75,000 hectolitres

Other breweries owned by the same company: also operates plants in Sault Ste Marie and Sudbury, Ontario.

Flagship brand: Superior Lager

### Oland Breweries

3055 Agricola Street
Halifax, Nova Scotia B3K 5N4

The Oland Breweries share a common ancestry with Moosehead Breweries (See Moosehead Breweries, Dartmouth, Nova Scotia), having both evolved from the back yard brewery started in 1867 by John and Susannah Oland in Dartmouth. John was killed in 1870 and Susannah died in 1886, but their heirs continued in the brewing business, with one branch of the family brewing in New Brunswick and the other in Halifax, Nova

Scotia. The Oland Brewery in Halifax (originally the Alexander Keith Brewery) was acquired by Labatt in 1971, but the Oland name was retained.

Annual production: 600,000 hectolitres

Other brewery owned by the same company: A subsidiary of Labatt Brewing, which also operates breweries in Edmonton, Alberta; London, Ontario; New Westminster, British Columbia; Winnipeg, Manitoba; St John, New Brunswick; St John's, Newfoundland; and La Salle, Quebec.

Major top-fermented brand: Keith IPA

Major seasonal brands: Keith's Dry, Keith's Light, Labatt's Blue, Labatt's Dry, Labatt's Lite, Old Scotia, Oland Export

## Pacific Brewing
6 Peacock Bay
St Catherines, Ontario L2R 7J8

Annual production: Under 500 hectolitres

## Port Arthur Brasserie & Brewery
901 Red River Road
Thunder Bay, Ontario P7B 1K3

This brewpub was founded by Frasier Dougall in 1988.

Annual production: Under 500 hectolitres

Flagship brand: Arthur's Lager

## Sleeman Brewing & Malting Company
551 Clair Road West
Guelph, Ontario N1H 6H9

This company was founded by John H Sleeman in 1834. John's son, George H Sleeman, managed the brewery until 1933 when, during Prohibition, he was caught smuggling beer into Michigan and was ordered to pay all applicable federal taxes and retire from the beer business. George Sleeman died in 1962. With backing from Stroh Brewing, in 1985 his great-grandson, John W Sleeman, once again incorporated the brewery.

In 1988 Sleeman Cream Ale, brewed according to the original family recipe, was once again available in Canada. The founder's intention in creating a Cream Ale was to combine the refreshing qualities of a German Lager with the distinctive rich taste of an English ale, without simply blending the two. Sleeman Cream Ale is a full-flavored, more lively brew with less bitterness than an all-malt ale and is known for its smoothness and creamy taste.

All Sleeman beers are all natural and free of additives and preservatives and are bottled in the Sleeman unique clear 'heritage' bottles.

Annual production: 200,000 barrels

Other breweries owned by the same company: Additional brands include Arctic Wolf, brewed under the Silver Creek Brewery label (available in Ontario, Atlantic and Quebec); and contract brews Nordik Wolf Light, Schlitz (draught and package), Stroh's and Stroh's Light.

Flagship brand: Sleeman Cream Ale

Major top-fermented brands: Sleeman Cream Ale, Sleeman Original Dark Ale

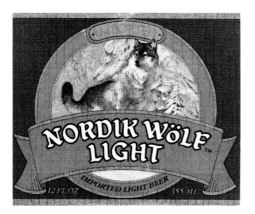

Major bottom-fermented brands: Arctic Wolf, Silver Creek Lager, Sleeman Premium Light, and under license from abroad: Nordik Wolf, Schlitz, Stroh's, Stroh's Light

Major awards received: Ontario Chamber of Congress: Outstanding Business Achievement Award, 1991; Monde Selection (Belgium) 1992: Sleeman Cream Ale (Gold Medal), Silver Creek Lager (Grand Gold Medal); Toronto International Food & Beer Show 1991-1992: Sleeman Cream Ale (Gold Medal), Silver Creek Lager (Silver Medal)

## Tapsters Smokehouse Grill & Brewery
100 Brittania Road East
Mississauga, Ontario L4Z 2G1

This brewery was founded in 1987 in what is now the Holiday Inn Toronto West.

Annual production: 230 hectolitres

Flagship brand: Tapsters Dark Lager

Major top-fermented brands: Tapsters Dark Lager, Tapsters Light Lager

## Thornbury Brewing
90 King Street
Thornbury, Ontario N0H 2P0

Annual production: Under 500 hectolitres

## Tracks Brewpub
60 Queen Street East
Brampton, Ontario L6V 1A9

This brewpub was founded by Henry Markand and Alan Knight in 1987 in the former Brampton Knitting Mill, which are adjacent to the railroad tracks, hence the name.

Annual production: 1100 hectolitres

Flagship brand: Old Mill

## Upper Canada Brewing
2 Atlantic Avenue
Toronto, Ontario M6K 1X8

This brewery was founded by Frank Heaps in 1985.

Annual production: 40,000 barrels

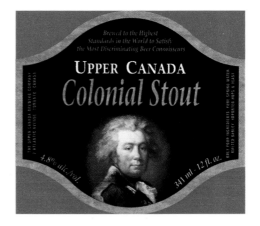

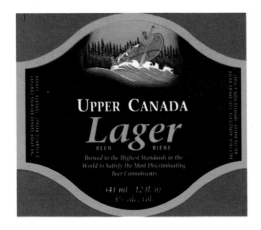

Flagship brands: Upper Canada Dark Ale, Upper Canada Lager

Major top-fermented brands: Lager, Light Lager, Rebellion Strong Lager, Wheat, True Bock, Point Nine

Major bottom-fermented brands: Colonial Stout, Dark Ale, Pale Ale, Publican's Special Bitter

Major seasonal brands: True Bock, Wheat

Major awards received: Monde Selection: Grande Medaille D'Or; International Wine, Beer & Cheese Show (Toronto): Best Lager

## Vancouver Island Brewing
#24 Vinefera Bar & Grill
150 Eglinton Avenue East
Toronto, Ontario M4P 1E8

This brewery/restaurant was founded by Der Lin in June 1992.

Annual production: 6000 hectolitres

Flagship brand: Vinefera Cream Lager

## Wellington County Brewing
950 Woodlawn Road West
Guelph, Ontario N1K 1B8

This brewery was founded in 1985 by Dr David Morrison, with Charles MacLean as the first brewer.

Annual production: 8000 hectolitres

Flagship brand: County Ale

Major top-fermented brands: Arkell Best Bitter, Black Knight, Imperial Stout, Iron Duke, Special Pale Ale

Major bottom-fermented brand: Premium Lager

Major award received: Five Stars by the *Ontario Beer Guide:* County Ale

# GLOSSARY

**Ale:** A top-fermented beer that originated in England as early as the seventh century and which was made with hops after the sixteenth century. It is fermented at temperatures ranging between 55 degrees F and 70 degrees F (13 degrees C and 21 degrees C), somewhat warmer than those used to ferment lager. It is the primary beer type in England and among North American microbreweries, but extremely rare elsewhere. It is, however, a close cousin to the German **altbier**. Subtypes include pale ale (which is actually much more amber than pale lagers), brown ale and India pale ale, a beer developed in the nineteenth century by English brewers for export to the Empire.

**Altbier:** The German equivalent of English or American 'ale,' literally a beer made in the 'old' way (pre-nineteenth century) with top-fermenting yeast. It is indigenous to Düsseldorf, Germany and environs. Virtually unknown in the United States after Prohibition, it was reintroduced by several microbreweries in Oregon and California during the 1980s.

**Barley Wine:** In Britain, ales with alcohol contents approaching that of wine (up to and surpassing 10 percent by volume) are called barley wines.

**Barrel:** A container for beer, at one time made of reinforced oak, now made solely of stainless steel. Also a unit of measuring beer which equals 31 gallons, or 1.2 hectoliters.

**Beer:** A general term for *all* fermented malt beverages flavored with hops. The term embraces ale, lager, porter, stout and all other types discussed herein. Ingredients include malted cereal grains (especially, but not limited to, barley), hops, yeast and water, although early English beers were unhopped. Subtypes are classified by whether they are made with top-fermenting yeast (ale, porter, stout, wheat beer) or bottom-fermenting yeast (lager, bock beer, malt liquor). Generally, top-fermented beers are darker, ranging from a translucent copper to opaque brown, while bottom-fermented beers range from amber to pale yellow. Because of their English heritage, top-fermented beers are usually drunk at room temperature, while bottom-fermented beers are served cold.

**Bier:** The German, Dutch and Flemish word for beer.

**Bière:** The French word for beer.

**Birra:** The Italian word for beer.

**Bitter:** A full-bodied, highly hopped ale (hence the name) that is extremely popular in England but much less so elsewhere. Bitter (or bitter ale) is similar in color to other ales, but it lacks carbonation and has a slightly higher alcohol content.

A noun used in England to identify highly-hopped ale. Originally it was probably short

**Opposite:** *Pike Place Pale Ale and Stout are produced by Pike Place Brewery of Seattle.*

for bitter ale. The less-used antonym is 'mild,' also a noun, which implies a lightly-hopped English ale.

**Bock Beer:** A bottom-fermented beer that is darker than lager and which has a relatively higher alcohol content, usually in the six per-cent range. Bock originated in Germany and most German brewers still brew it as a special supplement to their principal product line. An especially strong, dark lager occasionally, but not necessarily, produced in concordance with spring festivals. A seasonal beer, it is tradi-tionally associated with spring festivals. Prior to World War II, many American brewers pro-duced a bock beer each spring, but the advent of national marketing after the war largely eliminated the practice of brewing seasonal beers. In the 1980s, several breweries began to reintroduce bock beer. The male goat (*bock* in German) is the traditional symbol of bock beer. Subtypes include **doppelbock**, a bock espe-cially high in alcohol, and **maibock**, a bock marketed in conjunction with May festivals.

**Brasserie:** The French word for brewery and also for a small cafe.

*Above: **The bar at picturesque Spinnaker's Brewpub in Victoria, British Columbia offers Spinnaker's own Mitchell's ESB as well as other fine beers.***

**Brewing:** Generically, the entire beer-making process, but technically only that part of the process during which the beer wort is cooked in a brew kettle and during which time the hops are added. Following the brewing, beer is fermented. (see **Fermentation**.)

**Brewpub:** A brewpub is, by definition, a pub or tavern that brews its own beer on the premises. Until the 1980s, as a holdover from Prohibition laws, it was illegal in most states and Canadian provinces to both brew beer and sell it directly to the public on the same site. Subsequent changes in local laws have rescinded these outdated restrictions and have made it possi-ble for brewpubs to become more widespread. A brewpub differs from a **microbrewery** in that its primary market is under its own roof. Some brewpubs bottle their beers for sale to patrons and for wholesale to retailers, while some microbreweries also operate brewpubs, so the distinction between the two is somewhat blurred. Both, however, share a commitment to their own unique beers, and most brewpublicans entered their trade out of a love for brewing and an interest in distinctive beer styles.

**Cervecería:** The Spanish word for brewery.

**Cerveja:** The Portuguese word for beer.

**Cerveza:** The Spanish word for beer.

**Cream Ale:** A blend of ale and lager invented in the early twentieth century by American brewers.

**Diät:** A German word for lager low in carbohydrates originally developed for diabetics. It is *not* a 'diet' or low-calorie beer.

**Doppelbock:** A German word literally meaning 'double bock.' Although it is not nearly twice as strong as **bock**, it is typically the highest alcohol (over seven percent by volume) beer style brewed in Germany but lower in alcohol than English **Barley Wine**. In naming practice, doppelbocks are given names ending in 'ator,' such as Celebrator, Salvator or Optimator.

**Draft (Draught) Beer:** A term which literally means beer that is drawn from a keg rather than packaged in bottles or cans. Designed for immediate use, draft beer is not pasteurized and hence must be kept cold to prevent the loss of its fresh taste. Draft beer is generally better than packaged beer when fresh but not so as it ages. Some brewers sell unpasteurized draft-style beer in cans and bottles, which must be shipped in refrigerated containers.

**Dry Beer:** A pale lager in which all the fermentable sugars from the original malt have been converted to alcohol. In order to conclude the process with a beer of acceptable alcohol content (roughly 3.2 percent by weight), a brewer must start with less malt. Hence, dry beer has a low original gravity and will have very little flavor unless it is more heavily hopped than typical beers. The process is similar to that used by brewers to produce light beer, and the results are very similar. In fact, most American mass market lagers, including light and dry beers, are very similar in taste. Beer in which all fermentable sugars are fermented was developed in Germany and Switzerland in the 1970s as **diät** beer, a beer designed for diabetics.

**Dunkel (Dunkles):** A German adjective used to describe a dark lager, usually in the sweeter Munich style.

**Eisbock:** A German term that originated in Dortmund and applied to especially flavorful and powerful light-colored lagers.

**ESB (Extra Special Bitter):** A term that originated in England for describing a brewer's best highly-hopped bitter ale.

**Export:** This style evolved when the brewers in Dortmund, Germany began transporting beer to other markets across the continent. In order to withstand the rigors of travel, they produced a beer that was well hopped and slightly higher in alcohol. As such, the Dortmund lager as a style is known as 'export.' Dortmunder lagers are traditionally full-bodied but not quite as sweet as the beers of Munich, though not as dry as a true Pilsner. Beers identified as such are not necessarily brewed specifically to be exported, although they often are.

**Fermentation:** The process by which yeast turns the sugars present in malted grains into alcohol and carbon dioxide. Chemically, the process is written as:

$$C_6 H_{12} O_6 \rightarrow 2\ C_2 H_5 OH + 2\ CO_2$$
(glucose)      (alcohol)      (carbon dioxide)

**Gueuze:** Blended Belgian lambic beers not containing fruits.

**Hell (Helles):** An adjective used to describe lager that is pale in color.

**Hops:** The dried blossom of the female hop plant, which is a climbing herb *(Humulus lupulus)* native to temperate regions of the Northern Hemisphere and cultivated in Europe, the United Kingdom and the United

States. Belonging to the mulberry family, the hop's leaves and flowers are characterized by a bitter taste and aroma. It has been used since the ninth century as the principal flavoring and seasoning agent in brewing, although it had been prized before that for its medicinal properties. In addition to its aromatic resins, the hop plant also contains tannin which helps to clarify beer.

Different strains of hops have different properties and much of the brewmaster's art is in knowing how to use these properties. For example, one strain may be particularly bitter to the taste without being very aromatic, while another strain might be just the opposite. The brewmaster will blend the two in various combinations just as a chef will experiment with various seasonings before settling on just the right combination for a particular recipe. Hops also serve as a natural preservative.

**Ice Beer:** Developed and patented by Labatt in Canada, ice beer is a pale lager which is quickly chilled to sub-freezing temperatures after brewing but before final fermentation. The result is the formation of ice crystals in the beer, which are removed to produce a beer with roughly *twice* the alcohol content of typical mass market lagers.

**IPA (India Pale Ale):** A type of highly hopped, but light-colored, ale developed in England in the late eighteenth century, IPA was designed specifically to not deteriorate in quality during the long voyage to India.

**Keller:** A German-style of packaged, unfiltered lager that emulates *vom fass* (on draft) beer.

**Krausening (Kraeusening):** The process of instigating a secondary fermentation to produce additional carbon dioxide in a beer. Some brewers will first ferment their beer in open containers where alcohol is produced and retained, but the carbon dioxide escapes. The second fermentation, or krausening, then takes place in closed containers after a first fermentation (whether that first fermentation took place in open or closed containers) and is used to produce natural carbonation or sparkle in the beer.

**Kriek:** A Belgian lambic flavored with cherries. Probably the most popular of the fruit lambics.

**Lager:** This beer style accounts for well over 90 percent of the beer brewed and marketed in the world (outside England). Specifically, it is a clear, pale beer fermented with bottom-fermenting yeast at nearly freezing temperatures. The fermentation period is also longer than that for ale and hence the name, which is German meaning 'to store.' Lager had its origins in the heart of central Europe in an area that the author likes to call the Golden Triangle. This triangle is so named because of the golden color of lager itself and because of the success that brewers had with this product when it was first developed for widespread commercial sale in the early to middle nineteenth century. The corners of the Triangle lie in Munich, Prague and Vienna, the capitals, respectively, of Bavaria (a state of the German Federal Republic), Bohemia (Czech Republic) and Austria.

**Lambic:** A style of beer fermented with special strains of wild yeast indigenous only to Belgium's Senne Valley. One of the world's most unique native beer styles.

**Lautering:** The process of straining wort in a lauter tun before it is cooked in the brew kettle.

**Lauter Tun:** The vessel used in brewing between the mash tun and the brew kettle. It separates the barley husks from the clear liquid wort. The barley husks themselves help provide a natural filter bed through which the wort is strained.

**Light Beer:** Introduced in the mid-1970s by nearly every major brewer in the United States and Canada, light beers are by definition reduced-calorie lagers or ales. They also have a slightly lower alcohol content than comparable lagers or ales.

**Opposite:** *Saranac Adirondack Lager is the flagship beer of FX Matt Brewing of Utica, New York.*

**Maibock:** A bock beer brewed for release in May.

**Malt Liquor:** A bottom-fermented beer, it has a malty taste more closely related to top-fermented ale than to lager, which is bottom-fermented. Malt liquor has a much higher alcohol content (5.6 to 6.5 percent) than lager.

A term imposed by the American government to identify beer with an alcohol content above five percent. It is not actually a true beer type, as the term may be imposed on ales or lagers. Some larger American brewers produce very pale high-alcohol lagers and call them malt liquors.

**Malting:** The process by which barley kernels are moistened and germinated, producing a 'green malt' which is then dried. This renders the starches present in the kernel soluble. If pale beers are to be produced, the malt is simply dried. If dark beers are to be produced, the malt is roasted until it is dark brown. The malt is then subjected to mashing.

**Mash:** The substance that is produced by mashing.

**Mashing:** The process by which barley malt is mixed with water and cooked to turn soluble starch into fermentable sugar. Other cereal grains, such as corn and rice, many also be added (rice contributes to a paler end product

**Below:** *The fine products of Sierra Nevada Brewing of Chico, California.*

beer). After mashing in a mash tun, the mash is filtered through a lauter tun, whereupon it becomes known as wort.

**Microbrewery:** By definition, a microbrewery was originally considered to be a brewery with a capacity of less than 3000 barrels, but by the end of the 1980s this threshold increased to 15,000 barrels, as the demand for micro-brewed beer doubled and then *tripled*. A **brewpub** is, by definition, a pub or tavern that brews its own beer on the premises.

**Märzen:** Originally this German term was used to describe a reddish lager brewed in March and set aside for summer. The style is now brewed for autumn consumption, particularly in connection with Oktoberfest.

**Near Beer:** Non-alcoholic beer which originated during the Prohibition era in the United States and which is still in production.

**Pasteurization:** Though this term has come to mean the heating of a substance to kill harmful bacteria, the process was originally proposed by Louis Pasteur as a means of killing yeast to end fermentation and hence end the creation of alcohol and carbon dioxide (carbonation). Nonpasteurized beers are no less sanitary than pasteurized beers.

**Pils:** A German term for pale, Pilsen-style lagers.

**Pilsener or Pilsner:** A pale bottom-fermented lager beer originally associated with the city of Pilsen, Bohemia (Czech Republic) where it was first brewed in the early nineteenth century. The term is often used interchangeably with the term lager, although pilsners are technically the palest of lagers. Pilsners are the most widely known and widely imitated lager type. The Plzensky Prazdroj brewery in Pilsen brews Pilsner Urquell ('Pilsner from the original source'), which is considered the definitive pilsner, although the term has become generic.

**Porter:** A dark, sweet beer brewed with top-fermenting (ale type) yeast that was developed in London in the late eighteenth century and revived by American microbrewers in the late twentieth century. It took its name from the city's porters who had taken an immediate fancy to it. Similar to but sweeter than stout, it is a dark beer of moderate strength (alcohol, five to seven percent by volume), made with roasted unmalted barley.

**Prohibition:** The process by which a government prohibits its citizens from buying or possessing alcoholic beverages. Specifically, *the* Prohibition refers to the period between the effective date of the 18th Amendment to the US Constitution (16 January 1920) and its repeal by the 21st Amendment. Repeal took effect on 5 December 1933, although it passed Congress in February and the sale of beer was permitted after 7 April 1933.

**Rauchbier:** A lager with a wonderfully smoky flavor which uses malted grain that has been roasted over a very smoky beechwood fire. Indigenous to the Bamberg area in southern Germany, rauchbier literally means 'smoked beer.' As such, the grain is not only roasted to a dark color, but it takes on a distinctive smoky flavor as well. Smoked beer, which is rare outside of Germany, is generally served with meals including smoked or barbecued meats, rye bread and certain sharp cheeses.

**Reinheitsgebot:** A German purity law enacted in 1516 that permits only malted barley, hops, yeast and water to be used in the brewing of beer sold in Germany. Though it has no jurisdiction outside Germany, many North American brewers follow it, and some use the fact that they meet its guidelines as part of their advertising. Since Germany's admission to the European Community, the Reinheitsgebot has not been legally binding since 1987, but German brewers still proudly follow it.

**Sake:** A fermented beverage that is a cousin to the family of fermented beverages we call beer. Sake originated in Japan, where it is an important national drink. Several sake breweries have existed in both California and Hawaii over the years, but the only remaining

American commercial sake brewery is in Hawaii. Sake is brewed from unmalted rice and is not hopped. The resulting substance is clear and has a 14 to 16 percent alcohol content. In contrast to beer, which is drunk either chilled or at room temperature, sake is warmed before drinking.

**Steam Beer:** A term that originated in San Francisco during the Gold Rush era to refer to beer that was produced with bottom-fermenting yeast but fermented at 60 degrees F to 70 degrees F (15 degrees C to 21 degrees C) rather than the temperatures required for true lager fermentation. Fermentation was allowed to continue in the kegs and the escaping carbon dioxide that resulted from the tapping of the kegs is the possible source of the term 'steam' beer. In any event, the term steam beer is now a registered trademark of The Anchor Brewing Company of San Francisco, brewers of Anchor Steam Beer.

**Stout:** A dark, heavy, top-fermented beer popular in the British Isles, especially Ireland (where Guinness Stout is more popular than Budweiser lager is in the United States). It is similar to porter, though less sweet. Its alcohol content ranges from four to seven percent.

Stout is a dark, creamy beer produced with top-fermenting (ale type) yeast. Stout is the prominent beer type in Ireland and is widely available in England. Also brewed occasionally by microbreweries in the United States, it is not nearly so popular in continental Europe. Guinness, brewed in Dublin and London, is the definitive stout of the Irish type. It is also brewed under license in many places throughout the world. English brewers, such as Samuel Smith in Tadcaster, also produce oatmeal stout in which oats are used along with barley malt.

**Tesguino:** A type of corn beer produced by the Indians of Mexico and the American Southwest prior to their contact with Europeans.

**Wheat Beer:** Beer, by definition, is a beverage derived from malted barley. Other grains, such as rice and cornmeal, are often used in less expensive, mass market brands as a cheaper source of starch, but this practice is frowned upon by discriminating brewers and consumers. Exceptions are made in the case of oats in English oatmeal stout and with wheat in American wheat beer, German **weissbier** and Flemish **witbier**. Both the German and Flemish terms are literally translated as meaning 'white' beer. This is a reference to the light color of the beer and the fact that it usually has yeast particles in suspension and hence it is cloudy, transluscent and lighter in appearance than if it were transparent. In Germany, weissbiers that are cloudy are identified with the prefix *hefe* (yeast) as hefeweissbier, or simly hefeweiss.

**Weissbier:** A German word literally meaning beer that is white (weiss), but actually implying a style of pale-colored, top-fermented beer made with about half wheat malt. It is typical of Berlin and northern Europe. A **hefe-weiss** beer is a weissbier in which yeast sediment remains in suspension in the beer. Weissbier is also known as **weizenbier**, but should not be confused with **wiesenbier**, which is a festival beer that may or may not contain wheat malt.

**Witbier/Bière Blanche:** Flemish/French literally meaning white (wit/blanche) beer. It is brewed using over half wheat malt. A cousin to German weissbier, witbier is indigenous to the northern, Flemish-speaking areas of Belgium.

**Wort:** An oatmeal-like substance consisting of water and mashed barley in which soluble starch has been turned into fermentable sugar during the mashing process. The wort is cooked, or brewed, in the brew kettle for more than an hour and for as much as a day, during which time hops are added to season the wort. After brewing, the hopped wort is filtered and fermented to produce beer.

**Yeast:** The enzyme-producing one-celled fungi of the genus *Saccharomyces* that is added to wort before the fermentation process for the purpose of turning fermentable sugar into alcohol and carbon dioxide.